Praise for *West Winging It*

"Of all of President Obama's staffers, Pat Cunnane was definitely one of them. . . . But seriously, Pat tells a funny, moving story about working in the White House that is a must read for anyone who misses having Barack Obama as president."

—Dan Pfeiffer, cohost of *Pod Save America* and former senior advisor

"As the only human who has worked with Pat in a real White House and now a fake one, I have the authority to tell you to read this book. It's good. And inspiring. And funny."

—Kal Penn, star of *Designated Survivor*

"Sharp, funny, and true, *West Winging It* is a super fun journey for any reader—and for me, a wonderful trip down Memory Lane."

—Alyssa Mastromonaco, *New York Times* bestselling author of *Who Thought This Was a Good Idea* and former deputy chief of staff

"Pat Cunnane captures the feeling that anyone with the opportunity to occupy a desk in the West Wing should have: astonishment at their improbable good fortune, and awe at the responsibility that comes with it. *West Winging It* is a fun, poignant reminder that the best part about working in the Obama White House was the people working with you, and knowing that everyone was there for the right reason: to try to do as much good, for as many people, as we possibly could."

—Jay Carney, former press secretary

"*West Winging It* is the compelling true story of Pat Cunnane, who proves a talented, funny tour guide from his desk outside the Press Secretary's office. Pat reminds us that the responsibility and privilege of a job in the West Wing should be fun, even if it's not nearly as glamorous as it looks on TV."

—Josh Earnest, former Press Secretary

"With all that's going on in Washington these days, it's refreshing to read about the lighter moments inside a somewhat more normal White House."

—Rob Reiner, actor and director

"[A] fitfully funny, often earnest insider's look at the Obama era . . . a warm and observant portrait of what it's like to work for the White House . . .When he's truly candid, Cunnane nails it."

—Kirkus Reviews

"A fond look back . . . has the snappy, sunny vibe of a period that ended less than two years ago but seems like another century."

—*USA Today*

West Winging It

AN UN-PRESIDENTIAL MEMOIR

Pat Cunnane

GALLERY BOOKS
New York London Toronto Sydney New Delhi

G

Gallery Books
An Imprint of Simon & Schuster, Inc.
1230 Avenue of the Americas
New York, NY 10020

Certain names have been changed, whether or not so noted in the text, timelines have been condensed, and several individual characters are composites.

This Gallery Books paperback edition November 2018

GALLERY BOOKS and colophon are registered trademarks of Simon & Schuster, Inc.

Interior design by Bryden Spevak

Manufactured in the United States of America

10 9 8 7 6 5 4 3 2 1

The Library of Congress has cataloged the hardcover edition as follows:

Names: Cunnane, Pat, author.
Title: West Winging It : An Un-Presidential Memoir / Pat Cunnane.
Description: First Gallery Books hardcover edition | New York : Gallery Books, 2018.
Identifiers: LCCN 2017055266 (print) | LCCN 2018014264 (ebook) | ISBN 9781501178313 (ebook) | ISBN 9781501178290 (hardback)
Subjects: LCSH: Cunnane, Pat, author. | Presidents—United States—Staff—Biography. | Obama, Barack—Friends and associates. | United States—Politics and government—2009–2017—Humor. | BISAC: BIOGRAPHY & AUTOBIOGRAPHY / Presidents & Heads of State. | BIOGRAPHY & AUTOBIOGRAPHY / Personal Memoirs. | HUMOR / Topic / Political.
Classification: LCC E907 (ebook) | LCC E907 .C87 2018 (print) | DDC 973.932092—dc23
LC record available at https://lccn.loc.gov/2017055266

ISBN 978-1-5011-7829-0
ISBN 978-1-5011-7830-6 (pbk)
ISBN 978-1-5011-7831-3 (ebook)

For Stephanie

Contents

CAST OF CHARACTERS

Denis McDonough, chief of staff (2013–2017). The highest-ranking employee of the White House. The president's gatekeeper. Everybody's boss.

Dan Pfeiffer, communications director (2009–2013), senior advisor (2013–2015). In charge of the president's message and later his broader strategy, taking over for senior advisors David Axelrod and David Plouffe. My boss.

Jennifer Palmieri (JPalm), communications director (2013–2015). My boss.

Jennifer Psaki, communications director (2015–2017). My boss.

Jay Carney, press secretary (2011–2014). Also my boss.

Josh Earnest, press secretary (2014–2017). Yep, my boss, too.

Eric Schultz, principal deputy press secretary (2014–2017). Second in command to the press secretary, called on to brief in his absence. Also, the White House "fixer." Sort of my boss.

Howli, Jay's assistant and then director of message planning. Responsible for planning the president's events.

Brian, director of operations. Responsible for maintaining dignity throughout the West Wing.

Bobby, assistant press secretary. Responsible for managing press related to homeland security.

Matt, assistant press secretary. Responsible for managing press related to education and other domestic issues.

Marie, press assistant and press wrangler.

Antoinette, press assistant and press wrangler; later the deputy director of Hispanic media and Josh's assistant.

Desiree, press assistant and press wrangler; later, special assistant.

Peter Velz, press assistant and press wrangler; later, special assistant. Basically everybody's boss.

Jimmy, staff assistant.

Nana, my spunky grandmother.

PROLOGUE

The Beginning . . .

November 8, 2016, began like any other big night in Obama World: with chicken fingers and waffle fries. The tradition went back to the earliest days of Senator Obama's campaign for president, passed down from Chicago to Washington, DC, from Houlihan's to the White House Navy Mess. Throughout two terms, before Oval Office addresses to the nation, on debate nights, and before the president's State of the Union addresses, we called down to place an order, or four.

The West Wing had been buzzing all day. Staffers popped in and out of their regular meetings, their jackets and sweaters adorned with "I Voted!" stickers. Like everybody else, my attention was elsewhere, on anything but the matters of my regularly scheduled meetings. The polls, the swing states, the footage of long lines and allegations of voter intimidation—the stuff of Election Day overtook the usual rhythms of the daily working West Wing.

Everybody asked everybody else the same question: "What are you hearing?" Of course, nobody was hearing anything. There was nothing to know yet. I wanted to find David Simas, the White House political director, but figured it was too early to ask.

The night would be historic, but for now, our energy needed to be bottled. It was a waiting game.

My mom admits that there was a certain energizing kick in her interest in the 2016 election cycle, too. And it had nothing to do with her own reelection campaign to the Pennsylvania House of Representatives. Instead, it had everything to do with the pride she felt in the eight years of the Obama administration and all that Barack Obama stood for and accomplished. "Don't bother me with what this president did not accomplish; that list is far shorter," she would say.

It also had a lot to do with motherly pride and her very real melancholy: a sadness to see it end. She and my dad were pleased that I had taken their advice—freely and given often—to remain at the White House until the end. "Stay, and turn the lights out."

But most of all, her energy had to do with the powerful bookends of Hillary Clinton, a public servant, way ahead of my mom, at the top of her baby boomer generation, running for—and going to become—president! And it had been fun campaigning for Hillary with her own five-year-old granddaughter, Aubrey, my niece, who was predictably adorable, surprisingly quick-witted, and very, very outgoing. She was a natural-born politician.

Aubrey had been to five White House Easter Egg Rolls on the South Lawn. "I can't wait to see the bunny and Barack-Obama," she would always say, all one word. When I would gently warn her that she might not see him one year—that it was a crowded event—she would reply matter-of-factly, "Of course I'll see him. It's his backyard!"

She would tell him to his face, "I love you, Barack-Obama!" And she did. But it wasn't just President Obama whom she loved. Hillary Clinton held a special place in Aubrey's heart as well. She once piped up with an important question for Hillary at an intimate town hall meeting, asking what Hillary would do about trash on the playground. Hillary responded with kindness, calling Aubrey by name. "Trash on the playground? Well, I worry about that, too!" That sealed it. Aubrey threw her considerable clout behind Hillary.

My mom was sure to meet up with Aubrey on Election Day, to bring her into the polling booth to vote—not just for her grandmother but also for her "friend" and the first "girl president," Hillary Clinton.

My mom wasn't on the ballot in DC, where I met up with my wife, Stephanie, outside the White House to find our local polling place, but I was filled with pride just the same—voting for Hillary and watching what it meant to Stephanie to wear her arrowed Hillary shirt around town and to work. No shirt for me, though. In the White House, we had been warned by the lawyers: no political paraphernalia. Not even an "I'm with Her" button was allowed on premises.

Stephanie and I cast our votes. I called my mom on the way back to work. Things looked good, she said. Like Hillary's, her victory was all but assured.

As I waited for my two phones, one for work and one personal, to clear the X-ray machine, I smiled at one of the regular Secret Service agents. "Thank God, it's finally over!"

"Nothing's over yet."

"Yeah, guess you're right," I said. "Nothing more we can do but wait."

Around seven thirty in the evening, staffers started to crowd into Press Secretary Josh Earnest's office, festooned with Kansas City Royals gear and photos of his young son. The chicken fingers were good. The waffle fries were perfectly salted. There was nothing to worry about.

Picking up some alcohol from my desk, I bumped into a few friends, who mocked my clothing. I hate suits and had been pushing for Casual Fridays since the 2014 midterms. This Tuesday had a decidedly Friday vibe, so I'd changed into jeans and a sweater—"victory casual"—for the watch party. The only problem was that the buttons near the neck were out of whack, and I had to make a choice: Do I risk choking myself, or do I show, according to some friends and all of my bosses, "too much chest"? I chose the latter. "What's it matter?" I said to a colleague. "It's all over anyway. We're done here. Time to pass the baton to PIW."

For more than two years, I'd referred to Hillary as "president-in-waiting." I'm a worrier by nature, but it was always clear to me that she would succeed President Obama. The week before, the White House had begun making plans for the visit of the president-elect. I'd scribbled in my calendar: "Thursday, POTUS will meet with HRC."

The returns started rolling in shortly after the first of the chicken fingers had vanished. Donald Trump was up in the electoral college 19 to 3. I turned to the group and joked, "Oh no, we're losing!" Of course, we were fine. But it was a little disturbing to see the actual check mark of victory next to his smirking, copper-colored face.

The beer and bourbon flowed. Some of the early returns from the bigger states started appearing on the screen. Too close to call. Trump up. No problem: the Democratic-leaning counties hadn't reported yet. Ohio. Florida. North Carolina. We did what any sports fan does when he needs to regain the mojo. We switched positions. Around nine o'clock, a group of us went into the Rose Garden and did breathing exercises.

Back in Josh's office, texts, calls, and conversations blurred into a jumble. Pennsylvania. Michigan. Wisconsin. Still, nothing had been called. A few staffers—including some of the First Lady's aides—and I walked through the basement of the White House and into the East Wing. The Map Room, where a year before I had debated Jerry Seinfeld about the funniest way to end his interview with the president (he won), was dark. The Diplomatic Reception Room, so often filled with dignitaries, Olympians, and entertainers: empty.

We passed the Family Theater by way of the East Colonnade, hurried down an East Wing hallway, and entered the First Lady's office. It smelled beautiful, floral. I must have shown signs of distress, because Lauren, the First Lady's deputy press secretary, told me to sit in the First Lady's chair. After all, Mrs. Obama had been the standout surrogate of the cycle. Lauren and I, after working together for years, had realized only recently that we'd lived together on the same ship—circling the globe as part of a study-abroad program called Semester at Sea during the first four months of Obama's presidency. That seemed so long ago now.

Surely, the First Lady's chair was where things would turn around. I tried to take my mind off the moment. My mom's results had come in, and I remember telling the group she'd won her re-election big. We celebrated. We needed something to cheer. I called my mom on the walk back from the First Lady's office toward the West Wing. She spoke in a hushed tone, like she didn't want any-body at our house in Pennsylvania to hear. "I just want everyone to leave," she said of the partygoers filling her election-night bash at our home, each guest in varying stages of shock.

At 10:21 p.m., somebody got a notification that Ohio had been called for Trump. The remaining viewers in Josh's office were pacing nervously. One of the longtime White House press aides, Peter Velz, left to comfort a despondent speechwriter. Behind closed doors, away from the news, they began reading aloud a history of the White House.

At 11:07 p.m., North Carolina was called. I left to finally find David Simas, who was analyzing the results as a number of other staffers huddled around his conference table staring at a torrent of tweets. Hoping for reassurances, I found only disbelief and grim predictions. I tried to imagine what the president might say if the night wore on like this, but I couldn't hear his voice.

At 11:23 p.m., the Republican governor of New Jersey, Chris Christie, then responsible for leading the potential Trump transition, phoned the woman seated next to me. There was a deep silence following the call. At 11:30 p.m., Simas said Hillary had a 33 percent chance of winning but that "everything has to go right on a night where nothing has gone right."

A small blue fish swam in circles on a nearby desk.

Slightly dazed, I wandered away, not knowing where to go next.

The Rose Garden is dark at midnight, and quiet. As November 8 turned to November 9, it was also empty. I was alone, drinking bourbon from a cracked plastic cup. I walked off the Colonnade, crumbled absurdly to the ground, and realized that I was in the very spot where I had taken a knee four years before to propose to my wife, Stephanie, my grade school sweetheart.

This is ironic, I thought, seated on the grass, head tilted toward the glowing west wall of the White House. Or, maybe, by definition, it wasn't actually ironic. Much like Alanis Morissette, I was never totally clear on what was and was not ironic. The bourbon wasn't clearing it up. I didn't care. I got a text from my hometown neighbor Sean, but my phone died before I could respond with false confidence. I pulled out my work phone—one of America's last BlackBerrys—but it had an error message unlike anything I'd seen before.

On the way out of the West Wing lobby, I bumped into a staffer who had been in Simas's office.

"What's Simas saying?" I asked.

"She's not going to get there."

1

Warehouse to the White House

Nobody knows really what they're doing, and there's two ways to go with that information. One is to be afraid and the other is to be liberated.

—CONAN O'BRIEN

My parents walked me to my first day at the White House.

I know how absurd that sounds and, yes, how ridiculous it was. But they were excited. And I was nervous. It was just four years before, in 2006, that they had traveled with me to my first day of college. What business did I have at the White House? I was out of my depth. Beyond a knack for writing, I had few skills that would translate to success at the White House: a tenuous grasp of technology, a limited understanding of government. I had never used Microsoft Outlook. Hell, I didn't even know how to make coffee.

My nerves faded for a moment at the back entrance to the Eisenhower Executive Office Building (EEOB), with my parents looking on from beyond the black wrought iron gate below. I was distracted by the remarkable, imposing EEOB—a French-inspired building constructed over the course of almost two decades in the late nineteenth century—which originally housed the Departments of State, War, and the Navy. In 2010, 122 years later, I learned that it was home to the majority of White House offices. As I ascended the stairs, American flags flying overhead, something stirred inside of me—swelling with each step.

You would think it was patriotism, right? Wrong. My twenty-two-year-old self was a bit irked. I had applied for a White House internship, not an Eisenhower Building internship. Plus, Mark Twain once called the structure "the ugliest building in the country." And I kind of agreed.

Of course, I hadn't been scammed, I was just ignorant. The EEOB is made up of hundreds of offices, from communications, press, and domestic policy, to legal counsel, correspondence, and foreign affairs. It includes the vice president's ceremonial office, as well as numerous secure rooms called Sensitive Compartmented Information Facilities—SCIFs, for short. After the assassination of President John F. Kennedy in 1963, President Lyndon Johnson continued to work out of the EEOB as a sign of respect for his fallen predecessor. Roosevelts, plural, had worked there. Wars were planned there. The EEOB is where much of America's business gets done, for better or worse. My office was across the hall from the room in which Richard Nixon recorded many of his fateful tapes during the Watergate crisis that ultimately brought down his presidency. In 2010, I didn't have a handle on the history. The place, and the president for whom I was working, were still abstractions to me. I failed to appropriately value the vaunted halls that I rushed through.

Room 181, like most of the offices in the building, featured huge windows, soaring ceilings, and staffers at regal, dark wooden desks. I was situated next to three such staffers, none of whom was thrilled to have an intern stationed so close to them. They were nice, of course, but busy responding to reporters from across the country:

"POTUS has taken into account those figures."

"Sure, we can get you that as soon as POTUS returns from OMB."

It sounded like gibberish to me. I was listening to someone's call, trying to glean something—anything—but it was almost impossible. I overheard: "He's the OPE POC for LGBT and AAPI issues for POTUS."* They were speaking a different language. I did my best to hide my confusion.

My primary goal was to stay out of their way on day one—to make a good, quiet impression.

Following the rush of morning news and journalists' queries, room 181 fell into what I would learn was a rare silence, interrupted only by sudden bursts of desktop typing or a fit of coughing. We were in an early-afternoon lull, the silence seeming to grow by the

---

* Translated from White House speak: "He's the Office of Public Engagement point of contact for LGBT and Asian American and Pacific Islander issues for the president."

minute. I thought about saying something—we'd all exchanged pleasantries in the morning, but I hadn't said a word in almost an hour. It was an opportunity to showcase my personality, maybe make a joke or bring up some popular movie. I thought about it a bit more and decided against speaking. Instead, I planned to jump into the conversation once somebody else piped up.

Unfortunately, it was my computer that piped up before I had the chance. A pop-up advertisement overtook my ancient desktop. The speaker had been set to booming, and the words rang out crisp and clear:

"Hey, everybody, I'm Justin Bieber!"

Every staffer in the room turned to me. The words echoed off the towering ceiling, reverberating through the room. I maintained my back to my new office mates but could feel their glares piercing my thin façade of competence. I scrambled for the mute button. Couldn't find it. Bieber kept going.

"Catch me at the Verizon Center!"

After singing about tickets being on sale, Bieber literally began busting moves on my desktop, dancing on my dignity. My hands were shaking on the mouse, and I couldn't locate the *X* that's usually in the top right corner of the browser. Unfortunately for me, this was one of those crafty ads with the hidden Close Out buttons. I did the only tech-savvy thing in my repertoire and punched control-Alt-delete into the keyboard.

Mercifully, I had an excuse to leave, avoiding eye contact all the way out the door. It was time for my security briefing in the South Court Auditorium on the ground floor. On my way into the auditorium, which looked like an Intro to Communications college lecture hall, I got my first glimpse of the West Wing from inside the gates. I watched as a couple of generals exited their black, armored Chevy Suburban SUV and scurried into the basement entrance of the West Wing—presumably toward the Situation Room, which would be immediately to their right as they walked in. Of course, I didn't know any of that at the time and wondered what it must be like in there. The West Wing. *Wow,* I thought. *I guess this really is a White House internship.*

Still, I was too preoccupied with the Justin Bieber disaster to let the moment sink in. What did they think of me in 181? What were they saying?

Our security briefing began with a spot of tough love. A Secret Service agent took the room by surprise: "Congratulations," he said. "You're sitting in the cherry on top of every terrorist's dream cake."

He was about as subtle as my nana.

• • •

"I was baptized a Democrat, not a Catholic."

That's what my nana wanted everybody to know. Whether she was strolling out of St. Luke's Church, her local parish, with the monsignor or, more likely, sparring with a neighbor or grandson, you needed to know—above all—Joan Cunnane was a Democrat.

The only thing Nana likes more than talking about politics is arguing about politics. When she thought your point was particularly useless, or your argument unsound, she'd give a quick huff, smile to herself, and then look up from the tattered playing cards splayed across her gray laminate countertop. When Nana took her attention away from her never-ending game of solitaire and peered at you through the smoky haze of her 1980s-era kitchen, you knew she had you dead to rights.

And when she held a beat before speaking, shuffled over to the stove, and cranked the burner to ignite her cigarette, you knew she was about to light you up. Now, if she turned down the ever-present drone of MSNBC—God forbid—just to be sure you could hear her argument, well, we grandkids learned to run.

Nana is not known for subtlety. She once proudly ended a fifty-three-year friendship with her beloved Hazel upon learning that her longtime neighbor was sympathetic to Sarah Palin. I watched her say "Goodbye, Hazel" from her kitchen counter. Never spoke with her again.

However, Nana is known for playing favorites, something I've benefited from since day one. The morning I was born—November 22—was the twenty-fourth anniversary of President Kennedy's assassination. Upon picking me up for the first time in the hospital room, she exclaimed:

"I got my JFK back!"

My mother, Madeleine Cunnane, was reeling from a labor that had lasted twenty-two hours. I was big and overdue and unwieldy. I required a suction machine as well as, eventually, forceps, which—when he finally pried me free—sent the doctor flying across the room. I was bruised and my head a little misshapen temporarily from the forceps. Still, Nana saw only a little Kennedy. My mom wasn't feeling Camelot and found the comment ludicrous. In fact, she rolled her eyes so far into the back of her head that there was some worry the doctor would be needed to retrieve them. She looked over to my father for affirmation that what his mother, Joanie, had said was outright bizarre.

But my dad—my nana's favorite son—didn't notice. He was blinded with excitement. The moment he saw my eyes open, he screeched, "Oh my God! He's a genius!"

Turns out my dad, P. J. Cunnane, lived the first twenty-nine years of his life under the impression that human babies—like kittens—spend the first few weeks after birth with their eyes closed. He thought that I, his firstborn, eyes wide open in minutes, was enlightened. He would learn quickly that he was wrong.

I thought about how off base my dad's prediction had been as the Secret Service agent who reminded me of my nana droned on about safety. At that moment, my first day, I couldn't be bothered by bombs and wasn't worried about weapons. My reputation was already shot, and all I could think about was how to revive it.

When I returned to the office, I considered telling a self-deprecating joke but figured not landing it was too risky. I was already on thin ice with hot blades—better to build back slow. My plan: ask an informed question. I would prove that I was engaged; that I cared about what was going on around me. There was a term that had thrown me off all day. I didn't know if it was an obscure department or a piece of legislation or what. Sure, I could have googled it, but then nobody would know that I was a serious person here to learn and to do a good job.

But who to ask? There was Steve. He sat in the corner and had a proclivity for reacting—laughing, groaning, bemoaning—to whatever came across his computer screen. I could already tell that the obvious intention there was for somebody to ask him what was up. He was a prompter. Then, as soon as someone inevitably played his or her part and inquired, he would take to reading the entire article word for word. A few interminable minutes later, somebody would eventually say "Crazy," and somebody else might add "Interesting." Only then would everybody be able to get back to work. I wasn't going to ask Steve.

Dylan was another option. He sat an office over. I would come to know that he took his job so seriously that it was hard at first to get more than a one- or two-word answer out of him if it wasn't mission critical. I'd been warned early on that he also tended to internalize anything negative said about President Obama, letting it build up until he exploded at five in the afternoon with an inventive, impressive, expletive-laced tirade aimed at whomever had most recently taken an unfair shot at his boss. Dylan, however dedicated to the cause, wasn't right for the question either.

Then there was Matt: a longtime aide who joined the campaign early and took on key roles at a very young age. I didn't know much about him other than the fact that he had good hair—and he wasn't too much older than I was, which surprised me given that he seemed to have a vital job. In fact, I was beginning to learn that a lot of young people had important jobs. Despite some heavy typing and aggravated huffs now and then, Matt seemed the most approachable. Like, maybe we could one day be friends. I figured we might have something in common. And when I heard him talking about basketball, I knew he was the right choice. So I geared up for my question, clearing my throat. It was time to create a new narrative for myself in the office.

"Hey, Matt."

He looked up from his screen and swiveled his chair to me. I took a breath, remembering that there's no such thing as a stupid question, and proceeded confidently:

"What's a POTUS?"

I had created a new narrative for myself, all right. I knew from the way the room reacted—even before Matt answered—that stupid questions do, in fact, exist.

"President of the United States, Pat."

I wanted to get as far away from the White House as possible, to leave the city entirely. I felt like running back to my parents' hotel. I thought maybe my first instincts about living in DC—*not to*—had been correct.

• • •

In May of my senior year of high school, I was enrolled—nonrefundable deposits and all—at two universities. A couple things about this: one, pretty sure it's against the rules; two, it's definitely a colossal waste of money. Still, maybe I could have gotten around those roadblocks and attended both schools—if not for the fact that they were separated by more than a thousand miles.

Back then, it seemed my mom and I were even further apart,

at least metaphorically. We couldn't agree. I had been accepted early to Georgetown University. My parents were ecstatic, as they were about all things related to Washington. They had a thing for DC—were infatuated, even—and wanted desperately for my two brothers and me to be, too. My mom was adamant that I seize the opportunity presented to me by Georgetown, but my heart was set on the University of Miami. The choice was even clearer after my back-to-back campus visits: the lush, palm-tree-lined entrance to the University of Miami, juxtaposed with the winter drear of Georgetown's Gothic, gray buildings; the campus pool at UM, contrasted with the campus graveyard at Georgetown.

It didn't hurt that my girlfriend, Stephanie, was headed with her twin sister, Victoria, to Miami. Stephanie and I had met in second grade. I developed a crush quickly—okay, instantly—but kept quiet. It was a slow burn. For years, I kept up the crush, captivated by her from afar. Popular, but not one of the *popular girls*, Stephanie was the quiet, beautiful brunette. And in seventh grade, five years after I had first laid my prepubescent eyes on her, I got word she might be interested in me. Our mutual friends literally pushed us together outside the library. Finally face-to-face, I asked, "Will you be my girlfriend?"

Six years into my relationship with Stephanie, my mom and I were three months into a battle of wills about my school choice; if the past was any precedent, my chances of outlasting Madeleine Cunnane weren't good. Harry, my middle brother, is testament to that.

When Harry was a sophomore in high school at St. Joseph's

Preparatory, in Philadelphia, he decided—against the wishes of my parents and his better sense—to get a substantial tattoo on his side, just below his armpit. Standard fare for a first tattoo: something about "Living today" and "dying tomorrow." And a cross. I caught wind of it through Facebook and ratted him out—but just to my dad, who I knew wouldn't much care. Nevertheless, my mom found out (Harry, I swear it wasn't me) and devised a plan.

She took a blue Bic pen to her right foot and wrote in elegant cursive, "De La Salle": an ode to La Salle University—where she taught rhetoric and writing—and to St. Jean-Baptiste de La Salle, the patron saint of teachers.

Knowing the reality, the permanence, of his decision, my mom concluded that she wanted Harry to *want* to tell of his tattoo. So, following one in a series of what she liked to call "come to Jesus" meetings with Harry, she said, "Okay, Harry, I have something to show you."

And with that, my mom took off her shoe and sock, fully expecting Harry to see right through her farce. Maybe it had something to do with the dim lighting of the den, but Harry didn't question the authenticity of the "tattoo" on my mom's foot. He was just shocked—and impressed!—that his professor of a mother had inked up. In fact, he pulled off his shirt, revealing a tattoo the size of a football. More than that, he opened right up to her, telling the story of his own tattoo and asking where my mom went for hers and how much she paid. My mom, not knowing the first thing about tats, told him she went to a nice place out in Bucks County and paid $400.

"Ah, you got cheated!" Harry exclaimed, explaining that $400 was way too much for nine little letters. His guy would have charged only $35.

She didn't have the heart to tell him that her ink was temporary, totally fake. They had bonded. So she sustained the sham. At family parties, weddings, baptisms, Harry would tell cousins of her ink, and our mom would have to find a blue pen, run into the bathroom, and reapply. Eventually she just began each morning by reaching for a blue Pic pen at her bedside and coloring in the faded lettering below her toes. It was no longer about the tattoo; it was about bonding with her son, which might thereby help him to avoid these types of decisions in the future. Finally, she couldn't keep up the worry and the writing. The jig was up, but—in truth and out of character—my mom had grown fond of the tattoo. She wanted it.

My then-fifty-year-old mother googled "best place to get a tattoo," found the artist—Danny, the owner of Philly Ink on Kensington Avenue—under the El, and got her first and only real tattoo, exactly the same as her fake one. Harry was none the wiser for another few years, well after the tattoo had become real, when my mom finally fessed up.

All that is to say, as I thought through the endgame of my college battle with my mom, I knew her to be a worthy adversary—fully prepared to wait me out. I wondered what trick she had up her sleeve, or as in Harry's case, under her sock, for me. How would she get me to *want* to go to Georgetown? What trump card would she play to get me to deal?

By May, the whole community was looped into our ludicrous, First World ordeal. I got calls from aunts, uncles, grandparents, strangers—even my mom's boss, who reminded me helpfully that he had never made *his* mother cry. Things began to reach the boiling point. We circled the now-tired arguments—Georgetown was the superior academic institution; I was just following my girlfriend, Stephanie, to Miami—when my mom sensed an opening. She knew I had her just about beat, so she called on someone to come to her defense. A man of uncommon sense.

Larry King was one of my first great fears in life. Something about the dotted map behind him, his suspenders, and those pointy shoulders spooked me. One of my earliest memories is covering my eyes when he came on TV each night. Fortunately, I had gotten over that particular phobia when, after our fight that May, my mom caught wind of Larry's guest for the evening: Phil McGraw, PhD, better known as Dr. Phil, psychologist of the airwaves. There they were, two old men who—despite their personalities and looks—had become TV mainstays ready to field questions from the troubled public.

"I'm calling in," my mom said matter-of-factly. This was her trump card. Here it was, her fake tattoo.

"Go ahead. I'm sure you'll get through," I answered sarcastically.

The first caller was distressed, seeking counsel from Dr. Phil about the sudden loss of her husband. The next caller recounted life in his double-wide trailer. He just couldn't get ahead, and things weren't going well with his wife. I was confident that my mom, stuck on hold, did not have a problem that rose to the same level. We were safe, until:

"Hello, Philadelphia!" the suspendered king of dry CNN talk bellowed to my mom. "You're on the air!"

Stunned, she began to delineate our dilemma: "My wonderful boy Patrick has been accepted to Georgetown and the University of Miami . . . whatever shall we do?"

Double-wides and death be damned: Where should Pat go to school? They cut my mom off before she could explain the crux of her concern: Wasn't it a parent's choice, especially if they were paying? Didn't it seem like I was simply following Stephanie; that I hadn't given it real thought? And what about DC? They wanted me in DC.

Too bad. It was Larry's show. And he was ready to judge.

Larry explained that although he never went to college, Miami held a special place in his heart. He got his start in radio in South Florida. Miami, he thought, should have the edge.

The doctor chimed in next: "Ya say he's a good boy, right? It's not like he's gonna be runnin' drugs outta Colombia." Apt reasoning, I thought, and Dr. Phil moved to conclude: "Pack yer bags because yer headed to Miami. Yer gonna love the stone crabs!"

At this point, my freshly tattooed mom shouted into the phone that Phil was a "quack." Unfortunately, she had already been muted—and I was already on my way upstairs to pack my bags and google stone crabs. Washington, DC, was out. For now.

• • •

My first day as a real White House staffer was February 1, 2011. I moved one room down from my previous spot, to room 183, I think. Toward the end of my internship, I had learned of an opening on staff, and I applied to the most entry-level position available on the White House communications team: media monitor.

The role of the media monitor is simple: Watch the news. Scan the shows. Pull clips. Keep your bosses informed. Much to my surprise, and to the chagrin of some of my office mates, I got the job—joining a tired army of sunlight-deprived kids in their early- to mid-twenties (I was twenty-three); an overworked, ambitious bunch of media monitors strewn about the city and on both sides of the political spectrum.

The White House had one media monitor at a time. My predecessor, Andrew, was a force. He rose at five o'clock and pulled clips, sometimes more than a thousand in a day, until late into the evening. He worked weekends. Andrew was the gold standard of media monitors. A few days before I started, he was written up in the *New York Times* as one of the best monitors across the capital. No pressure, I thought. He seemed to thrive on the news—fueled by breaking bulletins. He never took a day off.

Until one day he was forced to. Probably not surprisingly, Andrew was hospitalized for exhaustion. By the time I started as an intern—a year and a half into the presidency—Andrew had to be on his last legs. The position should really be a one-year gig; a rite of passage to slightly less onerous and very slightly higher-level things.

Still, for my first few weeks, we both monitored the news. On my first day, Andrew sent more than eight hundred clips. I sent three. Matt helpfully alerted the entire office to this tally via email. But I had an excuse: I was busy filling out an SF-86 form, an extensive security document needed for the FBI's official background check, which was still under way—even though I had already been granted clearance to the White House grounds and was officially a White House employee.

The questions weren't particularly difficult to answer. No, I'd never had the impulse to overthrow the government. No, I never knowingly harbored a terrorist. Drug abuser? Nope. I was asked to list every country I had visited and the exact dates of my trip. Suddenly my innocent semester at sea seemed like a liability. The queries seemed endless. And lying on these things is a felony, so I did my best not to misremember anything—there would be consequences, I assumed. Over the next few weeks, I would get texts and calls from friends, friends of friends, and many family members who had just received a visit from the FBI about me.

I was just a media monitor, a professional copy-and-paster who had basically fallen into the gig. But I was learning that the White House was serious business—at all levels—and that the media monitor position was more crucial than I thought. Turns out, it's the lowest-level job with the highest level of name recognition within the White House. As a monitor, your name bombards every consequential member of the administration's in-box all day long. Everybody, from the top of the administration down, gets to know you—or at least an idea of who you are. I went by the name Pat, and for the first few months, a good portion of the staffers I worked with, but never saw, thought I was a woman.

You were expected to start sending emails the moment you entered the office—an initial morning batch of a couple hundred, including online articles from the *New York Times,* the *Wall Street Journal,* the *Washington Post*, and dozens of others—before allowing for a quick midmorning break. Eventually I got the hang of things and took over as the only monitor so that Andrew could move on.

At the request of—okay, maybe with the approval of—one of my bosses, Jen Psaki, I started my mornings later than Andrew, something that didn't sit well with many in the West Wing who were used to the clips pouring in around five o'clock. Mornings were stressful. I darted into the office, always feeling behind already, anxious every second I wasn't sending a clip. But once I got out the first dozen news items, I hit a rhythm and got one to two per minute to the team. Only then did I feel that the day was under way.

For security reasons, the White House complex would restart all of our computers every few days. I dreaded the weekly reboot. Because they were essentially antiques, and due to the sophisticated security measures taken, our computers often took twelve to fifteen minutes to restart fully. And I couldn't plan to wake up earlier that one day each week, because they often varied the reboot day. So there I would be—sitting in front of a loading screen—getting no credit whatsoever for being at work. Would Axelrod or Pfeiffer or Jarrett think I was slacking off?

After all, I just wanted people to think I was doing a decent job—and I had no intention to go back from where I'd come.

• • •

"Good work, Pat-rick. Really nice, Pat-rick."

I nodded, smiled at the recognition of my work, and finished pushing the box of plaid princess line jumpers across the concrete floor.

During summer break from the University of Miami, I took a job in a warehouse owned by my parents' close friend and our next-door neighbor, Sean, whose office in Northeast Philadelphia was on the same road as my dad's bicycle warehouse. I had worked at my dad's place the summer before, so a second warehouse gig made sense. I was an experienced bike-box mover; how much harder could school uniforms be?

Apparently, it was a snap, given that Caroline, my supervisor, was heaping accolades on me right from the jump. Caroline was a pleasant, middle-aged woman who regularly wore company products: school sweaters, khakis, plaid skirts, the works. She was seriously impressed with my abilities and seemingly wanted to be crystal clear in her compliments. She kept using my name—my full first name—even when it was just the two of us in the room.

"That's perfect, Pat-rick," she said as I slid the last of the morning's boxes into place and prepared for an outdoor lunch in the sunshine of a warm June afternoon. Contented with a job well done, I found a shaded spot below the lone tree off the corner of the parking lot, took a seat Indian-style in the grass, and ate alone in silence.

Sean, a successful, sarcastic man with a penchant for pranks, caught a glimpse of me as he walked to his car. My first memory of Sean, who had become a very close family friend, was "Mischief Night" many years earlier. He arrived at our house decked out in black, clutching a gasoline-powered leaf blower with a special gizmo attachment that held a roll of toilet paper in order to get maximum height and coverage while TP'ing an unsuspecting neighbor's trees or house. For those who didn't grow up in the Northeast, Mischief Night is the evening before Halloween when young people—in my case, supported by older people like Sean and my dad—went out and did dumb things.

Sean waved to me as I finished my sandwich under the tree. I returned the friendly gesture from my seated place in the grass, and he shouted across the lot:

"You look like a dim-witted Buddha!"

If only he understood how well I was doing inside. I knew as soon as Caroline reported back to Sean, he'd have to eat his words. Dim-witted? Yeah, right!

I largely kept to myself the rest of my first week, put my head down and did the work, determined to keep impressing Caroline one box at a time. Finally, on Friday morning, I thought it was time to shove my success in Sean's face. I burst into his corner office and provided an update.

"Caroline has been pretty positive so far. I could be looking at a promotion really quick."

"Is that right?" Sean asked, propping his feet up on his desk.

"Just don't get too comfortable in this office; that's all I'm saying." Then I attempted to pull off that quick double-knock-on-the-door thing as I departed, but it didn't quite work; and I lingered a second too long after the double knock.

Sean stared at me. "Why are you knocking?"

"No, I was just trying to—it was like a see-you-later type thing."

Despite the stumble in Sean's office, my success continued that afternoon with Caroline. She kept up her flattery, as well as her overuse and painful overpronunciation of my name. Eventually I took a break in the back of the warehouse in the middle of that Friday afternoon. The cavernous room was silent but for the hiss of the industrial lighting overhead. Suddenly that hiss was punctuated by a familiar sound: flip-flops thumping against the floor. Sean was en route, getting closer. Walking with Caroline, he approached with a smile.

"So, Caroline—end of week one—how's he doing?"

Caroline's eyes lit up. "You would be amazed, Sean!"

I was safe. *Who's the dim-witted Buddha now?* I asked myself smugly. She continued:

"Patrick's doing as well as anybody else here. He's fitting in and keeping up and—"

"Caroline, let me stop you right there," Sean, in his gravelly voice, interjected with a smirk. "Pat's not actually intellectually challenged."

My jaw nearly hit the concrete floor. Caroline was mortified. Sean had told the staff to watch after me, that I was "special." It was a con that had lasted five days. I had no idea what I would do next, but I knew I needed to get out of the warehouse and find a place where I wasn't the punch line to everybody's jokes.

• • •

At the White House, a few months in, I finally felt like I was getting the hang of things. By then, Andrew had been promoted. I had developed a routine and was beginning to get a sense for the way the news worked. What interested people, what mattered, what didn't. And sometimes, most importantly, what shouldn't have mattered but would likely catch fire online. That was the rapid-response part of the job, sniffing out future problems, regardless of how inane, and getting them in front of the staffers best equipped to handle them.

Often, that staffer was my boss, Dan Pfeiffer, one of President Obama's most trusted advisors. Ultimately, Dan was responsible for dealing with anything said about the president—online, in print, or on TV—which made him very invested in the media monitor. Dan had served as an intern in the Clinton administration, and, when I started, was the White House communications director. As monitor, I saw him only for short gusts when he would burst into the offices of the EEOB, making his rounds to visit the staff that didn't sit in the West Wing. He was typically funny, clearly very smart, and seemed to switch from socially awkward to the witty life of the party with ease. He always had a take on the topic of the day, and it was usually better than yours. Ultimately, Dan was the archetype "Obama guy." Hardworking to the point of physical consequences, Dan rose at four in the morning and eventually had a ministroke at a dinner with reporters. (He's fine.) Like his boss, the president, he loved basketball, hip-hop, being right, and electoral politics.

I didn't know any of that initially. In those early days, I remember Dan mostly for walking swiftly, just ahead of a staff assistant, Jimmy, who dripped of competence and meticulousness. Like most assistants at the White House, Jimmy helped run his principal's life at the expense of his own. Jimmy was dedicated, determined, and—I would learn—in need of a new gig.

Dan was constantly clutching a rectangular white notecard with "White House" written in regal blue lettering at the top. Jimmy used to review the card often. I would come to know that those cards, usually filled with a dozen or more meetings he needed to attend that day, were highly coveted over in the West Wing. Staffers scrambled to get their hands on them—status symbols, really—hoping to jot their to-do lists on the matte-finish cards rather than on the smudge-inducing glossy cards. I'd learn the difference later. For now, my focus was on my computer. The news.

One of the more common DC news cycles—and a personal favorite of mine—went like this: newsworthy event is reported on; reported event is reacted to by pundits and columnists; reaction to reported event is reported on and reacted to by other pundits and columnists.

A few years before I started, this cycle could have taken a week to play itself out. In fact, the head of the White House Research Department, Ben, used to tell stories of his time as a media monitor in Washington. This was before the internet took hold. As he told it, he would be up through the night, literally cutting out (you know, with scissors) headlines and stories from newspapers, gluing them together, copying them, and leaving stacks on his coworkers' desks before dawn. When he would tell these archaic tales, I imagined him in an old-timey plaid hat with the tiny brim that grandpas like to wear, ink splashed across a pair of worn overalls. The guy is only ten years older than I am, but in the age of Twitter, it felt like there was an eternity between us. You see, while that usual cycle—event, reaction, reaction to reaction—would take days just a few years before, now, thanks to Twitter, it cycles through in just a few hours. Over and over. Every day. No wonder Andrew was hospitalized.

The job was already beginning to wear on me when I learned that the FBI still hadn't even concluded my background check. In late March, I got a call from Sean, who relayed to me that he had just been interviewed. He said the agent asked several questions about my girlfriend's family, but other than that, the conversation was straightforward. Stephanie's family is Italian American. They retired early following the sale of their successful, eponymous family business: a supermarket chain called Genuardi's. Sean assured me that the investigator's questions were likely nothing—completely standard—and that the rest of the interview went very well. In truth, I was thrilled that the FBI had interviewed him; that my position was consequential enough to merit federal investigation. It was the ultimate revenge for his prank in the warehouse, I thought.

A couple days later, just as I sent out the last of the morning clips, Stephanie called.

"Pat! They're here with guns, the FBI! They're searching my parents' house."

I exploded out of my seat and rushed into the hallway as Stephanie continued, frantic: “They keep talking about the Mob. I don’t know what to do!”

I was shaking. This couldn’t be right. But I knew that the FBI had been asking questions a few days before, poking around. I didn’t have any answers for Stephanie but promised to get to the bottom of it. I hung up, knowing no recourse. I told one of my supervisors what was going on. I needed to be away from my desk for a little bit. There would be no clips for a few minutes. I had some news of my own to deal with. My supervisor, shocked, told me to keep her posted. I realized who I needed to call.

Sean picked up on the first ring. “What exactly did the FBI ask you about the Genuardis?” I demanded.

“I’m not sure. I don’t think it was anything too serious,” he responded.

“Well, it is serious!” I yelled. “They have guns!”

“Pat, Pat, Pat.” He tried to calm me down, but I was panicking. “Hold on a second.” Then he seemed to click me onto speakerphone. I could hear commotion on his end. His next sentence came out clearly:

“Look at the calendar, jackass.”

I pulled the phone from my cheek and waited for the screen to illuminate. The dateline gave it away. Stephanie was in on it.

April 1, 2011.

My coworkers had seen me fretting, frantically pacing the hall outside our office, shouting into the phone. All for nothing, a joke. It was my biggest embarrassment since asking Matt what a POTUS was shortly after blaring Justin Bieber throughout the office, and

I was frustrated with myself for falling for another Sean prank. I should have had my guard up on April Fools' Day. I was more determined than ever to prove myself a competent, if not good, media monitor. So when the summer of 2011 rolled around, I seized the opportunity to work late; to contribute in a time of supposed crisis.

Washington was mired in the debt ceiling debacle of 2011. For years, raising the debt ceiling had been routine, immune from partisan negotiations. But Republicans had taken back the House the year prior and were intent on upending those economic and political norms. I was told to send every tweet, no matter how seemingly mundane or tangentially related to the debt ceiling debate. The White House needed its most precious commodity: information.

I think Dan had Andrew's hospitalization in mind when he emailed me one night around midnight, telling me to stop sending clips—individual tweets, really—for the night and to get some sleep. I was proud to be a part of the team and grateful to get an email from the boss, but the high of feeling like I was contributing wore off quickly from my perch in the EEOB. It became tiresome, stuck sending endless tweets. It was hard to comprehend that what I did mattered when my job was so straightforward: copy-paste-send. It didn't feel entirely different from moving boxes in a warehouse.

Worst of all, most of the tweets said the same thing—namely, nothing—about an opaque partisan dispute that I was sure would work itself out just like every other manufactured Washington crisis. I didn't know that in the West Wing, they weren't so confident that things would be okay.

Obama would say years later, in his last official interview as president (coincidentally enough, with Dan on his popular White House podcast *Pod Save America*), that this was one of the most frightening, frustrating periods of his presidency. "It was a very realistic possibility," he said, "that we would be in a situation where technically we were in default—in uncharted territory." The votes didn't seem to be there among Republicans to avoid defaulting on the debts of the United States. Jon Favreau, Obama's chief speechwriter for the entire first term, had begun drafting the speech should it happen. Just across the driveway. To Obama, it was the scariest moment of his presidency.

To me, on the other side of West Executive Avenue, directly across from the West Wing, it was hard to get a sense of the gravity. It could be isolating in the EEOB—especially for the media monitor, given that you are essentially tethered to your desk from the moment you enter the building to the minute you race home. It was as if I were watching my favorite show for fifteen hours every day—*Seinfeld*, for instance—only to be reminded periodically that my office was on set, and that the misadventures of Jerry, George, Elaine, and Kramer were taking place all around me every day. I couldn't help feeling like I was some sort of odd mixture—caught between staffer and spectator—as tangential as the tweets I was sending every fifty-five seconds.

On the other hand, many of the EEOB's employees crossed West Exec multiple times a day to check in with the West Wing. That's where you could truly get a sense of how grim things had become. You could measure the depth of concern by the number of closed doors. Such was the scenario in 2011, even if I couldn't sense it from my computer station. Truth be told, I hadn't even seen the president in the six months since I was an intern. But I did what I was told, kept plugging away, clip by clip.

It was during this period that I bumped into Dan while departing the West Wing one night around nine o'clock. I was walking my Fuji bicycle along West Exec, ready to dash down Pennsylvania Avenue toward my apartment near the Capitol, about a fifteen-minute ride, where last night's Domino's pizza was a perfect twenty-two-hours cold. Dan and I made small talk. I didn't think much of it, but I would learn that I made an impression.

A few days later—as I hit my nadir—the White House posted the salaries of all administration employees online. Seven months after the *New York Times* had written glowingly, and deservedly, of my predecessor, the *Atlantic* took an interest in the unique position as well; only this time, I was at the helm, and its take was slightly different than that of the Gray Lady's. The magazine posted a blaring, bold headline that read: "White House Posts Salaries: What's a Media Monitor?" Then, jokingly, it accused the White House of burying this news on a Friday afternoon because we "wanted to give the press the smallest possible window of opportunity for follow-up questions about the White House media monitor, what he does, and why he makes $42,000 a year." You'll note that $42,000 was the minimum salary for the Communications Office at the White House.

It was an embarrassing article, but, hell, at least it was a bit of recognition, which certainly didn't bother me. The thing that did bother me? I wasn't the one to catch the news clip.

Andrew had sent it to me.

That's when I realized I'd never live up to the standard set by my predecessor. It wasn't even his job anymore, and he was still outmonitoring me. I couldn't imagine getting to the point where I'd media monitor myself right into the hospital. And that's what you needed to thrive in the position. My successor, Hannah, had it. Before she was promoted, she did a stint in a cast, her wrist undone by excessive copying and pasting, the repetitive pinky-index action of the CTR+C, CTRL+V. Talent, motivation, enthusiasm. Something was missing for me. I was beginning to long for my days in the warehouse. The sense of accomplishment, of moving hundreds of boxes from one place to another, the ability to see and touch your progress. Looking at my Sent email box didn't provide the same level of pride. Media monitoring, though a fantastic experience and one I am grateful for to this day, never came naturally to me. I wasn't good at it.

Fortunately, sometimes at the White House, you fail up.

Unbeknownst to me, Dan had laid the groundwork for me to move on shortly after our encounter that night on West Exec.

"Pat looks like death," he told his deputy the next morning. "We need to find him a new job."

And so the process of finding me a new position began. The Obama White House, vaunted for many reasons, was not known internally for having a highly functional human resources department—at least in the early years. The typical next step for a media monitor is to researcher, or press assistant, or if you're lucky, press wrangler, which meant sitting on the front lines in the West

Wing and—incomprehensible to me at that time—traveling with the president. I barely spoke about it with friends or family, too worried that I might jinx something; that my bosses would realize that I had no business in the West Wing. Were they truly going to pull me away from my corner in the EEOB and put me right on set? Didn't anybody realize I was an imposter?

You see, I didn't start out working for him in Chicago. I wasn't indoctrinated into Obama World from the start. I wasn't around during his days in Springfield, the capital of Illinois, or in the United States Senate, or even on the 2008 campaign—so I wasn't introduced to Barack Obama the state senator or Barack Obama the US senator. I came to know of Barack Obama the same way the rest of the world did. From thousands of miles away. As the most famous man in the world.

• • •

My nana knew the name Barack Obama before I did.

She was on to his charm, hopeful for his vision, even as I was just trying to get through high school and then college.

Of course, as the 2008 Democratic presidential primaries ramped up, I saw the crowds grow by the day. I watched the nightly news slowly begin to take him more seriously; this upstart underdog from the South Side by way of Hawaii and Indonesia. Yes, I remember where I was when he delivered his first famous convention speech (Cape May, New Jersey) and what I felt—my first flicker of real interest in politics—as he laid out his belief that there are better days ahead. ("Why can't this dude be president?") But beyond those seventeen minutes in July 2004, I didn't think of him until 2007—I was nineteen—when my nana turned down the volume on MSNBC and asked me a question.

"What do you think of Barack?"

I hadn't yet given the upcoming election much thought, but Nana wasn't waiting for me to answer. She tapped her cigarette in her ashtray and told me the way it was going to be.

"Barack is going to be president. I love him. I consider him my son."

• • •

I don't remember well my interviews for the press wrangler position. I know I was nervous to meet the new press secretary. After all, I knew Jay Carney only as the Jay Carney from TV. I hadn't dealt with famous, or at least *DC-famous*, people in the EEOB, and certainly wasn't prepared to be interviewed by one for a job. Hell, I was nervous just walking into the West Wing. It's not something I pictured when Barack Obama caught my attention in 2004, and certainly not what I anticipated for myself when my nana told me about her new "son."

Still, my luck rolled along. All of the conversations were fairly pro forma; I had the inside track on the position. And I got it.

After word had spread that I was moving, I returned to my desk in the EEOB to find a package of stickers: Justin Bieber collectibles. It was a lighthearted jab that made me feel like I was a part of the team; that maybe I had finally broken into Obama World. This was a shot of confidence I would need as I made my way to the West Wing for the first time, a place I would spend more time over the next five years than any apartment or condo I would live in. It would become my new home. I had seen the president a number of times as an intern, but nine months as a staffer in the EEOB, and I had yet to cross paths with him. That was about to change in a big way.

• • •

First, though, Sean was in town and wanted to take me out to dinner to celebrate my promotion. In DC for a meeting with a local high school about its uniform needs, Sean was unusually sincere on the phone with me, genuinely impressed by the promotion and the move to the West Wing. Dinner would be his treat. He'd pick me up in front of the regal Willard Hotel. It's said that the term "lobbyist" is derived from the Willard's lobby, which makes sense given the hotel's prime location between the Capitol and the White House, just a block or two away.

I made my way down Pennsylvania Avenue around eight o'clock, waiting on the corner out front of the Willard. I was wearing a dark suit, like usual. A cab lurched to a stop in front of me, and the back door swung open. I slid in next to Sean, already in the back. He shook my hand formally and stated his name, like we were just meeting.

"Sean. How are you? Patrick, right?"

I guessed he was finally treating me like an adult—maybe the promotion had something to do with it—so I played along. Shook his hand. "I'm doing well," I said. "A little tired."

"I bet so!" he said. "How's the West Wing?"

I was still very much adjusting to the pace of the West Wing, the frenzy of it all. We were halfway down Pennsylvania Avenue, our cab driver clearly speeding. "Ah, you know, it was nuts in there today."

The cab driver, shaking his head in disgust, glanced at me in his rearview mirror as he zigged through traffic, making remarkable time.

Sean asked our driver, "Can you believe this guy works in the West Wing?"

At this point, our driver became very uncomfortable, wanting nothing to do with me or Sean or the conversation. Unlike basically every other cab driver in the city, apparently, ours didn't enjoy talking about politics. So I turned to Sean and focused my answers on him.

"It was a little rough today."

Now the cabbie looked horrified. Undeterred, I continued.

"Everybody was all over me in there."

My head jerked forward as the driver threw the car into park; we were out front of another hotel bar, where we would grab some food and a drink to celebrate. Sean helped me out of the cab, which I found unnecessary. As the cab pulled away, I remarked on how disinterested—disgusted really—our driver seemed about the White House. "He must hate Obama or something."

Then Sean smiled, and my heart sank. He told me that as the cab was rounding the corner to the Willard, he pointed me out—standing on the corner in my suit—and, right before picking me up, told the driver that he was excited and a little nervous:

"I've never picked up a DC prostitute before."

I had gone from the warehouse to the White House, yet I was still the butt of the joke.

2

In the Buffer

We are all on a highway to hell for all of eternity.

—WOMAN ON MEGAPHONE
OUTSIDE THE WHITE HOUSE

Barack Obama burst into our office. He was pissed.

I hadn't seen him like that. Heck, I hadn't seen him at all—not since I was an intern. To me, he was still the figure—from the news and forthcoming textbooks; from the clips I pulled by the thousands—whom I'd heard about in my nana's kitchen and from strangers no matter where on Earth I traveled, the very embodiment of the globe's hope for the future.

"What in the hell is going on?"

Jimmy shot out of his seat the instant the president exploded in, grabbing Dan from his office. "Mr. Pfeiffer!" he exclaimed in a kind of whispered screech. Nobody ever called him Mr. Pfeiffer.

The president was fuming over the ongoing payroll tax cut debate, which had gripped DC. Most pundits agreed that Obama and the Democrats were on the correct side of this one—both in terms of policy, but also, especially, when it came to the optics. Democrats had proposed a tax increase on individuals making more than $1 million per year, while Republicans were allergic to a tax hike on the rich and preferred spending cuts. It was seen—like almost everything between Congress and the White House—as a proxy issue for the next election. Republicans were hesitant to allow POTUS a "win" as the 2012 campaign heated up.

I didn't understand any of that when Obama erupted into our humble bull pen. I was brand new to the place. I had only just crossed West Executive Avenue to the West Wing. I half stood, nearly bowed—I hadn't thought to ask about the proper protocol—and then I noticed that nobody but Jimmy was on his or her feet.

The West Wing was filled with a new cast of characters for me. Bobby sat in front of me. A former college football player, he was the kind of guy who is exceedingly cool from afar but endearingly nerdy when you get to know him. He had a Clark Kent look—tall, square-jawed, trendy glasses—but his love of cats and photography made him feel more approachable. He volunteered during the 2008 Pennsylvania primary in the Press Office under Matt, who, on his first day, asked him to write a media advisory. An hour later, he still hadn't finished, so Matt asked him what was up. Bobby hesitated and then said, "So . . . what's a media advisory?" It wasn't quite so bad as me asking Matt what POTUS stood for while already working at the White House, but Bobby had come a long way from that moment.

Howli sat to my right. She was smart, fun, and—because we started in the West Wing on the same day—sympathetic toward me. A big-sister type. Howli began on the 2008 campaign as an unpaid fellow before graduating to a field organizer in North Carolina. She could talk with equal aplomb about red carpet fashion and issues of voting rights and gerrymandering. She was extremely open—and, whenever possible, I tried to follow her lead.

She and Bobby were doing their best to keep working even as the president propped his hand on the back of Howli's computer and laid down the law for Dan and Jay. I followed suit, sliding as quietly as I could back into my seat. *Look busy*, I thought, as I pulled up a Microsoft Word document and typed a variation on the same fake sentence over and over until the president cooled down.

He wasn't screaming. He didn't need to. He was using his presidential privilege to make a point—raising his voice just a bit. Crystal clear. Message received.

But to me, his words blurred together, sounding a bit like the adults in a *Peanuts* cartoon special whenever Charlie Brown is in the room.

I hadn't been around him much yet. So far, my first week in the West Wing had been overshadowed by the birth of my first niece, Harry's daughter Aubrey, up in Philadelphia. Still, I sensed an odd joy in the president's contained outburst—a glint in his eyes, glad for the opportunity to loosen his tie and vent about Washington. I just hoped desperately that no reporters would amble in at this less than presidential moment.

As a newly minted press wrangler, I was beginning to learn the ways of the West Wing, the White House press corps, and our little piece of real estate perched between the president and the press. I would spend my tenure in the West Wing here. We called it Upper Press, a small suite of shared desks between the James S. Brady Press Briefing Room and the Oval Office, about thirty feet from each, situated somewhere between historically remarkable and utterly regular.

There are a series of four Norman Rockwell paintings that hang on the outer wall of Upper Press. Each frame depicts the scene in the White House waiting room—the West Wing lobby—in the early 1940s, when Franklin D. Roosevelt was commander in chief. As you near the Oval Office: newsmen huddle with an administration official; celebrities of the era hope for face time with the president; military leaders prepare their briefings.

In the fourth and final painting, we see the door to the president crack open.

Just as Rockwell's *So You Want to See the President* illustrates what it's like on the periphery of power, I was beginning to understand that my own story of proximity and history was just getting started as, for the first time, Millennials helped run the country.

I was in frame. Sort of. But I had a lot to learn.

The first thing I gathered was that the reporters who came to the White House each day were free to enter our offices as they pleased. We were a kind of buffer zone between POTUS and the press.

Now, the official meaning of *buffer* within the White House is the space between the president's stage and his audience—typically six to ten feet deep, cordoned off by a bike rack or blue pipe and drape, and built into nearly every presidential event. During my time with the president, the area was filled with the press pool, Secret Service agents—and me. It's the angle from which photographers can get the "hero shot": a from-below portrait of a president or candidate speaking from the podium. During his presidential campaign, Donald Trump often did not let reporters into the buffer because he was not comfortable with the way his chin looked when photographed from below. I doubt President Obama had an opinion one way or the other, but we in the Obama Communications Department—the folks tasked with thinking about such matters—loved that angle and photo. We were blessed with a handsome principal, which made our jobs, superficially at least, somewhat easier. So the buffer was important to us.

And our place in the unofficial buffer of the West Wing was crucial. Just as we encouraged reporters to take up positions by the stage at events and rallies on the road, they often spilled into our workspaces in the West Wing without warning, which is why I was concerned that a journalist would walk in on POTUS as he hammered out his frustrations. To move beyond Upper Press, reporters needed explicit permission, and they required—and rarely received—an escort by a White House staffer. It all added to the complexity of an already bizarre place. The Communications Office and the Press Offices, known as Upper Press and Lower Press, respectively, are situated directly between the president's office and the press corps's stomping grounds—equidistant, a sometimes fuzzy zone of its own that I was still getting used to as the president wrapped up his diatribe.

I noticed Pete Souza, the president's photographer, snapping photos from down the narrow hall, capturing a few of the countless behind-the-scenes moments for which he would become famous. The best of the bunch were turned into "jumbos": blown-up photos of President Obama hung throughout the West Wing and the EEOB. They switched them out every two weeks. There was always a new favorite to look at while walking from meeting to meeting.

Initially, I was alarmed at the president's visit, but it turned quickly into something else. I felt honored to see Barack Obama this way. Gone was the polished politician smiling in front of an adoring crowd. Vanished was that silhouetted figure waving to a world that viewed him at best as a once-in-a-lifetime leader or at worst as a once-in-a-lifetime orator from Kenya—but most certainly not like he was that day in our office. At that moment, he was just a frustrated guy trying to get stuff done. This wasn't artist Shepard Fairey's iconic *Hope* Obama; this was something better.

As quick as he came, he was gone.

The president's visit set our room abuzz. Jay and Dan scurried into Jay's office. "I'll have Josh come up," Howli said, picking up her phone.

Josh Earnest was Jay's principal deputy and almost certainly the next press secretary. He was like everybody's big brother, widely respected for his great hair, clean jokes, and dedication to the president. Josh always had a sense for how to handle the day's problem, no matter how big or small. I once had Josh edit a Yelp review I was thinking of posting about my car dealership. I suspect the president counted on him for slightly more pressing topics.

Josh made his way up in moments and slipped into Jay's office. As Josh closed the door behind him, Jimmy sat down and exhaled a breath he'd seemingly been holding in for minutes. Bobby let out one of his catchphrases, "Whoa, doggy!" and I closed my Word document. My perception of the president had been altered forever. Turns out I wasn't working for some sort of rhetorically gifted robot, naïve as that notion may have been in the first place. I was learning that Barack Obama was something else entirely, something far more complicated and much more impressive.

• • •

Joe Biden was what you would expect—in the best possible sense. On my very first day in the West Wing, somewhat lost, I watched as the vice president approached from down the narrow hall off the main lobby of the West Wing. I froze, a deer in headlights. Quickly, I turned to get out of his way, scooting through the large, dark wooden door to the lobby. I looked back; he was close now. Biden seemed to almost be saying something, but there was no way he was talking to me. He wasn't quite near enough that my holding the door wouldn't have been awkward. Plus, I thought he would be making a left to head down the stairs, not a right into the lobby with me. I continued. The door slammed behind me with a crack that echoed through the lobby.

On the other side of the door, I heard as clear as day: "What? Am I talking to a door here?"

I was mortified. I did not want to get on Biden's bad side. You see, he reminded me a great deal of my own grandfather, my "pop-pop," who is also a close talker and seems to know everyone, the de facto mayor no matter where he is. Like the vice president, Pop-Pop likes to grab your arm when he talks to you. Quick with a quip. Ready to route the conversation back to being Irish. Because of these similarities—or more likely in spite of them—Biden was on my nana's short list of acceptable politicians. In fact, she loved him. Maybe more than my actual pop-pop, her husband.

So I loved him too. It was hard not to. The vice president had a saying—one among many, but this was his most important—that his mother taught him: "Nobody is better than you, but you're better than nobody." From what I saw, he lived that creed every day, from the way he gave the time of day to everybody, no matter his or her status, to the bathroom he chose to use. Sometimes I would end up at the urinal next to him in the West Wing basement lobby bathroom—a four-stall, two-urinal affair with low ceilings and white marble—one level below Upper Press and the Oval Office. Exiting that same bathroom one afternoon, I watched as President Obama, back from a political speech, sauntered down the hall. Suddenly Biden burst into the basement lobby entrance, calling out, "Hey, boss!"

He darted down the hall to catch him and put his arm on Obama's back.

"That was great out there today!"

"Thanks, Joe. I had fun," the president responded as they rounded the corner together. This was years before the Obama-Biden memes took the internet by storm, but the veep bounding down the hall after his "boss" was a meme come to life. It was a charming reminder of why people love the guy so much—and why I hated offending him, especially on my first day.

After slamming the door in his face, I did the only thing I could think of. I ran back to my half desk in Upper Press and emailed his press secretary to apologize. She said not to worry about it—that I'd get used to things like that.

• • •

For an office space no more than thirty feet from the Oval, Upper Press is ordinary, uninspiring, and cramped. Composed of three offices, four desks out in the open, and nine people, things were tight. In the bull-pen area where I sat for five and a half years—I'm proud to say longer than anybody else in the Obama administration—there were four desks, two of which were shared, as well as a bastard of a printer, a fax machine that hadn't been used in years, and multiple TVs tuned permanently to the quad: a White House station that bombarded us simultaneously with CNN, Fox News, MSNBC, and Bloomberg News.

I would find that our office fit in with the rest of the West Wing, where square footage hardly squared with the complexity or the prominence of the place. Even as the need for more offices and additional personnel grew over the years, the building's footprint has remained stubbornly the same. It's a maze of narrow, "jumbo"-lined windowless hallways connecting understated waiting areas to small offices and overcrowded conference rooms.

Occasionally, older journalists would meander up our tight hall—taking full advantage of the fact that none of us had doors—and recount what notable people had sat where and when. They particularly liked to remind Howli that she was sitting in Diane Sawyer's old seat, and that George Stephanopoulos was right here, and Rahm Emanuel over there.

"I heard John F. Kennedy used to work over there, too," I wanted to say while pointing toward the Oval.

The Office of the White House Press Secretary, which is one of the largest in the West Wing, is the exception to the cramped rule, featuring a couch, working fireplace, large desk, table, and chairs, as well as a wall of digital clocks displaying the current times in hotspots across the world, from Cairo to Moscow, to Beijing, to Jerusalem. That's where we gathered as a group for morning meetings, staff parties, and special occasions such as State of the Union addresses or to watch election returns.

The deputy communications director and the communications director each had significantly smaller offices, despite the fact that the communications director outranks the press secretary. At first, it was hard for me to tell where everybody ranked; all I knew was that everybody outranked me. Bobby and Matt often asked Dan if they were technically allowed to fire me. His answer normally depended on how the day was going, but "You're fired, Pat" became a familiar refrain around the West Wing.*

* Similarly, writing "Friends, colleagues, Pat" became a frequent way to start an email. And saying it became a traditional method of entering a room.

So Dan was ultimately in charge, but in our world, it made more sense for the press secretary to occupy the bigger office, as he spent his mornings being briefed by between four and eight deputies and assistants such as Amy Brundage, who before becoming a deputy communications director was responsible for press about the economy (no small task in the early days of the Obama administration), and Ned Price, who was in charge of national security press. Matt and Bobby were a part of those prebriefings, too. They would volley mock questions back and forth in preparation for the daily press briefing just down the hall, through Lower Press and past the sliding blue door to the podium in the Press Briefing Room.

Lower Press was the slightly grungier—though they would say the "tougher"—version of Upper Press. They had three offices, too, but those doors slid; no hinge. In the winter, their heater never worked, and in the summer, mosquitoes loved Lower Press. Those who sat there were beholden to a large, automatic sliding door that opened to another automatic door that swung open to the Colonnade, known mostly for famous photos of American presidents walking with leaders from around the world discussing affairs of state. It's a grand, stately walkway, befitting the business that gets done on it.

But when the president departed from or returned to the South Lawn via Marine One, the Colonnade was also the corridor for the fuel fumes that wafted from the helicopter up the Colonnade and into Lower Press, swamping the eight or so staffers in its stench.

In the past, Lower Press had been described in the media as a kind of frat house—a young men's club—but by the time I moved over to Upper Press from the EEOB, the gender balance had roughly equaled out in our sister office down the hall. Josh and Amy, two of Jay's most crucial deputies, had offices there. Matt—the Matt who knew me as the guy who loved Justin Bieber and didn't know what a POTUS was—had moved in. Marie and Antoinette (yes, these are their real names) sat next to each other as you descended into Lower Press.

Marie, Antoinette, and I had started as interns and fortuitously made our way over to the West Wing. Antoinette, from the Bronx, was often affectionately referred to as a "wise Latina" and sometimes as a "saucy Latina" by her colleagues. I knew her as the staffer who understood how to work the system. If you needed something accomplished—from better food at the mess to better press for the president—Antoinette wasn't going to let anything get in the way of getting it done. She ended every day with the nonironic pronouncement "It's been a pleasure serving the American people with you today." Marie, the pride of Cranston, Rhode Island, was a whip-smart Duke University graduate with a hummus obsession and a—perhaps related—perennial stomachache. We would become wrangling partners for the 2012 campaign, traveling together on each trip, for every stump speech, "OTR" (on-the-run, or unannounced) stop, or closed-press fund-raiser. She was beloved around the White House and among the press—reporters had to do their best not to groan audibly when they'd learn that I was their minder instead of Marie.

Jimmy made the quick trip down the ramp from Upper to

Lower Press often, because they had the lower-tech printer that was more suitable for reprinting Dan's ever-evolving schedule card. After POTUS's visit, Dan's day was blowing up, and a reprint was in order. Dan and Jimmy shared an archetypal boss-assistant relationship in the West Wing. Like so many West Wing duos, theirs was a bond built on shared anxiety, mutual fear, and—ultimately—friendship.

Most assistants in the West Wing last roughly eighteen months to two years before they move on. As the third year starts, a psychological wall seems to come down. Frustrations once manifested in hushed whispers and hidden eye rolls come to light through slammed phones and abrupt exits. Scheduling changes are taken as a personal affront, and adjustments made only begrudgingly. For the most part, White House senior staffers did a good job of recognizing the wall and doing right by their assistants: promoting them internally or throwing their considerable weight behind their candidacy for an external gig.

Dan had seen that I was at that point on West Exec. He used to say often that it was important to take care of the junior staff "to prevent a coup." It was getting to such a point for Jimmy, too, though he did his best to hide it. Jimmy, who seemed always to have a sense for trajectory, related a story to us once. He was eleven, and upon completing the school year, he approached his subpar teacher—pencil case surely in hand—and said, "The most just thing to come out of this year is the fact that I will move on, and you will stay here." Suffice it to say, Jimmy was struggling to rein in rampant frustration at this point in his seemingly stagnant tenure. Smart and driven as he was, Jimmy was ready to put his talents to more substantive use than scheduling, no matter how important that scheduling may have been. He tried to cover: he was as chirpy and cheerful on the outside as he was infuriated and foiled on the inside.

Back from Lower Press, he settled into his seat, largely hidden behind his massive computer screen. Trying to dust off his irritation at yet another reprint, he asked, "How was your weekend?" and began reorienting his mug of razor-sharp pencils. Jimmy never used the No. 2s, but apparently the chief of staff had once said that those with sharpened pencils were to be taken note of. Jimmy had dozens.

"Oh, it was pretty good, thanks," I replied without volleying the question back to him. Not because I was rude, but because I already had a pretty good idea of how his weekend had been.

As I delivered my canned response, I teed up an email to some coworkers. The subject line contained only a period, a part of the language in the West Wing. It conveyed that the body of the email was going to be snarky and best not to be opened in front of others. Into the body of the note, I typed:

"It's Tuesday."

Yes, Jimmy had a habit of continuing to ask how your weekend was well into the week. Late Wednesday afternoon remains his official record. Rumors swirl that the question was posed midmorning on a Thursday once, but that's something I can neither confirm nor deny. I thought better of sending the note, what with the Presidential Records Act mandating that work emails be stored and eventually released publicly.

It can be easy, even for the most earnest employee, to forget when chained to a desk fifteen hours per day that said desk occupies some of the most valuable real estate in the world. It happened to me. It happened to everybody. That's why visits from the president—even when he was pissed—were so vital: they provided a kick in the pants. A reminder of where we were and why.

• • •

"Got any snacks?" Pete Souza bellowed from down the hall, camera in hand.

We always had treats because reporters were constantly dropping them off. They tended to pile up on top of the fax machine that never got used. Cupcakes, donuts, rum cake, cookies, and the like. The holidays were the best—or some would say the worst—when we would be showered with chocolates. The Russian reporter used to bring vodka; one time he brought a bottle with Barack Obama's face on it. Howli asked if we ought to get it swept for listening devices. Jay, who'd worked as a reporter for *Time* magazine in Russia, burst out cackling. "Where would they hide a bug in vodka?"

I laughed thinking of the Russians listening in. This was a few years before we realized just how active the Russians aimed to be at our highest levels of government.

One of our favorite photographers, Doug, brought his famous pretzels with Hershey's Kisses baked right in. Word spread quickly through the West Wing when the pretzels were in play.

"These don't have nuts, right?" Pete tried to confirm as he grazed through piles of boxes containing chocolates and candies. He popped a piece in his mouth and headed for the hallway. "I love it when he gets fired up like that!" he said with a sly smile, referencing the president's earlier flare-up.

As Pete exited, Brian, the director of Oval Office Operations, swung through the door to our office, the one that connects to the hallway outside the Roosevelt Room and the restrooms. Not the one I sometimes shared with the vice president, but the single men's and women's restrooms situated midway between the Oval Office and Upper Press.

Brian, always dressed impeccably, was the unofficial arbiter of style around the West Wing. Officially, he was charged with ensuring that the president's in-house events ran smoothly and that the decorum—from the Oval Office to the East Room—was upheld.

"Jesus, who's been in the men's room recently?" he called out, swinging the door open like Kramer bursting onto set. "Disgusting!" It was becoming a thing. Brian was determined to root out the West Wing pooper.

Schultz sauntered in next, grossed out. "I have a flag about the men's restroom," he said, which sent Brian sprinting back into the hallway to get a handle on things. A "flag" was something that could become a thing, and a "thing" was code for a "problem." And when a flag became enough of a thing, there was only one person to call.

Eric Schultz was the White House fixer. He relished—indeed,

encouraged—the inevitable comparisons to Kerry Washington's character on the TV drama *Scandal*, the male version of Olivia Pope. Truth is, he was talented enough for it to be so, but for those of us who dealt with him daily, we knew him as a lovable combination of Dwight Schrute from *The Office* infused with the wiles of Dan Egan from *Veep*. In fact, the folks who worked at *Veep* met with Schultz before their show aired to nail the eccentricities of Washington's elite. Schultz rushed through personal pleasantries so perfunctorily that they weren't pleasant at all. He loved perks and was uncomfortable around babies. Like many Washingtonians, he could be transactional by nature, but he had a good heart, and he was as gifted and sophisticated a press person as you could find anywhere. When things went haywire, the White House often turned to Schultz. He would know what to do, which is why he was a regular member of the "red teams" that popped up in preparation for complicated rollouts or in the wake of pseudoscandals. He had the right combination of drive, discretion, and decency—mixed with an entertaining flair for the dramatic.

Noticing the open box of candy, Schultz continued, calling out, "Did I get screwed out of snacks again?" Throughout his tenure, Eric was known for simultaneously trolling for treats around the West Wing and for his fruitless pursuit of a personal trainer across DC who would be willing to put up with his hectic schedule.

Velz, a persnickety press assistant famous for his eye rolls reflecting a thinly veiled sense of superiority, and for overseeing the communications interns, sighed. "They're from the interns."

"And what am I, chopped liver?" Schultz demanded.

"Can you even name an intern, Schultz?" Howli asked.

"No, but that's because none has ever made an impression on me," he replied with his signature head swivel and a quick check of his watch. A nervous tic.

"Schultzy, I was one of your interns," Velz reminded him. This warranted a major eye roll.

Without missing a beat, and with the knack for spin that made him so valuable, Schultz retorted: "And I don't want to take all of the credit, but look how well you turned out!"

"There it is!" Desiree interjected. "A white man trying to claim credit for a minority's success." (Velz's mother is from Thailand.) Desiree was my desk mate and good friend—though neither of us would admit it. She started with the Obamas as an intern very early on and was a standout member of the advance team before moving into her role as a wrangler and, later, as a special assistant in the West Wing. An African American woman my age, Desiree had a habit of turning her quick wit on me.

Upper Press was a diverse work environment, though no thanks to me. For a few years, aside from the press secretary, I was the only white guy working there. And for the duration of my time, women outnumbered men. Diversity in our workplace never seemed forced. It felt organic, like the pool of talent drawn to President Obama came from every background imaginable. Our differences were our strength, but they also provided plenty of opportunities to call out one another, to erupt in mock indignation, or to have a little fun at one another's—or our own—expense.

There was an openness to talking about race in the office, and there were many jokes we could all get into comfortably. But there were some we couldn't, and Desiree was particularly skilled at screeching the conversation to a halt when I overstepped, or, more frequently, when she could pretend I did for the good of the room. I was the foil, after all.

"Yeah, Schultz, do you really feel comfortable taking any of the credit?" I asked. "I'd say that's red-zone material, right, Desiree?"

Red zone is what somebody would inevitably announce when things were going south in Upper Press; when we were veering into awkward or potentially offensive territory. Now, given that I was considered a repeat offender, Desiree kept a Post-it note between us titled "Red Zone." She tallied—often unfairly, to my mind—each time I crossed the verbal line. I was desperate to get somebody other than myself a tally.

"No, Pat. This is one thing that you—as a straight, white, privileged man—do not get to be in charge of. You don't dictate tallies to me. In fact, that in and of itself is red zone!"

Schultz, foraging through the food, ignored us both and turned to Howli. "I have something for your boss. It's timely, so if you could get me a few minutes, that'd be great. 'Kay, thanks."

"He's in the Situation Room. And this better not be about Louie."

"Totes! T-Y, T-Y!" Schultz shouted to Howli as he dashed down to his small office in Lower Press, donut hole in hand.

Louie is Schultz's dog.

• • •

Bo and Sunny, the First Dogs, liked to rustle around what we called the "burn bags": they looked like trash bags, after all, and we threw a lot of uneaten food from the press into our regular trash cans. These free-standing brown paper bags with burnt orange lines zigging and zagging around them were strewn throughout all of our offices. They were meant to collect our work-relevant papers, especially anything that was sensitive or classified. When we ran out of use for a particular document, record, or page of notes, we'd "burn-bag it." That was a misnomer, however, as the glorified trash bags weren't all sent off to be scorched into oblivion. Some turned into a catch-all for relevant and semirelevant documents that we didn't know how to discard.

The two Portuguese water dogs had free rein of the place, bounding up and down the stairs, barking their way through the Outer Oval Office and into Upper Press. During the day, when the First Family wasn't in the residence, Dale, a longtime, trusted employee of the White House grounds, helped to mind them. As head groundskeeper, he was always on the move, which made him a perfect fit for helping to tire out the dogs. Sometimes they got loose, though, without Dale close behind, and went foraging for food.

Bo had done just that, inspecting the trash can by my desk, sniffing the remnants of a "Chocolate Freedom": an extravagant chocolate lava cake with soft-serve vanilla ice cream in a cup on the side, prepared by the White House Navy Mess. (Upon ordering one for himself after his famous interview with President Obama on the internet talk show *Between Two Ferns*, comedian Zach Galifianakis asked if the Chocolate Freedom was named after Obama himself. It wasn't. Rumor had it that it was made of French chocolate, and in the madness surrounding "freedom fries" and France's opposition to the invasion of Iraq, the George W. Bush White House deemed it the Chocolate Freedom.) We looked for any excuse to order them: somebody's last day, a birthday, whatever.

I lunged for Bo the instant I saw him getting too close to the Freedom, determined not to be the staffer responsible for killing America's First Dog. Schultz popped in as Bo was leaving, sans chocolate. "How come I can't bring Louie into the West Wing?"

"Because you were never elected president of the United States, Schultz," Bobby reminded him.

I liked when Schultz bore the brunt of the office's sharp sarcasm and acerbic wit. Usually, I was the primary and, most would say, easiest target, but Schultz's misadventures were often a nice distraction for my office mates.

"Your boss still isn't back?"

"I'm sorry, Schultz," Howli said. "Jay's still in the Sit Room. He's getting briefed on Syria, but I'm sure your problem is just as important."

I was ready to lay into Schultz—to ask specifically what he needed and make fun of him. Surely, it couldn't be as important as Syria, and, more likely, it was a ridiculous request or pet project. But before I could, Jay walked in, back from the Situation Room. Matt followed behind him from Lower Press.

"Hey, you guys ever notice who Pat looks like?" Jay asked.

What movies are out right now? I wondered to myself. Maybe he had seen a movie star the night before who reminded him of me. Who would it be? I was kind of excited to find out.

"Bashar al-Assad."

That didn't sound right.

"Whoa, whoa, whoa—wait a minute," I said.

Bobby pulled up a photo of the Syrian dictator. Jay, Matt, and Josh gathered around.

"Holy shit, you're right," said Matt, delighted at yet another opportunity to mock me.

When a problematic story hits the press, there's an immediate decision to be made in Upper and Lower Press: respond, let it be, or wait and see. If you think the story is a blip, that it will wash away within the next news cycle, it's best not to give it extra oxygen and more life. Better to leave it alone, to die out in the crowded news environment all by itself. Now, if you think the story has "legs," that its impact will be more meaningful and destructive, it's best to respond quickly.

I knew immediately that Jay's joke was a problematic narrative. And I could tell by the response of my Upper Press colleagues that it wasn't burning itself out anytime soon. It had legs, so to speak. I took the first approach. I responded immediately. A flat-out denial.

"No way!" I declared. "I am far better-looking than he is. This is a joke, right?"

"I can kind of see it," Howli added sheepishly. That's when I knew this would truly stick, and that I was in trouble. Howli was usually protective of me, quick to give me the benefit of the doubt and play good cop.

"You're like the handsome version," she added, trying to make me feel better.

"Much more handsome," I insisted.

"You know he's also a brutal dictator," Bobby said.

"Okay, can we at least say I'm the handsome, nondictator version of Assad?" I pleaded, just hoping for a correction at this point.

"Nope. Sorry, Bashar," Jay said, laughing all the way into his office.

Bo scampered back to my desk as Jay closed the door, but somebody shooed him away. "The First Dog shouldn't be associated with a ruthless dictator."

• • •

My Uncle Bob knew all about the power of presidential pets.

In the mid-1990s, he volunteered every Wednesday in the Eisenhower Executive Office Building, where he read, sorted, and coded mail for President Bill Clinton. There was one permanent staffer in the group, and the rest, like my Uncle Bob, were volunteers—teachers, police officers, veterans—just hoping to help out. After a few hours of reading and cataloguing, the volunteers would grab a bite to eat at a local bar. Then my Uncle Bob would drive back up to Philadelphia, arriving home around two in the morning. The trip was worth it to him. He loved the idea of playing a part, however small, at the White House.

Still, he sometimes needed a reminder about what he was really doing there, so he approached the permanent staffer and asked him if he ever got to see the president.

"I saw President Carter once," the man said with a smile. *Oh, brother,* Uncle Bob thought. This did not portend much of a chance for his next ask, but he plowed ahead anyway.

"Well, it's really cool here, and I love it, but do you think President Clinton might ever come up here, say hello? I think it might mean a lot to the group."

"No, I don't think so," the staffer replied.

And just like that, Bob went back to work. *Worth the shot*, he thought as he continued chipping away at the pile of mail in front of him. By the end of the next Wednesday's session, my uncle had largely forgotten his request and was just happy to be involved, when the staffer asked for everyone's attention. "Excuse me, everybody." Before heading out the door to their usual spot for late-night food and a story or two, the group turned back intently.

"I have some exciting news."

Now he really had Uncle Bob's attention.

"And I know Bob's going to be particularly happy about this. We have a very special guest coming next week . . ."

The other volunteers looked at Bob, sharing smiles. He was practically bursting at the seams. My uncle adjusted his tie, ready to make a quick statement of his own after the staffer completed his announcement. *My request got to the president*, he thought, astounded.

"Socks the cat will be stopping by!"

You would think they might have been disappointed, but you

would be wrong. The group of volunteers cheered, a high five or two slapped out, and they departed for the evening—excited for what the next week would bring. Everybody dressed a little bit better than usual the following Wednesday. Uncle Bob wore his newest tie. Everybody brought a camera. They were distracted reading letters that night, shifting anxiously in their seats. Finally, the door creaked open, and a young female staffer from the West Wing entered with a crate. It was the same kind of crate Uncle Bob used to drag his cat to the shore in the back of his sedan.

The young woman popped open the cage, and the critter crawled out—black and white with green eyes, just like they had seen on TV. The woman sat on a chair with Socks on her lap, like Santa Claus. The volunteers assembled into an orderly line, ready to crouch down and get their photograph taken with the famous feline. It was ridiculous, but the team was hypnotized. Socks was something, anything—a tangible piece of history. He was the president's cat!

The room was buzzing even after Socks had long departed. But as the afterglow burned off, Uncle Bob realized the whole thing was absurd. That didn't stop him from recounting the story repeatedly. In fact, I remember as a little kid on the way to first or second grade hearing my mom excitedly retell Uncle Bob's close encounter with the First Cat. I used to brag about Uncle Bob's Socks visit at recess, probably to Stephanie back in grade school.

Now I was chasing Bo out of my trash can, passing him on the Colonnade, and staging "BOTRs"—first dog drop-bys for special guests or volunteers, not unlike the Socks the cat fiasco. Another reminder, albeit a furrier, less imposing one than Obama himself, that I wasn't in any old office—and that despite the remarkably familiar nature of our interoffice dynamics, we weren't pushing paper at Dunder Mifflin in Scranton.

"Could you imagine if the press knew that Syria's dictator was sitting thirty feet from the president?" Bobby asked me with a glint behind those glasses.

No matter how embarrassed I felt as I continued to get labeled as the doppelgänger for one of the world's most evil men, I knew that I was someplace special.

3

Lower Press

Where the press is free and every man able to read, all is safe.
—THOMAS JEFFERSON

Peter Velz was stationed temporarily in Lower Press. We needed him on the front lines fending off the deluge of requests rushing in from reporters. They were coming in fast, sliding quickly through the blue door from the Briefing Room. One journalist seemed more agitated than the next. Everybody wanted a word. An explanation. It was a time of great stress in the West Wing.

It was time for our annual holiday party.

Returning from the brief Thanksgiving break at the end of November always proved one of those I-can't-believe-I-work-here moments. Year after year, as I would walk into the West Wing lobby, fresh from home in Philadelphia, the fragrance of the newly cut Christmas trees and looping garland would hit me: Christmas at the White House. It was hard not to get into the spirit. Volunteers from across the country, mostly moms in aprons and holiday sweaters, scurried from room to room decorating the People's House.

Like Manhattan's Rockefeller Center in December, anticipation was in the air—a keenness to mark the year's end. Thanksgiving was an appetizer. A real break was in sight. Soon the president would be wheels up for Hawaii. But first we had to get through the three-week slog. Washington would struggle to finish its business, and the White House would host two parties every day—for press, representatives, celebrities, staff, or stakeholders (a DC term for a bunch of people of differing degrees of bearing)—each afternoon and evening.

We in the Press Office and the communications shop were responsible for two of those parties: one primarily for print reporters and the other mostly for broadcast television reporters.

As was the case every previous year, space for our receptions was tight; we couldn't accommodate everyone. Still, every member of the press wanted an invite. They were entitled to it, they thought, and never ceased to be shocked that there might not be space. It didn't matter that some of them hadn't been on the White House's eighteen-acre campus since the previous December, when they'd done the same bidding they were now doing with Velz, pleading for an invite and excoriating the powers that dared restrict their holiday spirit.

Schultz was situated comfortably behind his sliding door in Lower Press, but still within earshot of the constant conversations between Velz and the press; the wheeling and dealing for a spot—*Pretty please!*—to the White House holiday party. Schultz, like the rest of us, was just glad he wasn't the one dealing directly with the invites.

Velz was the man for the job. He had a process. He had three interns helping, sorting photo cards on the floor, alphabetizing invites. He created a sense of order in handling the dependably pesky press, who had a knack for posing questions others might have been too embarrassed to ask. The debacle was predictable and some of the meltdowns memorable:

"Am I not important enough to get an invite?"

"My job depends on going! Can you please add me?"

"Do you know who I am?"

And the thing that really separated reporters from the rest of us: they always remembered to follow up.

Like a skilled fencer, Velz swatted down most requests adroitly, quickly consulting his behemoth color-coded Excel spreadsheet: Invited. Not invited. Wait-listed. Next!

One notable last-minute guest who had been wait-listed and then approved, a card-carrying member of Old Washington's elite, tried to push his luck. He had been approved as a special case, invited on the agreed-upon precondition that he not receive a picture with the president. That's because POTUS and FLOTUS stood for more than three hundred photos nearly *every night* in December as the parade of holiday parties wore on. We refused to add further to the president's pain by tacking on any more photos at the eleventh hour. But this guest decided to sneak past three interns and into the photo line, where Velz stopped him.

"Just one quick picture, please," the man pleaded, his date by his side.

Where I would have broken, Velz didn't even bend.

"You were invited by Eric Schultz on the condition you wouldn't receive a photo. He told you this, correct?"

"Yes, but—"

Velz sternly cut the man off again. "No, unfortunately I can't allow it. You're free to enjoy the party upstairs, but we won't be able to provide a photo." Velz turned away, on to more business. Additional fires to put out.

I was impressed. Velz thrived in this environment; his natural ability to gatekeep was part of what made him a good press wrangler. Schultz, known for cutting last-minute deals, wasn't as adept at turning away people. He scooted up to Velz. "That was a DC-VIP you just dismissed—there goes my invite to his legendary brunch!"

Velz didn't bat an eye. He'd been dealing with requests from important people (usually self-proclaimed) for two months. Reporters sometimes tried to play the race card. Or the favorites card. But Velz stood firm. He would say, "I can offer you a White House Christmas card."

Truth is, we weren't responsible for the bulk of the invites to our parties. We let the newspapers and networks decide who they wanted included on the invite lists, precisely so we wouldn't be perceived as playing favorites or for rewarding positive coverage. All we had was a number, dictated to us by the Social Office. We told NBC how many people it could invite, and the network gave us a list of names. So too for Fox News, the *Washington Post*, and the rest. Somehow that never seemed to sink in for the reporters who flocked to Lower Press in the lead-up to the receptions each year. That's because they knew we did cut "drug deals" on the side, adding a few friendly faces and longtime reporters or crew members—the lower-level folks with whom we actually worked but who were left off of their bosses' lists in lieu of media executives from New York and Los Angeles.

They hoped that they might be the recipients of one of those side deals, too. We were all dependent on one another, after all.

Depending on the story of the day—or moment, for that matter—the press corps can be your ally or your adversary. There are the usual suspects: the TV anchor who thinks he's a budding hotshot; the breathless TV reporter always desperate for "just two seconds" of your time; the grizzled still photographer who knows more about the place than anybody else. They wanted the scoop, and we wanted to shape the message, which fused a relationship that could be mutually beneficial or detrimental—but always dependent.

The White House holiday receptions served as a kind of culmination of that year's mutual dependence. A night to let loose, imbibe the boozy eggnog, marvel at the tree in the Blue Room, or talk in the East Room about things other than pool sprays, embargoes, and background quotes.* It wasn't all fun, though; the Social Office required that members of the communications team staff portions of

* A pool spray is a staged opportunity for the press to quickly cover a person or event.

our parties. Velz typically tasked me with the photo card table for an hour or two. That's where reporters and their dates picked up name cards just before heading into the Diplomatic Reception Room (Dip Room) for their photo with the president and First Lady.

Most of the riffraff had been snuffed out by the time people reached our table in the basement Cross Hall of the main mansion, marked by its long, piercing red carpet and arched marble walls. One photographer did come close, though. She sneaked a second guest into the party: her newborn child. Now, she didn't smuggle the infant in through the metal detector unnoticed, but no staffer to this point was willing to stand up to the mini party crasher.

Velz didn't blink: he made her choose between her stowaway baby and her appropriately RSVP'd adult guest. (She chose her husband; I don't know who she left her baby with.) Mercifully, Velz handled her before she made it to me at the card table.

So my only concern was remembering names—or bullshitting my way through interactions until the reporter's name popped into my mind, and I reached for the appropriate card. There were plenty of instances when I knew I just wasn't going to remember no matter how much small talk we did, so I'd put my head down, pretend not to see who was next in line, and shout, "Last name!" The reporter would say his or her name, and I'd look up with a smile. "Oh, hey, man, didn't see you there!" I'd say, handing over the card. "Enjoy your photo!"

I was gearing up for my turn at the table—the party had just begun; photos would start soon with the president and First Lady—when I saw one of my newest coworkers, a charming, smart woman named Crystal, in the Cross Hall. Crystal was the rarest of White House assistants: she never got rattled and rarely showed frustration. She was savvy in the best way. I headed to her as I scarfed down one of the White House's chocolate cookies baked to look like Bo, which was sort of ironic, I think, given that Bo could have died eating one. There was always a line for those in the State Dining Room, and I knew to snag them early. And I needed one tonight.

Our receptions were on weekday nights. And this weekday had been particularly difficult. As usual, Washington was still struggling to get its business done. Congress was breaking toward another week of brinksmanship, threatening to shut down the government once again. It wasn't a banner day in the West Wing. We had cracked into the aforementioned Russian reporter's vodka and were sustaining ourselves largely on Doug's famous chocolate pretzels. Nobody was in the mood for a party.

I tried to lighten things as I reached Crystal.

"Hey, don't take this in any kind of a *way*," I prefaced, already provoking her unease. I should have stopped right there. Sentences that start this way don't end well. But I continued: "Do you watch *Black-ish* on ABC?"

At that very moment, our nation's first African American president strode in, exhausted. We made eye contact, and he shook his head. He couldn't have heard me, I thought. Even if he had, there was nothing wrong with my question, right? It was totally normal banter between colleagues. I loved the show and wanted to see what Crystal, a young black woman, thought. Oh, who was I kidding? I looked like an ass.

I was always curious: What must the president have thought, walking around the White House and seeing twenty-five-year-olds essentially running the place? What would Americans have thought if they knew that terrifying, wonderful truth: that their hopes and dreams rested in the hands of a bunch of twentysomethings? Mostly, I'm sure the president was proud, impressed by our professionalism, rejuvenated by our energy, grateful for our optimism. But that general sense of pride had to be punctured at least weekly by interactions like these: reminders that, yep, you're the leader of the free world, but you've got a bunch of Millennials who actually make the place go.

Another good impression, I thought to myself as the president turned the corner to his elevator for the two-story ride home, tired after a long day of work, with the weight of an impending government shutdown bearing on him. He would have just a few minutes for dinner with his family before heading right back down to take three hundred photos with strangers.

"What kind of a question is that?!" Crystal shot back the moment POTUS was out of sight. "You been having some of that eggnog, or what?" She feigned exasperation. I begged her not to tell Desiree. Crystal had a superb knack for deadpan humor. "Do I go around asking you what happened on *How I Met Your Mother* last night?"

• • •

Many hundreds of journalists claim to be White House reporters, but there are maybe a hundred regulars who make up the true press corps: the reporters, photographers, producers, camerawomen and -men, audio crews, and radio correspondents whom we saw day in and day out on the North Lawn of the White House and in the West Wing. They keep watch over the place, dutifully monitoring the goings-on, witnessing and participating in history. The White House is their office, too.

In fact, President Obama, or any president, for that matter, couldn't walk between his office and his residence without passing the Briefing Room. Situated between the West Wing and the People's House, the Briefing Room's location is a reminder of the crucial role of the press as intermediary between the president and the public. We hold briefings there, but it's also a workspace for reporters on deadline and a location from which TV journalists broadcast their reports.

Pebble Beach, named for its once-gravelly, muddy, outdoor mess, is a collection of tented press stand-up locations where television reporters film their daily dispatches, often for the nightly or morning news shows. But traffic flows to and from the area at all hours of the day, as reporters, producers, and camera crews try to keep up with the all-day demands of MSNBC, Fox, and CNN. It was a visible reminder that the business had changed—that the media were evolving, trying to keep up with the increasing demand for news, or what passes for it, in the attempt to fill the void.

When I first started in the West Wing, Pebble Beach was obscured by a massive, mysterious hole in front of the main lobby, where the driveway used to be. The hole required a temporary, elevated walkway to and from Pebble Beach and the main entrance for press and staffers at the northwest gate on Pennsylvania Avenue. The moat-like mystery hole, given its prime location under the feet of dozens of reporters as they made their way to and from work each day, was the cause of much speculation, especially among the press.

The General Services Administration, the agency responsible for managing government buildings, provided a bland statement about renovations to the West Wing's standard systems—electrical, for instance. That take was met with healthy skepticism among the press. Frankly, most of us who watched the hole grow wider and deeper for more than a year weren't buying it either. Not when giant hunks of concrete were lowered into the abyss right outside our windows. We figured it was security related but knew better than to ask. Like anything having to do with the protection of the place, it was beyond my pay grade. I just hoped there might be room for me in what I assumed was an apocalypse-ready bunker.

If our space in the West Wing is tight, the press space is tighter still. Reporters are stationed behind, and beneath, the Press Briefing Room. Five, six, sometimes seven members of an outlet—the Associated Press or CBS News, for instance—squeeze into booths no more than ten feet deep that are separated by slender glass doors. In the midst of the crammed glass compartments, there's an open space where a metal sign hangs from the ceiling. This is "Stills Country."

The "stills" are a rotating crew of still photographers, a cast of characters who range in age from late twenties to early sixties. By and large, these are the living historians of the White House. Some have taken thousands of flights on Air Force One, working for the bulk of their lives—over a number of presidencies—in the bubble. They're from the *New York Times*, the Associated Press, the Reuters news agency, Agence France-Presse (AFP), and a revolving group of additional outlets from across the country and around the world. They move like a pack, and when it's just the men, they verge on the vulgar. They are as dedicated to having a good time as they are to doing a good job. They make the place more fun.

Stills don't "take pictures." They "make pictures." And they adhere to a strict code of conduct among themselves. Yes, they'll jostle for position on the rope line, but they respect that their peers need to make the shot as well, and they'll help a photographer if he or she is in need. Making space. Advocating for one another. Working as a team. It was all a part of the code. There are infamous stories, mostly from the distant past, about what happened when a photographer or some other reporter in the pack broke the code. One of my favorite photographers, a genteel older man with a sweet affect and shy charisma, was said to have opened a competitor's luggage during an overseas trip and relieved himself on the contents of the bag. Nobody quite remembers why he supposedly did it, but all seem to understand the frustration that can build over days, weeks, sometimes months on the road.

Fortunately, the crew had evolved by the time Obama took office, graduating to harmless pranks when I met them, such as teasing newer reporters into thinking big news was just around the corner. To a new press wrangler, though, a trustworthy still photographer can be a godsend, as a few were to me. I often looked to

Doug—the bald, friendly leader of the pack—for advice. As I was still getting my footing, he'd give a subtle nod, flagging for me that something was amiss: a Secret Service agent was blocking the shot, for instance, or a newer reporter was creeping too close to the president. Most of all, the stills are a remarkably talented bunch, and their work regularly lands on the front pages of the nation's largest newspapers—above the fold.

We trusted the photographers. They were the nucleus of the president's press pool.

Press pool was a term—like *POTUS* on my first day—that I had heard thrown around but never truly understood until I became a wrangler, tasked with herding the pool from place to place and country to country.

There were variations for in-town pool versus out-of-town travel pool, but the basic gist is this: a group of reporters, camera crew, and photographers traveled everywhere with the president, from foreign trips and domestic rallies, to rounds of golf and birthday dinners in DC. There were five stills, four writers, a radio reporter, a sound tech, a cameraperson, and a producer.

The pool, established during the Eisenhower administration, was born out of simple logistics: not everybody who wanted to cover the president could. There's not enough space, and most outlets can't afford the expense of doing so in the first place. So this group of reporters *pools* its talents, time, and resources to cover the president continuously. Its purpose is straightforward: report and record what's happening with the president.

Sometimes they record real history—swearings-in, Papal visits, the State of the Union—but more often, they're around "in case." When there are date nights, parent-teacher conferences, midnight arrivals of Marine One, their purpose is understood and unspoken and often grim. Truth is, the pool is around in case something goes wrong around the world or in the president's protective bubble. After all, any picture of the president could be the last. That's when they're really recording history: those flashes of intrigue or tragedy that play in our public conversation for years.

The pool was there when President Kennedy was shot in Dallas; it's how a devastated nation, and my distraught nana, were kept informed as their president fought for his life. So, too, the pool fed footage to the country in the aftermath of the 1981 assassination attempt on President Ronald Reagan in Washington. It's how we know of President George W. Bush's immediate reaction upon learning that we were under attack on September 11, 2001. The pool—including then–*Time* correspondent Jay Carney and favorite photographer, Doug—was aboard Air Force One, the only plane in the sky, as America considered its next move.

A similar moment—a stark change of course—could replay itself at any time, but that was easy to forget while sitting in the food court at JBA, short for Joint Base Andrews, the US Air Force facility where the president's planes were stored and where we departed on countless domestic and overseas trips. But when the weekend rolled around, assuming there wasn't snow on the ground, there was a good chance we were headed to JBA for a different reason.

It was a wrangler's worst nightmare: Obama loved to golf.

We in the Press Office often said he just enjoyed the chance to take a walk outside. That was the company line, and it was certainly true, but to use a frequent Obama-ism, "what is also true is" that the man had become somewhat obsessed with the game. Many weekends, he'd try to squeeze in a round or two. And, naturally, the pool was always along for the ride. I would sit with them in the food court for five hours while the president played. It was the bane of whichever wrangler had "weekend duty"—especially for me. I'm an avid golfer, and I would much rather have been on the links than watching the pool scarf down junk food at creaky cafeteria tables. One of the producers who frequented the pool liked to try his hand at "eating around the world"—like at Epcot in Disney World, except with Taco Bell, Anthony's Pizza & Pasta, a Burger King, a knock-off cheesesteak place, and a fish sticks stand. He'd pile his tray high, one item from each spot, and dig in until I got word from the Secret Service agent stationed with us that the president was on the sixteenth green.

That's when we would head to the pool vans to link back up with the motorcade. The print reporter would send a note to the rest of the White House correspondents any time the pool or president made a move. They were called pool reports and went something like this: "The pool has moved to the vans; the president evidently wrapping up his nearly five-hour round of golf." That was about the extent of insight we wanted the pool to have. Golf was one of those "in-case" circumstances: if something went wrong, the pool was there. If not, I was to keep everyone at a reasonable distance.

We didn't like footage of the president playing golf.

A duffed chip or missed putt could draw out trite, stretched analogies to a failed policy or flawed rollout from a bored press pool. And if he striped one right down the middle? Well, then why is the president so good at golf? He was clearly playing too much golf and had too much time to practice his drives. Most of all, the right-wing media just didn't approve of the president playing golf, and the far-right-wing media personalities more specifically didn't approve of *this* president playing golf.

To keep the fodder to a minimum, we rarely let the pool film or photograph the president while he was on the course. Instead, we staged the pool vans about a block away. One summer afternoon, we lined up on the wrong block and missed the motorcade. That meant they couldn't report in real time exactly when the president left and when he returned. They wondered if something was up, worried that they were missing important news. They weren't. It was a routine drive home. Still, the pool let me have it in the van, yelling, bickering, complaining all the way back to the White House. I was pissed at them, but I also knew they were right.

"Where's the president now?!" That's what the print reporter in charge of writing pool reports called out every few minutes, both to do her job and to get back at me. It was like a back-seat driver asking "Are we there yet?"

"Where's the president?"

• • •

It was the same thing Josh was anxious about as he scampered to Upper Press on a similarly beautiful day the following summer. "Pat, I need a favor."

I had recently moved on from wrangling to writing—for me, golf trips were a thing of the past—and I was toiling away at my desk on the White House "daily message points," which I sent every day to stakeholders—from basketball legend Charles Barkley and POTUS's high school friends, to liberal economists and political pundits—anybody who we thought might spread the good word about the news of the day.

But this day was getting out of hand, and this was an all-hands-on-deck moment. Josh told me: "We don't know where the president is right now."

It was the summer of 2014, and the president was feeling a bit caged in. He wanted out of the bubble. We had developed a term for it earlier in the summer when POTUS veered from the preapproved path around the White House to greet tourists nearby. "The Bear is loose," we took to saying. In fact, that's exactly what the president told Jennifer Palmieri as he departed the White House with Denis. They were going to Dunkin' Donuts, we thought. The wranglers scrambled to assemble a pool and made a run for it toward Dunkin' Donuts. Half of the pool got left behind and was waiting out front of the West Wing lobby as I burst through the doors. The marine who typically guarded the door, opening it for everyone who walks through, was off duty, which meant the president truly wasn't in the West Wing.

Without stopping, I waved the pool to follow as we darted through the northwest gate and headed north toward Dunkin'. Just as we were about to cross into Lafayette Park, I spotted a commotion to our left, up Pennsylvania Avenue. It had to be him.

He was at Starbucks.

I did my best to keep the pool at bay, but it was pandemonium when we arrived. The pool crept close. "C'mon, guys, give me some space," the president asked, coffee cup in hand. Somebody asked what he'd ordered. It had to be tea. That's all he drank during the day. Rather than answer, he looked at me. "Let's test your wrangling skills." At that point, I started screaming at the pool, "Back up! Back up! Let's go, pool!" And every wrangler's favorite euphemism for "Leave this instant!": "Thank you, pool!"

The case of the missing president was solved quickly, but the ramifications lasted quite a bit longer. The Secret Service wasn't thrilled, and the press corps was up in arms. Unacceptable, they thought. The poor guy just wanted to take a walk, but it was a reminder that he couldn't. Yeah, Barack Obama could theoretically go for a stroll whenever he wanted, but the president can't. Thank you, pool!

These flare-ups often come off as petty press problems, and we were frequently frustrated by their fretting. But the White House Correspondents' Association, the group that represents the press and advocates for coverage of the administration, was right to push for more access. It was their duty to obsess over the pool's continued coverage. There's no law mandating that the president be covered continuously by a press pool. It's simply a White House norm, preserved by tradition. Like so many norms, it can be upended. That's why it needs to be protected every day, by the press, by the president, and by the people of the United States demanding to know what's going on, taking agency over their citizenship.

There's a reason it's called the People's House.

• • •

It's clear that the White House press pool plays a crucial role in our democracy, and if common sense prevails, it's not going away any time soon. But with an evolving media landscape, tight budgets, and shifting norms, change will come to the pool over time. Fewer individuals per pool, possibly. New, less traditional companies—BuzzFeed and who knows what else next—joining the ranks of the rotating outlets, for instance. The form it ultimately takes and when the pool evolves are less important than the basic function of the press pool continuing. That's a norm that should be an ironclad rule.

There is another White House custom that appears to be in limbo, its future considered by some to be on the chopping block.

The daily press briefing, even with its live feeds and miles of wires where the famous White House swimming pool used to be, can feel archaic, harkening back to a time when what was learned at the briefing drove the day; when the press secretary could steer the day's narrative from behind his or her podium.* That capability, for a number of reasons—some good, some not so much—has been diminished.

Still, Josh recently put it to me this way: "The daily briefing gives the White House an unrivaled platform to advocate and defend the president's agenda. It also gives journalists—as agents of the American people—the opportunity to ask skeptical, pressing

* Steering the narrative on *Saturday Night Live* does not count.

questions to hold those in power accountable for their actions and demand transparency into how that power is being used."

At its best, that's exactly what it does. Picture the first row in the White House Briefing Room: What do you see? Probably reporters jostling for attention, jotting notes, holding the president to account. And it's true: the first row is filled with reporters at their professional peak—many fulfilling a lifelong dream, years of diligent work in the making—grilling the administration, rooting out answers, sifting through half-truths and misspeaks, exposing evasions.

So, what's the problem?

Well, the Brady Press Briefing Room has more than one row.

The room has moved away from the gritty, wizened reporter—the Helen Thomas, a legend who questioned ten presidents from the front row—toward younger journalists looking to bigger and better things.* Somewhere along the way, for many, the White House beat became a stepping stone. Too often, the reporters are out for themselves or their network, which is understandable—just not ideal for getting at answers, insight, and the truth.

The regular White House TV reporters with whom I dealt when I first started as a wrangler were, for the most part, a gifted, driven bunch. Some of them would hit it big in just a few years: Chuck Todd became host of the vaunted *Meet the Press*, which my dad sits down to watch every Sunday and considers a "religious experience"; Jake Tapper was the breakout star of the 2016 election cycle; Savan-

* I recognize the same could likely be said of Obama White House staffers.

nah Guthrie went on to *Today* show fame; and Norah O'Donnell became cohost of *CBS This Morning* and a contributor to *60 Minutes*. Chuck, I remember, would pressure Jay and Josh about the press digs: mainly, he thought that the press should be allowed to dine at Ike's on the first floor of the EEOB, an unassuming office cafeteria named for President Eisenhower. It would be much easier than the press having to leave campus and go through security all over again, just to grab lunch. We never had a great retort. Our denial didn't make a ton of sense. Maybe it would have been the right thing to do.

Chuck and Jake, Savannah and Norah, aside, many TV reporters were and are rewarded for asking the same question that their peer has just asked, solely so there's footage of them asking it for their respective nightly news or cable outlet. It does nothing to further the debate or probe deeper for answers.

It can become an echo chamber; the questions can become the story. As one Lower Press staffer once put it bluntly to one of our favorite reporters: "You are self-fulfilling, vacuous whores."*

One TV reporter, a well-meaning, talented woman named Mandy, always needed just "two seconds." Two seconds from Jay or two seconds from Josh. Two seconds from anybody. Didn't matter what the topic was—Syria, the Affordable Care Act, gun violence—two seconds was all it would take, which was all the time cable news allowed for substance or policy reporting anyway, so it worked out.

* The staffer was teasing, of course.

In many ways, Mandy was cable news come to life. Breathless and quick, she was a walking headline ticker. When something was breaking in the news, she was often the first to breeze through our walkway into Upper Press, assuming, of course, that nobody had *two seconds* to spare in Lower Press.

She was usually followed closely behind by other members of the proven, traditional organizations that claim seats in the first few rows of the Press Briefing Room: the Associated Press, the *Times*, the *Post*, the *Journal*, the *Chicago Tribune*, and NBC News, for instance.

One evening, as the president was said to be pondering a military strike across the world, and we were waiting on word from our friends in the National Security Council for an update, my bosses were standing around in Upper Press, discussing the state of play: How would we roll out the decision to the press one way or the other? Who would we give the story to first? Should we do a background briefing? What were the talking points?

All good questions, but it was getting late, and I hadn't had a Mountain Dew in hours. I noticed the time: I had only one minute before it would be too late. The White House Navy Mess is a one-window pickup spot, run by the US Navy, that offers breakfast, lunch, and dinner—and of course, its famous chicken fingers and waffle fries. Staffers dialed from their desks—it was the one number nobody ever forgot—and placed orders. It was also where you could pick up snacks and coffee as well as soda, which was the only product we were allowed free of charge. I took full advantage, doing the Dew like it was a part of my job. But on this evening, I knew any second the man behind the counter would erect the wooden plank, concealing the mess's pickup window like it was never there. Closing time.

As I dashed down the hall to the steps to the West Wing basement toward the mess, I stopped dead in my tracks.

"Hello, Johnny."

There he was: a well-respected reporter from one of the aforementioned front-row outlets. He was loitering, slinking slowly back and forth by the top of the steps down to the basement. He had been listening in on my bosses from just beyond the hall, out of sight. He was startled as I came upon him, like I had walked in on him with his pants down. It was a breach, and he knew it. Scurrying to effect some semblance of normality, he pointed and smiled at a jumbo blowup of Obama hanging on the wall, like he had just stopped briefly to admire Pete Souza's latest work.

"You looking for anybody?" I asked suspiciously.

With that, he continued on to Upper Press. I took a detour down to Lower Press, where I found Marie.

"How long ago did Johnny pass through here?" I asked.

"Awhile, why?"

Johnny's actions forced a new policy. We instituted an unofficial yet crucial piece of protocol in Upper Press that Velz was in the unique position to execute. His seat aimed him directly down the hallway, so he was the first to spot approaching reporters. To alert the rest of us, he took to yelling the names of incoming reporters, greeting them loudly enough that, if need be, our sensitive conversations were hushed, our bosses' doors were quickly shut, and our close-hold (meaning not to be shared) desktop documents were minimized.

Whenever anybody from Politico headed up, Velz lost all sense of shame: "Politico's in the house, everybody! Hide the secrets!" he would yell good-naturedly, usually to self-deprecating appreciation from the reporter. Politico's assigned seat is toward the middle of the Briefing Room, near the *Hill*'s spot. Both of these outlets were founded to focus more on the day-to-day politics of Washington—mirroring the direction of cable news—than on policy. Sometimes more style than substance, the *Hill* newspaper and website was famous for its "50 Most Beautiful People" edition, one of those *important projects* I was tasked with spearheading for the White House.

Politico, the *Hill*, and others like them provided yet another perspective with which our press secretaries needed to contend. If, on its better days, the first row focused on substance, then there were these middle-row reporters ready to pick up the slack and pose questions that were purely political. To be fair, these outlets have recently stepped up their investigative and policy reporting in important, impressive ways, evolving slowly away from who's-up-who's-down reporting.

And beyond them, on the periphery of the room, without assigned seats, there were the hanger-outers; the usually-lovable oddballs who took up residence in the Briefing Room for no ostensible reason other than to be around.

There was a lovely older woman who had covered the White House for nearly fifty years. She liked to remind us that she was probably going to die soon, often visiting Upper Press before or after the briefing with a box of chocolates for the press secretary, who was usually in briefing prep or briefing wrap-up. "I just wanted to thank him for calling on me," she would say, handing me the box to pass along. Before ambling back down the ramp to the Briefing Room and then up the driveway, she often asked, "You'll come to my funeral, won't you?" Some thought her family needed to step in; she wasn't doing well and was in no shape to schlep through security and into the White House, where she would rarely get in a question. She struggled to walk, and her voice was softening. She was battling Parkinson's disease.

Truth is, the White House was important to her, and being in the thick of things was probably the best thing for her spirits. We appreciated what she was doing and why she was there. But that didn't make her comments about her upcoming funeral any less uncomfortable.

There were less sympathetic characters, too, elbowing their way to the margins of the forty-nine-seat Briefing Room. Christine had a hair-trigger temper. She was prone to paranoia, and wrote often of conspiracy theories and completely unfounded gossip about the staff. She once accused Velz of practicing "voodoo" against her. She was litigious, too. (I've changed her name, obviously.) Claiming discrimination, threatening to sue the White House and individual staffers—once for what she claimed was tainted tuna fish from the vending machine. Eventually the Secret Service stepped in. We didn't see much more of Christine after that.

There was Rickie the friendly part-time Uber driver and part-time political observer with a hard-to-find blog who occasionally fell asleep—snoring disruptively—during the briefings.

And then there was Goyal. Much has been made of the Briefing Room's resident Indian reporter without a paper for which to report. I knew him mostly as the friendly man who dropped by

Lower and Upper Press at least weekly with a plastic bag of inexplicably warm fruit and dented canned goods. It was a sweet gesture, even if the presentation left a bit to be desired. Sometimes the bag had to go right into the trash; more bait for Bo and Sunny to sift through. More often, somebody would grab the bag before walking home, ready to hand it off to the nearest homeless person. I liked to take the bananas home for smoothies.

Goyal made real waves throughout the West Wing when he brought a life-size, creepily lifelike bust of Mahatma Gandhi to my desk as a gift for the president. This was not something we could throw in the trash. It looked much too real, like it had been pulled from the costume department of a movie set.

I called Brian, the director of operations, to come over—I wasn't going to be the one to walk this over to the Oval Office—but he was tied up, so we hid Mahatma behind the door to Katie Beirne Fallon's office. Katie, one of my many bosses, was at a meeting. She was the deputy communications director at the time, just before taking over as the director of legislative affairs, the White House's chief liaison to Capitol Hill.

Emails began pouring back in, and we forgot about the little guy for a few hours until Katie returned from her marathon of meetings. She closed the door behind her. Then we heard a shriek as she blasted through her office door in terror.

Eventually Gandhi made his way throughout the West Wing, left on bosses' desks by assistants looking for playful revenge and in office corners to shock unsuspecting staffers. He even made it to the Resolute desk, where the president eyed him skeptically, a glare

Pete Souza caught for posterity and turned into a jumbo that hung in the West Wing. Goyal was escorted to the basement of the West Wing to see the photo and appreciate the impression he had made.

The bust wasn't the first time that Goyal had made his mark. It was said that press secretaries from previous administrations, when they needed to veer away from a problematic line of questions, would call on Goyal, who would, without fail, ask about the US-India relationship, sidelining whatever the rest of the room wanted to discuss. It was a creative form of filibustering that our press secretaries sometimes indulged. You never knew what you were going to get from the folks on the outskirts.

Goyal once asked Josh if the president was celebrating International Yoga Day. Josh, never one to sidestep a dad joke, leveled one of his best groaners:

"I think that question's a bit of a stretch."

As soon as Josh entered Upper Press, trailed by his deputies and assistants, all still laughing off the dad-joke-ness of it all, I accused him of planting the question to get in his punch line. He denies it, and I'm inclined to believe him. That room will ask anything.

• • •

A year earlier, as Jay Carney, Josh's predecessor, wrapped up his daily briefing, someone asked, "Jay, is there a red fox running loose on the White House grounds?"

That was my fault.

As I grew out of wrangling, I took on a kind of utility player role. I had started some writing, was taking on message- and event-planning responsibilities, and, every once in a while, I was tasked with "story management." That's what we called it when someone oversaw a specific issue or upcoming story. Bobby managed stories related to homeland security. Matt managed stories about education and other domestic issues. Amy was in charge of the economy.

I got stories about White House varmints.

The *Wall Street Journal*'s Carol Lee,* a White House regular, is an example of a reporter whose work sometimes caused us trouble, but who was a gifted reporter and a congenial person. We occasionally disliked her stories, but it never interfered with her working relationship with the White House staff. When I was a media monitor, I remember there was a hubbub over one of Carol's upcoming pieces. My bosses asked me to compile her latest twenty stories, to help prepare for her pending article and to get a sense of just how bad it would be. Still, we knew it was part of a reporter's job, and we did our best—though we often failed—not to take it personally. That's the way it was with many of the talented White House beat reporters: part of the natural, healthy tension.

In early 2014 Carol had an idea for a less controversial piece.

There was a fox that was said to be sleuthing about the White House in the evenings, darting between the shadows, startling staffers exiting late at night.

Carol wanted to do a deep dive on the sneaky fox, and her editors were interested. Josh quickly looped me in to the email. I was

* Carol is now with NBC News.

just the man for the job, he claimed. It was the first—and most successful—story I would ever deal with.

Managing a story involves seeing it through, beginning with getting a sense from the reporter of the direction and tone of the piece. Did the story need shaping on our end, or was it best left alone? To shape a story is to engage with it. You can do that on a number of levels. White House officials can speak to the reporter "on background," meaning that the content of what they're saying can be reported on but not quoted. What's more, the source is not to be named and instead referred to as an agreed-upon alias such as "a senior administration official" or "a source close to the matter."

Then there are on-the-record interviews in which the content of the discussion, including quotes, is free game, and sources are to be identified by their real names.* These become more complicated when the source is not accustomed to dealing with the press or when the source is high level.

While the fox story didn't need much shaping, we decided to engage because lighthearted White House content, without infringing on the president's time, can be hard to come by. We ran with Carol's idea. We would provide on-the-record sit-downs for the fox piece, but they would be straightforward, with folks like Dale, whose unofficial role of minding Bo and Sunny was eclipsed only by his official job as caretaker of the White House grounds.

---

* There is also "quote approval," meaning the interview is on background, but the reporter can follow up with requests for specific quotes she would like to use.

Carol had a sense that this story could be big. She asked for more sources and additional quotes. For a week, I went around asking everybody I came across if they had seen the fox, and if so, whether they would be willing to go on the record about it. I even took it to Brian in the Outer Oval Office.

"Do you mind asking the president if he's seen a fox running around his lawn?"

It was exactly the kind of question I would be tasked with asking the Outer Oval. Pointless, but part of my job. I didn't get an immediate answer, but Carol told me that the story was getting juicier—it had front-page potential—what with the wordplay possibilities and unorthodox nature of the thing. She told me the fox was going to get the special treatment: its own stipple portrait, the dot drawings for which the *Wall Street Journal* was famous.

I pushed Brian to ask the boss and eventually got an answer.

"I can confirm for you that the president has seen the fox, Carol."

It was the talk of the town the morning the exposé ran. Despite the frivolous nature of the story, I was riding high, collecting accolades for a job well done. My first story—okay, it was Carol's story—was on the front page. Blogs picked up the piece throughout the day. And that evening, the piece de resistance: the nightly news, the staple of American newscasts, was considering running with the fox story.

However, it turned out to be a busy news day. After all, the health care red team had been building to this day for months. They were working on Obamacare open enrollment, one of the president's top priorities. The health care exchanges had closed at the end of the prior month, and the numbers were just coming in. The news was good: our goal had been to sign up seven million Americans, but *eight million* had signed up for quality, affordable health insurance, many for the first time!

Good Obamacare news was even harder to come by than lighthearted White House fare. This was a major, and somewhat unexpected, win. A banner news day for the White House Communications Office.

Unfortunately, there's not a ton of space on the evening news, and both pieces didn't fit.

Which do you think made the cut?

The media monitor sent out the nightly news clips. Congratulations started to pour in. Jesse from the red team wrote: "We just learned that 8 million Americans signed up for health care for the first time in history, but it got bumped from the news for the White House fox. But, congrats to Pat."

• • •

It's easy to criticize the nightly news for bumping crucial Obamacare news—information that affects people's lives—for a silly story about a fox. But, the truth is, very often they're just giving the people what they want. That's not to say that there aren't some very broken things about the media, but their actions are driven largely by readers, viewers, consumers.

People don't want to read about policy. They want to read about people. It's part of why politics is so peculiar, too—why the personality of the candidate often trumps his or her ideas. We knew that, of course, which is why we went to great lengths to engage real people in the debate of the day and to "reach people where they are"—one of our mantras—whether that's on YouTube or a comedy show with Jerry Seinfeld. News media executives knew the same as we did, and that's where politics and media meet.

But there is also an important disconnect between the way the media as a whole is set up and the way government works. It's something President Obama often discussed. He would tell us, in good times and in bad, that the federal government is akin to an aircraft carrier at sea: it takes a long time to alter its course; turning around is difficult. Change—for better or worse—he would say, takes time.

Sure, history zigs and zags, but currents run deep, and ramifications, like ripples radiating from the engines of an aircraft carrier, can take a long time to hit.

That's a notion fundamentally at odds with the way the political media report now, in an age when who's up and who's down is determined by the end of every day, and when Twitter's hot takes decide the same thing by the minute. Although cable news has nothing but time to fill, reporters, anchors, and network executives all act as if they are running out of it. They rush. POTUS, on the other hand, understood that winners and losers are determined over months—decades, even—not minutes or days. That, to him, was a more appropriate, if impractical, measure of progress.

It's a belief that sometimes set up a clash between the president and his press team. It was our job to pay attention to what the media were doing every minute, while President Obama took a much longer view of the horizon—of politics, the press, and history. It would serve him well, especially toward the end of his second term.

News of the day rarely riled him up or even particularly interested him; somehow he was more engrossed in intellectual think pieces and deep dives on health care policy than Politico's latest accounting of who was up and who was down inside the Beltway. Sometimes I hoped he would snap a bit, maybe take a turn as Michael Douglas in *The American President*, talk about *serious problems* and *serious people*, and remind the world, "My name's Barack Obama, and I *am* the president."

But he was usually too calm, totally collected. Even when his staff was spinning out around him, he was the quiet at the center of the storm. The president's untroubled, logical demeanor often drew comparisons to *Star Trek*'s Mr. Spock. The big ears probably didn't hurt that comparison.

But there were exceptions to the Spock-like practicality when it came to the press, and they were usually personal. In February 2013 the *Washington Post* Style section ran an article titled "Michelle Obama's Posterior Again the Subject of a Public Rant." The story recounted the latest moron to comment on the First Lady's appearance and then delved into the historical precedent for such chatter and included quotes such as "She looks great for her age." There was also some *butt* wordplay. This was an example of a story written in service of an eye-catching headline. Click bait. None of this sat well with the First Lady's husband.

He erupted into Upper Press, mad as hell, ready to do a little ranting of his own. I hadn't seen him like this since I first started in the West Wing. At least I knew what to do this time: look busy, get to typing.

"It's totally disrespectful!" POTUS said of the piece to Jennifer Palmieri, who was then the White House communications director. JPalm, as we called her, was a wonderful boss, confident and shrewd and sharp, capable of holding her own in the face of a frustrated president.

She did her best to quell his temper. You can't undo the damage of a story with a correction, nor would one be offered, but the White House was equipped to let reporters and their editor bosses know when we thought a story was off base, incorrect, or—in this case—completely out of line and offensive. Still the president didn't take his annoyance public. There would be no Michael Douglas–like speech in the Briefing Room, no barrage of tweets. He vented privately, he got it off his chest, and he moved on.

It was, however, good practice for JPalm's next gig: running communications for Hillary Clinton's 2016 presidential campaign. It was precisely the kind of superficial coverage she would deal with every day.

• • •

We messed up a lot. We yelled at reporters; we nitpicked their headlines; we sometimes took out our frustrations on them, even when their stories were completely legitimate. And sometimes they were unfair to us, or they broke embargoes, or maybe they lingered a little too long outside our hall, listening in on private conversations.

But in a broader sense, for eight years, both sides—the president and the press—kept up the American covenant that says our press is free and that the People's House is theirs, too. As Josh says, "The briefing is about accountability and preserving trust between the White House and the American people." That trust is fragile. We've seen how it can be eroded, how the most powerful person on Earth can use his platform to sow doubt, impugn motives, and make us all a little less free.

Sure, we preserved the natural tension between the president and the press. But we preserved the trust, too. And an idea of objective truth as a foundation for debate. Josh liked to say that the briefing is a venue to make an argument. But that argument is fruitless without a set of facts from which to work.

Jay, as a former journalist at *Time*, knew better than most what it's like on both sides of the White House podium—and everybody who sat in Upper Press and Lower Press knew that we weren't the only public servants who came to work every day at the White House. That's why I was proud of the way Josh and Jay handled their responsibilities as press secretary.* They prepared for news-of-the-day questions, sure, but they also tried to be ready for whatever was on the minds of the dozens of individuals of varying degrees

* Robert Gibbs, Obama's first press secretary, left shortly before I moved to the West Wing. I didn't work closely with him, but I think he upheld the same bond that Josh and Jay did.

of aptitude and relevance spread throughout the Briefing Room's assigned seats and along its periphery. And I was always proud of the way they handled the standing-room-only reporters. Who were we to say who should or shouldn't come to the People's House and question us? They were treated with respect, no matter how ludicrous we found their questions.

The White House Correspondents' Association pushed us for more access; we pushed back. It's a conflict that will continue. The president's press team will always look out for the chief executive and his agenda first, and the press pool wouldn't be doing its job if it wasn't advocating constantly for additional access to the president and his team. We embraced our roles fully, but both sides always knew that the other wasn't the antagonist.

Still, the members of the press weren't our partners, either, which is why I suppose it wouldn't have been appropriate for Chuck Todd to march through the EEOB on Taco Tuesday at Ike's. It was important to preserve the natural boundaries—a buffer—that exist among the president, his staff, and the press.

But we knew something that we thought obvious; something we thought never needed to be said, but maybe it does:

The press is not the enemy of the American people.

As the vice president's mom would say: They're no better than us, and we're no better than them.

COMMON DC STORIES (SO YOU KNOW WHAT TO LOOK OUT FOR)

Think Piece. Often bloated, these deep dives are meant to rise above news of the day but frequently fall into the same daily tropes of Washington. Bad ones are overwrought, asking questions without offering meaningful answers. Good ones make you think about an issue or person in a different way.

The Obituary. Can refer to a policy proposal or a person; the press loves to declare the end, death, whether by sinking polls or looming scandal.

The Comeback. A natural companion to the obituary; the press is quick to equate a bounce in the polls or a well-done mea culpa to a full-blown comeback, a masterstroke of political brilliance—back from the brink.

Counternarrative. The media thrive on plot twists, and if no pivot is on the way, they sometimes manufacture one with a story positing that the opposite of what's happening is really happening.

The Oppo-Dump. Slightly repurposed from the research departments at the White House or any number of congressional offices, these are glorified press releases that friendly outlets—progressive and conservative alike—push out in the form of an independent article to further the intended narrative.

The Profile. From presidential candidates in the *Times* to White House junior staffers in their hometown papers, these are typically fluff pieces, but profiles can go sideways if not managed properly.

The Hot Take. Quick analyses, typically in terms of political winners and losers. They are basically tweets that become stories.

The Flyover Drop-in. Occasionally, coastal reporters will go on location to the middle of the country—"real America"—to highlight a few real people who embody the way Washington perceives America is feeling. Though these can be patronizing and overly general, the White House uses real people, too.

Stat Stories. Some reporters love stats and write entire stories based on the number of times the president has played golf or traveled on Air Force One, for instance, banking on other outlets to pick up the figures and run with them, often to their own conclusions.

Faulty Autopsies. Win or lose—debates, policy fights, elections—the media scramble to explain the results, sometimes in an oversimplified and underresearched way.

Palace Intrigue Pieces. Gossipy look-ins on the people behind the place, usually written when things aren't going well for the subjects of the article.

4

2012

I know 'cause I won both of them.

—BARACK OBAMA

I was never farther from the inner workings of Washington than the day in 2009 that Barack Obama was first sworn in: I was in the middle of the Atlantic Ocean.

Stephanie, her twin sister, Victoria, and I were on our way to Cadiz, Spain. It was the first leg of a thirteen-country itinerary through a study-abroad program called Semester at Sea. To some, the program is a joke: a forced, curated adventure servicing some sense of "culture." And I suffered no shortage of Semester at Sea jokes from my White House colleagues; Matt and Bobby particularly like to mention my "cruise." Of course, their take is partially true. But it's far from the whole story, at least for my trip, thanks to my future boss.

As with the previous twenty-three voyages, we on the MV *Explorer* departed the United States under the presidency of George

W. Bush. Yet unlike the previous eight years' worth of semesters, we arrived in our first port of call as Americans with a new leader, President Barack Obama.

As it turned out, it would make all the difference in the world.

On the second day of our voyage, January 20, the captain came over the speaker system: "Would everyone please power down their laptops?" It was the only way we could hope to have enough bandwidth to livestream the inauguration. We were hundreds of miles off the Eastern Seaboard, where history was unfolding and the world that we were about to explore was watching. We didn't want to miss it. This was one of those public occasions—only a handful in a lifetime; good and bad—that you don't forget. A true where-were-you-then type of deal.

Stephanie and I shuffled into a shipboard classroom, brimming and buzzing with students and faculty. We spotted an opening on the ground and took a seat. The buzz grew. Anticipation turned to excitement as the large projector screen at the front of the room sputtered to life. We caught glimpses of the pomp and pageantry: armored limousines waiting in front of the North Portico of the White House; Pennsylvania Avenue lined dozens of people deep. The National Mall was so jam-packed that only a high-flying helicopter could give it appropriate scope. We watched the First Families exchange pleasantries. The television reporters walked us through the protocol as the incoming and outgoing presidents began the time-honored and uniquely American tradition of peacefully transitioning the awesome power of the presidency from one person to the next and, in this case, from one party to another.

We burst into applause as President-Elect Obama stepped through the narrow door framed by the North Portico of the White House. A portal. The point of no return. He was on the way to become the forty-fourth president of the United States. When he returned in just a few hours to the White House, it would be his home.

On the MV *Explorer*, we hoped that our bandwidth would hold out as the seemingly endless motorcade made its way down Pennsylvania Avenue. On-air personalities told of the backstage commotion and machinations, the palace intrigue, the Grand Foyer and the East Room, and something called the Blue Room. They focused on the logistics of turning over the world's most famous home office in just a couple of hours. I couldn't picture it. In my mind, I had the midseason fine-tuned frenzy of Aaron Sorkin's *The West Wing*. The real West Wing was foreign to me.

But at this very moment, as removed from the goings-on of Washington as I ever would be, my soon-to-be friends, coworkers, and bosses were filling up what I could only imagine was Sorkin's empty set, streaming into the White House for the first time. A group of young people who bought into that "hope-y change-y" stuff. They traded in their campaign casual wear for suits, their personal phones for heavily encrypted federal government BlackBerrys. They were starting their own voyage. They had arrived. And now it was their job to turn promises into policy as, for the first time, Millennials moved into the West Wing.

Meanwhile, their boss was making it official in front of the Capitol. On the ship, we held our breath. The feed cut out, which offered an opportunity to look around the room. Many students were already crying; some were barely paying attention; others sneered that their candidate had lost. Yet most were overjoyed. The professors had a different look altogether. They were particularly compelled by the proceedings.

"Everything's about to change," one of them said during the frozen frame.

The feed popped back to life, eliciting relieved applause, which quickly gave way to raucous celebration when President Obama took his hand off the Bible, thanking Chief Justice John Roberts and stepping to the podium as our new president.

I didn't know him. Stephanie didn't know him. But we felt like we did. That was part of the magic of the 2008 campaign: the candidate's ability to connect, to strike a nerve. A positive nerve. We felt like we knew what he meant for our country. Like the reverse on several levels of the legendary Franklin Delano Roosevelt story. As historians retell it: At the time of FDR's funeral procession in April 1945, as the cortege carrying the president's coffin passed the crowds, one man broke down sobbing. A reporter nearby questioned the man, "Why are you crying so hard? Did you know him?"

"No," the man replied, "but he knew me." This simple comment captured President Roosevelt's extraordinary ability to understand the struggles of others.

For us, it was the same, only in the reverse. Not grief, but hope as far as the horizon stretched. And a real sense that this man knew me, knew us, and our hopes, our hurts, and our aspirations.

As Barack Obama took to the podium, the footage on our projection screen freezing and the audio faltering, our ship rocking and swaying, I swelled with pride. Stephanie did too.

In his red tie and dark overcoat, he addressed America and provided context for the beginnings of his time in power: "Forty-four Americans have now taken the presidential oath. The words have been spoken during rising tides of prosperity and the still waters of peace." I glanced out the window. Our waters were far from peaceful. "Yet, every so often, the oath is taken amidst gathering clouds and raging storms." He recounted our current crisis: two wars in the Middle East, an economy in freefall, and a planet in peril.

But he reminded us of how and why we would get through. "At these moments, America has carried on not simply because of the skill or vision of those in high office but because We the People have remained faithful to the ideals of our forbearers, and true to our founding documents. So it has been. So it must be with this generation of Americans." As he concluded his inauguration, some of us took to the ship's stern. Rather than look down at the chop where the water swirled and clapped harshly against the MV *Explorer*, we focused on the horizon, motionless and peaceful. Hope as far as the eye could see. Stephanie and I couldn't imagine a cooler spot to watch an inauguration than from the Atlantic Ocean.

Looking toward our first port of call, somebody shouted, "So, I guess we don't have to pretend to be Canadian anymore, eh?"

• • •

By the end of 2011, I was finally feeling at home in the West Wing—like maybe I wasn't such an imposter after all. I understood the cadence of the morning hustle and could predict the din of the press Briefing Room as we announced, "Two-minute warning. This is your two-minute warning for the press briefing." I'd caught on that two minutes usually meant five or six. I looked forward to the early afternoon lull, memorized when the mess line died down, and learned to always keep an eye tuned to the news. Underneath everything, I knew that any day could shift in an instant. And we began to feel like a family—for better or for worse. Bobby, Schultz, Matt, and Howli; Marie and Antoinette; Josh, Jay, Brian, and Dan—we were spending more time together than with our actual families. Rather than "you" or "the White House," I started to say "we" and "us."

But just as I was learning the ways of the West Wing, America was lurching toward its next presidential election. Before I knew it, the time had come to ramp up for reelection—to prove to the American people why any of us belonged.

President Obama often joked that he and his family were just renting, and that their lease would soon be up. He sensed the impermanence of it all, even as some of us—especially many of the Millennials—couldn't grapple with the thought that maybe there would come a time when we weren't working for this president in this building. It was all my adult self knew. I didn't want to grow up and enter the real world. At the very least, we had to put it off—for another four years.

Looking back on the 2012 presidential campaign can be a blur.

Everybody knows the top line: Mitt Romney, a seemingly out-of-touch Mormon millionaire, lost badly to President Obama in an election that centered on the economy. If you had asked me on that ship in 2009 about the 2008 election, I probably would have given a similarly concise, overly boiled-down wrap-up of the contest between Senators John McCain and Barack Obama. That's because I didn't have any idea of the long nights, the seven-day weeks, the many months that go into building those top lines that everyone remembers—and I had not yet felt the sting of the lowlights that everyone else forgets.

A billion bucks. A bunch of babies kissed. Repeated punch lines and perpetual rope lines. Worn slogans and endorsed messages. From West Hollywood to West Des Moines, and the Holiday Inn to the Four Seasons—across four very different seasons—2012 taught me what it actually takes to get a person elected president of the United States.

It started with a song.

"The more you see, the less you know."

I would rush from the motorcade, through the backstage pipe and drape, and toward the event site. The press pool would be right on my tail. We inserted ourselves into the buffer, crouched between the anxious crowd—weary from waiting—and the empty stage. The photographers readied their cameras and opened their laptops, spreading them across the floor. The cameraperson hoisted his hulking television camera up and over his shoulder. That was the routine. It's how every event kicked off.

The introducer—chosen by the campaign to make a brief statement before the president hit the stage—would end his or her brief remarks with the same phrase: "And now it's my honor to introduce the president of the United States, Barack Obama!"

A good introducer knew to hold a beat after "And now . . ." allowing the crowd to pull in its collective breath. Murmurs would shoot through the audience like lightning, as, for just a second, the introducer was in control. But as soon as he or she said "honor," the room would leap to its feet, letting out a raucous cheer on "introduce." By "Barack," the cheer would have overflowed into a deafening shriek. Only the most rhetorically gifted introducers could keep their attention long enough to even make it to "Obama!" before the floodgates opened, and the crowd had taken control of the room. All eyes would be on the corner where the pipe and drape meets the bleachers. For a moment, there would be nothing. A pregnant pause. The expectation boiling over. President Obama knew how to make an entrance.

Then it would begin.

The pluck of the electric guitar. Then the crunch of another one, building to something more. The mounting rumble of the drums. Those seated in the stands by the pipe and drape would see him first. Another cheer. The photographers would click away. To most of the crowd, he was still obscured—down on the floor level, shaking hands and waving. The expansive melody would take hold on the piano, escalating as he reached the bottom of the stairs.

"The more you see, the less you know."

U2's "City of Blinding Lights" served as the entrance theme for just about all of the president's campaign events, including his announcement in 2007 that he was first running for president, which took place at the foot of the Old State Capitol in Springfield, Illinois, where he served as a state senator; where Abraham Lincoln got his start in politics.

Rising, the song reached its crescendo in sync with the moment the president would crest the four stairs on the side of the stage. That's when he became visible to everyone in the arena, and the cheers overtook even U2. He would hug the introducer and put his arms in the air. For those of us who watched this spectacle unfold often two or three times a day, the cheers became a part of the song. The shrieks a fitting piece of the orchestra. His waving and pointing, an instrument to accompany the drums and guitar. All of this in service of the moment and the song, everybody—for a time—blinded by the lights.

And then he'd take to the podium and hush the crowd. The quiet would be pierced by the inevitable "We love you, Ba-rack!" and his automatic "I love you back!" Some laughter. Then he'd dig in, thanking his introducer, welcoming the crowd, pandering to the school's football team or jabbing at the city's basketball team. "If you have a seat, sit down," he'd say. "And if not, bend your knees. I'm gonna talk for a bit." And then he'd dive in, and I'd sit back in the buffer, my head against the bicycle rack that kept the crowd at bay.

I listened to hundreds of these speeches. His rhythm—rising, falling, repeating, culminating in an optimistic close or an earnest now-I'm-letting-you-in-on-the-real-answer moment—had become like second nature to me. It seeped beyond work. I remember

Stephanie editing a letter I wrote to our landlord; he didn't need to read about "hope" or "change," she said, he needed to fix our air conditioning!

Still, the speeches were always tweaked before delivery, so Marie and I would send each other the last three paragraphs of the remarks, so we knew what phrase to look out for and when to prepare the pool to move from the buffer.

During the campaign, Marie and I were on the road together constantly. We switched off: one of us minded the press pool and traveled on Air Force One; the other tended to the larger traveling press corps that followed Obama in a chartered plane and sat off to the side of the stage as the president delivered his remarks.

President Obama would inevitably turn his attention to his opponent. This would elicit boos, and the opportunity for him to deploy one of his favorite call-and-responses. "Don't boo!" he would cry out, waiting for the crowd to reply with him: "Vote!" From the buffer, I knew he was feeling good about the event if he slapped the side of the podium. It was his tell. By the time the first phrase in the last three paragraphs came about, he was usually on fire. He wasn't giving a speech anymore, he was delivering a sermon. Each word flowed into the next, each turn of phrase upped the ante until finally, his voice becoming hoarse and the crowd overtaking him, he would shout, "Thank you! God bless you! And God bless the United States of America!" He'd wave, and with a slap to the side of the podium, he'd be on his way to the buffer to shake some hands. As soon as Obama hit the steps, the music would return.

The familiar, driving beat of drums and then the ensemble

strains of the E Street Band took hold as I led the pool up to the stage, grabbed the president's remarks binder from his podium—and, for a flash, looked out from his previous vantage point, feeling for a fleeting moment the power of the president's platform.

"We take care of our own. Wherever this flag's flown. We take care of our own."

Bruce Springsteen's roaring chorus blared throughout the arena as a few lucky audience members joined the scrum by the buffer. They held out their babies for a lift and pawned off their books for a signature. It was hard to hear over the Boss's anthem—Americana at its finest—but I rustled the pool with hand gestures and nods. As the chorus wound down for the final time, I'd pull the pool back beyond the drapes, through the bowels of the building, and out to the motorcade, from where we'd come. On to the next stop. Wherever our flag's flown.

• • •

We did those events hundreds of times in service of one goal: reelecting President Obama. To do that, everybody—from the president to the press wranglers—needed to execute his and her jobs. For the president, his surrogates, and his senior campaign advisors, the job was clear: promote our policies while painting Mitt Romney as out of touch with the middle class.

Funny thing is, the Romney team had the exact same plan: to portray an aloof Obama who was hindering rather than helping middle-class Americans.

To us, Romney was a rich robot—not a bad guy, but not the right guy for Americans who don't own car elevators. To them, Obama was a big-government elitist who didn't understand the struggles of middle-class Americans or the burdens government imposes on them. To us, Obama had staved off a second Great Depression, saved the auto industry, and fundamentally rebuilt health care in a way that benefited tens of millions of Americans. To them, Obama was a failed president.

Those were the theses, and they were clear. Each campaign had a theory of the case about the opposing candidate. The months leading up to the election were about making the argument—over and over—until we could take a completed thesis to the electoral college in November. In the meantime, we took our case to the American people. Even by 2012, with the Obama campaign building on its success in 2008, social media would never be enough—and so the fourth estate was never out of sight or mind.

As we kicked into campaign mode, Josh took Antoinette and Marie and me aside and impressed upon each of us how crucial our role was. We were on the front lines; the Obama staffers most in touch with the press. He told us that it could be easy to forget—to think of ourselves as simply press wranglers or assistants—but that on the road, we represented the president. Small, seemingly meaningless miscues could spiral, sending things into a tailspin. "Let's not give anybody any reason to doubt our competency," he said. To me, that meant getting the little things right.

It's been said that campaigns are like start-ups on steroids. So there were a lot of little things to bear in mind. Thousands of people—staffers, volunteers, vendors—thrust together with a singular intention. The 2012 start-up was again based out of Chicago. There are strict rules bifurcating campaign staffers and White House officials, but a few people fell somewhere in between. A handful of senior aides, such as Dan, Jay, Valerie Jarrett, and others, were legally allowed to take part in the campaign in their official capacity as White House staffers.* Fewer lower-level staffers were allowed to travel with the president on the campaign. Marie and I were among the lucky few, fortunate to have been designated wranglers at the right time.

Our Secret Service hard pins, as they were called, provided universal and unfettered access to the presidential bubble. We had free rein of the place sans standard security checks. Our quarter-sized red or blue pins seemed a rather low-tech instrument for such a powerful measure of access, but off we went clapping our pins to our shirts—two cogs in the massive road-show machine that was the 2012 election.

By the time the campaign got into full swing, a dedicated press charter plane was put into effect, hauling dozens of reporters, producers, and crew wherever Obama went. Marie and I took turns. One of us would go on Air Force One with the smaller press pool, and one of us would go on the charter, which was the cushier gig. When with the pool on Air Force One, we needed to be on guard constantly—ready to relay information, parry questions, mind the

* All staffers were legally allowed to take part in the campaign in their personal capacity.

reporters, or make changes on the fly. On the charter, there was less to do; the White House travel office ran the show. My biggest worry on those flights was the hands-y middle-aged stewardesses who were a tad too attentive.

On the charter, there was a clear caste system. On-air talent, big-time print reporters, and experienced producers sat at the front, in first class. Cameramen, crew, as well as more junior reporters or folks from lesser-known outlets sat toward the back. Up front, conversations among those in first class often turned to which reporter would be named in the lead of the article should the plane crash.

The plane never went down. It typically arrived at the event site hours prior to the president and the pool. For outdoor sites, we'd hurry into great white tents, where the press filed their stories and where the buffet stood ready to fill up ravenous reporters and staffers. Reggie Love, the president's first "body man"—which is a DC term for the always-present person at the side of his or her boss ready with everything from a Tic Tac to classified documents—offered wise counsel about life on the road. "Eat on the plane or at the event," he told me. "Not both." I failed to heed his advice and ate my way through more states than I care to remember.

Really, it was the same nine swing states over and over again: Colorado, Florida, Iowa, Nevada, New Hampshire, North Carolina, Ohio, Virginia, and Wisconsin. Plus dashes to California for fund-raising.

Sometimes we took the road less traveled. In Iowa, we embarked on a three-day bus tour across the state. Iowa held a special place in the hearts of Obama people. The prairie-filled state had propelled him toward the presidency four years prior, and those who were there, including Obama, talk about that night like folklore. Politics at its best, they liked to say. We were back four years later to try and recapture that magic.

The president's hulking, armored black bus, complete with a presidential seal next to its impenetrable door, rumbled down narrow roads, bisecting dry cornfields and cresting rolling hills. Only at the top of those hills did it become truly clear: we were a behemoth of an organization, swooping down into Middle America, out of place and very much in the way. The giant vehicle—Bus Force One or Ground Force One, as it was known—was reduced to the size of a toy Matchbox car from my view in a vehicle toward the back of the motorcade. The president was trailed and preceded by countless police cars and motorcycles, nearly a dozen black Suburbans and numerous buses, one filled with Secret Service agents prepared to leap into action in an instant, and another stuffed with journalists ready to report. Our rolling presidential convoy kicked up a great deal of dust and dirt, drew its fair share of onlookers, and delayed locals just trying to go on about their lives.

But that's what we were after: the locals. We wanted interactions. Meetings with Middle America. Rolling through town in a tanklike bus wasn't the most relatable method of making connections, however, so we pandered to what unites so many Americans.

"Four more beers!"

As we crisscrossed Iowa, the chant rang out repeatedly. The public had recently learned that the White House was brewing its own beer: a honey ale and a honey porter. And the president was not above divvying out our stock, stored on Bus Force One, to local Iowans. Crowds particularly loved it when Obama was willing to have a drink at the bar with patrons. It was easy positive publicity for totally normal behavior. Polls in Iowa mirrored the national ones—a tight race—but Obama held the edge. We felt good. And the beer didn't hurt.

• • •

Even as the world obsessed over the election, I was fixated on something even more important. By 2012, Stephanie and I had been grade school, high school, and—thanks to the wise counsel of Dr. Phil and Larry King—college sweethearts. In all, we had been together for twelve years, half our lives. People were starting to ask about our "plans," which was code for "It's time to step up, dude!"

Marie and Antoinette were no different. They had been needling me for a couple of weeks to no avail about if and when I was going to pop the question. The first part was easy: yes, of course, I was going to ask Stephanie to marry me. The second part, the specifics of it all, was a bit blurrier.

Things came into focus the night of the state dinner in honor of David Cameron and the United Kingdom. Technically, because state dinners are reserved for heads of state (the Queen) rather than simply heads of government (the prime minister), this was actually an "official dinner." But it was grander than any state dinner the Obama White House had ever thrown. The White House set up a colossal white tent on the South Lawn, hidden beneath the limbs of massive trees and concealed from the outside by bushes and the South Lawn fence. It was rather like an elegant backyard wedding—if your backyard wedding was filled with celebrities and CEOs, dignitaries and diplomats. There was an old-timey trolley shuttling guests from the entrance reception by the East Wing to the main event a few hundred yards away. Everybody was dressed to the nines. Even we wranglers needed to dress up. I wore a dark suit that I pretended was a tux, while Marie and Antoinette wore floor-length gowns, which concealed their sneakers. (High heels are not efficient wrangling footwear.)

We ushered the press pool into the tent at the appropriate time—to hear toasts from President Obama and Prime Minister Cameron, as well as the first song or two from that night's entertainment, and Marie's favorite band, London's Mumford & Sons. I had never heard of them and therefore offered to depart with the first wave. I met up with Marie and Antoinette by the mess, but not the mess pickup window like usual. Because we were staffing the dinner, we were allowed to crash the fancier side of the White House Navy Mess: the exclusive wood-paneled room just behind the pickup window. Antoinette, who is nothing short of direct, asked what the latest was. "When are you going to pop the question?"

Maybe it was the formal wear and the dancing, the toasts and swanky tables. It could have been David Cameron's* charm or singer

* For years, a headshot of David Cameron hung above my desk, alongside one of network news anchor Brian Williams. I wasn't afraid to admit the man crush.

John Legend's very public displays of affection for his date, model Chrissy Teigen, just beyond the view of the press pool. Whatever it was, I was in the mood for a wedding of my own, and I decided to quit obfuscating in front of my friends. I was going to do it, I told them, which elicited quick, frenzied feedback: How, when, where?

"I want to do it here."

I had discussed with my parents as well as Stephanie's sister, Victoria, where to do it and landed on the White House. It was such a big part of my life and an increasingly important place to Stephanie, who was becoming more interested in politics and impressed by the president than even I was. Initially I worried that the Rose Garden was "cliché," but my parents told me to snap out of it; that I was nuts to even say such a thing. The Rose Garden it would be.

It's not that the rest of the White House community wasn't as supportive as Marie and Antoinette. Instead, some of my bosses and colleagues, as well as a reporter or two, simply had a different perspective, and they weren't afraid to share it. As the agreed-upon proposal date got closer, and the planning among Antoinette, Marie, and me picked up steam, Schultz would ask, "Don't you need a letter from your parents or something?" Matt and Bobby wondered whether "interns" were allowed to get engaged at the White House. Another boss called me "a child bride." We had to keep the plans hidden entirely from Brian, who would not have taken kindly to somebody putting the White House grounds—especially the Rose Garden—to use for personal, nonpresidential pursuits. If he came sniffing around, I planned to tell him that the

West Wing pooper was now wreaking havoc in the EEOB. Maybe he should go check into it.

We laid the groundwork weeks in advance. Stephanie was still living in Philly, where she worked for Fuji Bikes. So we switched on and off taking Amtrak or making the drive along I-95. I told Stephanie that the communications shop was hosting a spring party at the White House on Friday, April 6, so she would need to be in DC that weekend. I suggested she wear something nice—that she look good, which she didn't take as well as I'd hoped. I looped her on an email with Marie to talk through what each was planning to wear to the party. It was a long con. The most consequential trick I had previously played on Stephanie was in college, when my roommate Chris and I said we would cook dinner. Instead, we bought Taco Bell, repackaged it nicely on gourmet plates, poured the Mountain Dew Baja Blast into an elegant pitcher, and sat down to eat. An unwitting Stephanie was then forced to admit that she did not, in fact, hate Taco Bell as she so often claimed.

The stakes were higher for this sham. As Friday neared, my nerves increased, and by the morning of the proposal, jitters were jumping through me so much so that I couldn't sleep. I arrived at work earlier than normal.

By early afternoon, Jay couldn't help himself. He approached my desk, and I knew what was coming.

"I know, I know," I said, preempting him. "Bashar al-Assad, yada yada yada."

"No," Jay said. "I just heard today's the big day, and I wanted to say—"

"Oh, thank you," I said, feeling like an idiot.

"No, I gotta say, you don't look great."

"Huh? I didn't get much sleep," I protested.

"You should really go home and shave."

And so I did. I walked briskly up Sixteenth Street to the filthy studio apartment I was renting. Stephanie arrived early from Philadelphia as I was getting out of the shower, so I hid the ring box in my hanging sock cubby just before she walked in. My plan was to stay with Stephanie and walk back to the White House together. Then I received an email from Marie. The subject line began: "Don't freak out, but . . ."

I was absolutely freaking out. Marie explained that the president's schedule was shifting. We might miss our window and lose the light. I didn't have a backup plan, hadn't considered that something might not work out. I had gotten a bit too comfortable in the environment. A slow Friday could feel like a bit of a flophouse—like any office counting the minutes until happy hour. I neglected to consider, as I had learned time and again, that the tenor of the place can change in an instant, with fun plans scuttled just as quickly. To compound things, both my family and Stephanie's family were waiting at a nearby hotel to celebrate our Rose Garden engagement. They had come from across the country to be there. I shaved quickly, rustled through my socks and grabbed the ring, told Stephanie the party was delayed slightly due to a minor work emergency, and rushed back into the office.

The Oval Office looks squarely into the Rose Garden. Often, when the sun has only recently disappeared beyond the monuments and the Mall, the Oval remains alight, and the room's glow seeps through its sizable windows, partly illuminating the Colonnade and the Rose Garden, but not enough for my plan to work. I couldn't let it get to that point. The pictures wouldn't turn out well.

A Secret Service agent stands guard along the Colonnade whenever the president is in the Oval. I checked as soon as I arrived. The agent was there. But the Rose Garden was still bright. I consulted the president's private schedule again. He was supposed to be finished for the day. What could possibly be keeping the leader of the free world at work late on a Friday night, I asked Marie and Antoinette, irrationally frustrated.

"Calm down, Pattycakes," they told me. "It's going to work out."

I took a seat at my desk in Upper Press to try to do just that, but then coworkers who had heard the news started coming out of the woodwork, popping in from all corners of the West Wing. Jay walked in with Gene Sperling, one of the president's top economic advisors, and explained what I was about to do. Now, I hadn't previously worked at all with Gene—known around the West Wing as the Gene-Machine—but he piped right up.

"Can I offer you some advice?" he asked.

"Please."

"She might say no."

"That's advice?"

"Hey, I'm in politics," the Gene-Machine reasoned. "It's all about expectation setting."

I couldn't sit around any longer; time to get things in motion. I took a flier and, with time winding down, sent Stephanie a note to head toward the White House. I promised I would meet her at the northwest gate in front of Lafayette Park. As she made her way down Sixteenth Street, the president—mercifully—crossed from the Oval, down the Colonnade, through the Palm Room, and up to the residence.

Relieved, we took our positions. Marie dashed through the Briefing Room to grab Evan, a photographer from the Associated Press who'd agreed to surreptitiously photograph our engagement. Antoinette jogged out to the gate to meet Stephanie, and I took up a spot on the Colonnade. It was then that I realized, for all the crap they were giving me, much of the West Wing had stayed late on an otherwise slow Friday to help out. Ben Rhodes, a deputy national security advisor with many more important things on his mind, volunteered to block the double doors to the Colonnade, so that no one would interrupt our moment.

Stephanie told me later that she was annoyed with me for abandoning her at the apartment and doubly perturbed when I was nowhere to be found at the White House. She was mystified when Antoinette grabbed her from the gate, insisting on removing her security badge and taking her purse. But then Antoinette pushed her out to the Rose Garden.

I was waiting on the Colonnade. Truth is, I don't remember much more after this. I took her hand and walked her through a small clearing in the bushes toward the center of the Rose Garden. I spoke for what seemed like an eternity—in varying degrees of coherence—and then took a knee. I remember hearing the familiar click of a camera but didn't know where it was coming from. Stephanie doesn't remember what she said either, but she was nodding her head over and over, which had to mean something good. She said yes!

We walked back to the Colonnade and down to the Palm Room. I saw Marie and Evan the photographer jump from the bushes to the Palm Room to capture more moments. When we got to the Palm Room, we celebrated.

"This was my favorite wrangling job yet!" Marie exclaimed.

My family was waiting for us at the hotel, but as Stephanie and I stepped down into Lower Press, where everybody was waiting—Matt, Bobby, Howli, and others—I realized that I was developing another family. An Obama family. And I didn't want any of this to end.

• • •

Even in the afterglow of our engagement, as the White House felt more like a second home than an office, and just when I was finally getting the hang of things, polls and bumper stickers, attack ads and obnoxious buttons, were constant reminders that it could all come crumbling down on Tuesday, November 6, 2012. Even while Obama seemed to command a comfortable lead, Dan, Jay, Howli, and others—all more experienced political hands than I was—warned me not to worry too much when things tightened.

The gap between the two candidates would inevitably, and naturally, begin to close. After all, gaffes would be made. Many of the all-important undecideds would soon *decide* to "come home" and vote the way they usually did. Most of all, a close race—or the perception of a close race—benefits the media. So it would have to be. For months, the Obama campaign had capitalized on Romney's proclivity for goofy gaffes, foremost among them his attempts at appealing to Middle America by talking about how some of his friends own NASCAR teams, as well as his caught-on-audio comments about nearly half the country:

"All right, there are forty-seven percent who are with him [Obama], who are dependent upon government, who believe that they are victims, who believe the government has a responsibility to care for them, who believe that they are entitled to health care, to food, to housing, to you name it. My job is not to worry about those people. I'll never convince them they should take personal responsibility and care for their lives."

Now, that was a doozy, damaging in the way that the worst gaffes so often are: they provide seeming proof of a notion that many voters already have about a candidate. In this case, that Mitt Romney is rich and out of touch. And they can be boiled down into a quick turn of phrase rebutting the candidate: "I am the 47 percent."

Obama slipped up and flubbed a line that fit all of the same criteria. Campaigning in Roanoke, Virginia, as he was speaking about the unique opportunities our country and way of government has provided for its citizens, Obama told a hypothetical entrepreneur in reference to his hypothetical business, "You didn't build that." You didn't build that. I knew the second he said it, it didn't sit well. Sure, I understood what he was going for—that the hypothetical entrepreneur no doubt benefitted from America's infrastructure or technological advances from the military or any number of other benefits of living in the Land of the Free—but it didn't ring right rhetorically. And the Republicans seized the opportunity. *I did build that.*

The gaffes both candidates made during the summer of 2012 seem quaint when considered through the looking glass of the election that would follow, but on the trail, they haunted us into the fall.

Tension ratcheted up as the first presidential debate loomed in early October. Still, as I pulled into debate prep in Henderson, Nevada, I felt fine, buoyed by a seven-point lead in the polls and ready to spend some time *at* the pool—rather than *with* the pool. Meanwhile, the president and his team, with Senator John Kerry of Massachusetts playing Mitt Romney, ran through mock debates on a stage nearly identical to the one that waited in Denver. It's common practice to prepare for presidential debates secluded from the distractions of DC in a retreat-like setting. So our motorcade snaked along the highways of Henderson as always, but things took a turn—literally and figuratively—as we approached our hotel, with nearly five hundred rooms, about twenty miles outside of Las Vegas.

As we advanced, something was becoming abundantly clear: we were entering the hotel equivalent of a ghost town; a onetime luxury resort with no guests. No hubbub. Nobody lining the streets looking at us, zero signs waving, no clapping from supporters and no middle fingers raised by detractors. There was another way folks along the motorcade route expressed their displeasure with the president that was actually more offensive than the middle fingers: they would dramatically turn their backs to the motorcade as it passed.

It was a particularly effective form of silent protest, in that it really caught our attention. It irritated me every time. And yet it was also wonderfully American. To openly gripe about your leader, even in his presence, the kind of action that helped make America great in the first place. I got the sense that those middle fingers and turned backs didn't bother President Obama quite so much as they did me.

But there was no one to turn their backs on us as we continued along the vacant hotel grounds—driving through an overgrown, grotesquely unused golf course, and passing a vacant high-end shopping center constructed with man-made water features to look like it sat on a quaint river bluff in Europe. The ride was eerie. Like Disney World the day after the apocalypse.

I sent Marie a text: "This place is odd, right?"

She filled me in on some of the details. Turns out the resort defaulted on its mortgage during the economic crisis of 2008–09, which hit Las Vegas and its surrounding cities particularly hard. The city was coming back, but not as quickly as most would like. Insofar as the 2012 election—like all elections—was about the economy (stupid), and a referendum on whether the president had done enough to jump-start our economy, Henderson was a troubling spot to choose for the president to hone his argument for the American people about why his vision for economic growth continued to be the best one. It was the ideal dateline for a snarky think piece waiting to be written by one of the slightly bored journalists hanging around the hotel pool with me as the president worked diligently behind closed doors on his economic talking points.

We would have three days here. Three days for Obama to refine the rhetoric, adjust the arguments, memorize the statistics, and practice a punchy line or two—before stepping in front of seventy million Americans (plus the dulcet-toned Jim Lehrer, the recently retired *PBS NewsHour* anchorman) and the man who had been campaigning for months to put the president (and all of us) out of work. Three days before America really started to pay attention: *Do we want to keep this guy or try something new?*

It's a truism that most incumbents lose the first debate. Thing is, nobody told me that. So by the time our three days in Henderson were up, I was optimistic, confident as we landed in Denver, excited as we rolled down the cleared-out highway, that my boss would wipe the floor with Romney.

There were omens, though, that suggested we might be in for a surprise. First, our motorcade driver was nuts. The motorcade becomes so unwieldy in its length when traveling outside of DC with the president that we often rely on volunteers to drive many of the vans toward the back of the convoy. The driver assigned to the press van I was fortunate enough to ride shotgun in, bless her, did not understand the basic concept of the motorcade: the idea that, above all, we must stay together.

Now, these drivers are not pulled off the street and thrown keys; they are instructed exactly how to drive. We have an advance staffer fully dedicated to the motorcade. And I do mean dedicated. One of my favorite advance staffers, Tim Sneed, had developed a bit of road-show glory, known for his cowboy hat and the moniker Tim-Sneed-Motorcade, which was how most people referred to him. He packed dozens of Matchbox cars for every trip to simulate a miniature motorcade. There's a very distinct order into which the motorcade's vehicles are arranged. Absent a breakdown, there's no passing in motorcades—so the convoy is only as strong as its weakest rental van. In Denver, mine was the weakest link. We were delaying the cars behind us. I didn't want to be a back-seat driver, but we were threatening to chop the motorcade in two.

"You should really keep a little closer to the car in front."

From that moment on, she overcorrected, and every time the string of vehicles tautened, we'd nearly slam into the van ahead.

"Brake!" I'd yell. The reporters' cameras and laptops would go flying forward.

Eventually I had to stop looking at the cars ahead; it was too nerve wracking. So I focused on the billboards that went whizzing by until a striking advertisement loomed in the distance and grew larger as our driver lurched us forward. A darkened photo of a dour-looking Obama came into focus, shouting down at all of these swing-state passersby trying to get to work: "You didn't build that!"

I nearly refound religion on that ride. A photographer or two kissed the pavement when we pulled up to our destination. But we'd need more than faith for what would come next.

We knew we had lost the debate within the first ten minutes. Twitter said so, but I didn't need them to tell us. Truth is, my gut had dropped by the end of the two-minute opening statements. Each candidate had made a joke about it being President and Mrs. Obama's anniversary, but Romney's landed better; he actually got the bigger laugh. It was a precursor: his lines would resonate with the room all night. Obama seemed listless, whereas Romney came to play, finally on equal footing with the president. He "looked" the part. I had never been to a debate before and didn't really know how to watch one. So I took it in like a Philly sports fan. *We'll come back*, I kept telling myself. *This is our year. He's got to win.*

He didn't win.

"Let's get the hell out of here." Like two grousing Phillies fans trying to beat traffic, my coworker Nick and I darted out of the "spin room" (there was no spinning this in my mind) and dashed into a waiting car, where a Democratic volunteer would take us back to the hotel.

"What happened in there?" the driver asked.

"Nothing good."

Marie, on the other hand, was with the pool, rushing from the arena back to the vans. They all piled into the motorcade, where their volunteer driver had a different take. "Wow, he was great tonight!" It's easy to be blinded by partisanship, but this was such a decisive loss that even my nana was momentarily disappointed in *her* Barack. Still, Marie ran with it, nodding along in disbelief until the driver piled on, mentioning how proud he was of . . . Mitt.

Marie turned around to the reporters filling the three rows behind her and shared a moment of panic.

"Run!" Marie shouted.

They were unwittingly behind enemy lines. "Wrong motorcade!" They swung open the doors, sprinted down the road and barely caught up to the correct motorcade, where their driver, an Obama volunteer, was waiting nervously. She had been worried that the president's debate performance was so bad that everybody had jumped ship and literally climbed aboard the Romney bandwagon, leaving her van empty.

• • •

On Election Day 2012, our motorcade was a bit different. Rather than the bland vans to which we had become accustomed, our advance staffer Jeff hooked us up with a party bus that was more suitable for a bachelor party than a presidential motorcade. There was booze, swanky leather chairs lining the walls, and decorative lighting, as well as an impressive sound system and a mirrored ceiling. Marie, the pool, and I were grateful for Jeff's creativity. We would be in the van for many hours on November 6, 2012. Election Days are about active waiting—the party bus was a nice place to do it.

Obama had bounced back after the first debate knockout, and our side had finally begun to rationalize the subpar performance. Much of Democratic Twitter had melted down at first. In fact, Andrew Sullivan's take was so bleak that Dan put a moratorium on our media monitor (Velz at the time) sending around the *Newsweek/Daily Beast* writer's increasingly terrible analyses. Obama's predebate polling edge had been chopped in half, but we were still up, and our path to 270 electoral votes was much more clear than Romney's. The polls would need to be overwhelmingly wrong for things to go against us, and we had no reason not to trust the polls. So things looked good as we boarded the party bus, escaping the early-morning Chicago chill outside of President Obama's family home.

We'd been up since before dawn and didn't expect to sleep again until the next day. The long nights, ten-day travel stretches, the debates and commercials, the OTRs, bus tours, and slogans had all led to this day: America was voting! While we waited, we popped into a local campaign office for some phone banking. The president, in shirtsleeves and black-and-gray striped tie, took to the phones, greeting breathless volunteers and chatting on the phone (when they didn't ignore the call) with Chicago-area voters. Beyond that, we mainly waited. We asked: "What have you heard?" Nobody had heard anything. We wondered: "How are you feeling?" Everyone felt the same: nervous.

As the sun went down, the stakes went up.

Returns rushed in. I met Bobby, who took a few days off from the White House to volunteer for the final days of the campaign in Chicago. On Election Day, his primary task was finding the pool dinner, making him the most overqualified pizza boy on the planet. I met him to help carry the boxes. But when we arrived at the pizza shop, it was closed. The pool was hungry. And it was beginning to rain. Jeff had a backup plan and had food delivered directly to our bus. As we got back, damp from the deluge, word came down that the numbers looked good. Jeff, Marie, and I celebrated. Then my mom called: she won her first reelection to the Pennsylvania State House. One more thing to celebrate. As the night wore on, and the numbers continued to add up to what we thought would be a big win, the motorcade made its way to McCormick Place, the largest convention center in North America, and the site of the reelection speech as well as what seemed like the biggest party North America had ever seen. Music blared; we kept our eyes glued to our BlackBerrys. When would they call the election?

Just before ten fifteen local Chicago time, it happened. The election was called for President Obama. We had a party on the party bus, and waited some more. The president couldn't speak until after Romney had called and conceded. Jon Favreau sent the text of the reelection victory speech with a fitting all-caps subject line. Eventually we rushed into McCormick Place like we had so many times and so many places before—snaking backstage, beyond the drapes and into the event site, where we were met by massive blue drapes, countless waving American flags, and the most overjoyed, optimistic people you could cram into a convention center.

The president took the stage with his family as Stevie Wonder's celebratory "Signed, Sealed, Delivered, I'm Yours" blared. As his family dispersed to cheers and Stevie's last refrain concluded, the crowd erupted, chanting "Four more years!" so powerfully that the president needed to delay his start. The crowd was in control until Obama took over:

"Tonight, more than two hundred years after a former colony won the right to determine its own destiny, the task of perfecting our union moves forward. It moves forward because of you."

I turned around in the buffer, looked out at the sea of people behind me and thought back to four years before—a world away—watching a similar scene from the Atlantic Ocean. I knew the president meant what he said. Everyone—staffers, volunteers, voters—had a say in moving America forward.

"For the United States of America, the best is yet to come . . .

No matter what you do or where you go from here, you will carry the memory of the history we made together."

I didn't know what was next for me or where I'd wind up following life on the campaign trail, but I knew he was right. I would never forget this moment. This moment when politics seemed so big.

"The arguments we had are a mark of our liberty," the president continued. "Progress will come in fits and starts. It's not always a straight line. It's not always a smooth path." That much, as we would learn firsthand, was all too true. But there was no time to worry over that. We were focused on, as President Obama said, "what makes America great."

"I have never been more hopeful about our future. I have never been more hopeful about America, and I ask you to sustain that hope." His wasn't a call for blind optimism, it was a belief in "that stubborn thing inside us that insists, despite all the evidence to the contrary, that something better awaits us so long as we have the courage to keep reaching, to keep working, to keep fighting."

And just like that, he was finished. The campaign was officially over. And confetti rained down. Backstage, Marie, Jeff, and I bumped into the president and First Lady after the speech. He gave me a hug. I worried for an instant that maybe none of this was real. It was all going too well. But then the First Lady came up to me and sort of shimmied to the music, and I didn't know whether to sort of shimmy back, and so I just stood there like a moron. And I felt super awkward, which is when I knew it wasn't a dream. This was real life, though not the life I could have envisioned four years prior—and a world away—looking out with Stephanie over the vast, blue Atlantic.

• • •

The Blue Room of the White House is, well, blue. Sandwiched between the equally aptly named Red and Green rooms, the Blue Room was known best by members of our White House staff as the spot with the largest Christmas tree come December. During the marathon of holiday receptions, it was the place to meet on the crowded State Floor for some of the White House's infamous boozy eggnog, which was made by melting ice cream before pouring in too many types of alcohol to list. It was known to get the better of guests and staffers alike.

We planned to use the Blue Room for a slightly more presidential purpose on January 20, 2013.

Tradition holds that if the new president's swearing-in falls on a Sunday, it is to be handled as a small, private ceremony. The spectacle of the public inauguration is meant to follow the next day, Monday. Marie, Antoinette, Brian, and I had been working on the logistics for weeks. The oath taking would require only moments, but the timing had to be right. The US Constitution dictates it. More importantly for our purposes, the TV executives demand it. Every network planned to break in to its special programming and take the oath live.

We had to hit the mark.

For these most sensitive events and big moments, we brought

in an atomic clock: sturdy with red, digital numbers blinking the time. Atomic clocks are the most accurate timekeepers in existence, some with an uncertainty of just one second in thirty million years. That made us more comfortable. We knew that if our timing was off, then the schedules for the military's global positioning systems were wrong, too. I'm not sure why that made us feel better, but it did. Something about thirty million years and being in this together. So we liked our chances of hitting the mark at 11:55:00—five minutes prior to the Constitution's noon deadline.

The Friday before inauguration weekend, we got word that the president wanted to do a practice run. Stephanie and I hadn't noticed this on our Atlantic Ocean feed four years before, but I learned later that Chief Justice Roberts had fumbled the oath at Barack Obama's first inauguration. In fact, he had to visit the White House the next day for a do-over in the Map Room, just to be sure America's president was, in fact, president. We wanted to guard against similar problems the second time around. The First Lady couldn't make it to the practice, so we needed a stand-in. Somebody chose Marie. Now we just needed a book.

I had a copy of the comedian Sinbad's 1998 bestseller *Sinbad's Guide to Life (Because I Know Everything)* on my desk. Our go-getter of an intern Michael had just submitted an impressive book report* to me on what he'd learned from the book. Even though it might have been my bible, Sinbad's smash paperback was too thin to be a credible replacement for the real deal. So Marie ran down to

* Michael's book report was optional. He wanted to do it. Relax.

Lower Press and grabbed a more substantial stand-in, snatching the first of two books she spotted resting against the base of her desk. Then she ran upstairs to the Blue Room to pretend to be the First Lady. As our pretend chief justice got under way, she held out the book for the president to rest his right hand.

He gave her a quizzical look. "Hmm . . ."

Marie gasped. Had she accidentally grabbed *Fifty Shades of Grey*?

"*Life of Pi*?" Obama asked. He placed his hand on the cover and, before getting on with the practice run, gave his approval: "Good book."

Friday's rehearsal was a success. We spent most of Sunday morning prepping the Blue Room. The camera crew set up gear, and then did final sound and lighting checks. The residence staff removed the marble-topped wooden table in the center of the room. Marie and I waited, worried, and wondered how it would all play out. We answered the same questions over and over:

"Yes, we're still on time."

"Yep, the whole First Family will stand with him."

As the clock hit 11:30:00, the room began to fill: the pool was in place, and a few lucky members of the president's extended family filtered in. There were just a few staffers in the room. Marie and I eagerly anticipated the official start to the second term.

At 11:53:00, I gave a two-minute warning to the producer standing next to me. I triple-checked that my phone was muted. It was. Remembering that it had gone off the week before, interrupting our meeting in the Roosevelt Room, I quadruple-checked. I didn't think the lighthearted, ineffectual whimsy of the *Curb Your Enthusiasm* theme song would play well over the president's oath of office.

Two minutes later, the president hit his mark, the oath went off without a hitch, and Barack Obama's second term officially began.

It was difficult to wrap my head around the idea that I was in the room—a few paces away—on the periphery of history. I did my best to take it in.

To not let it slip by for granted.

To stretch it as long as I could.

I knew firsthand what this moment in the Blue Room meant to folks a world away.

5

Office Politics

I padded the book immensely. I probably would eliminate chapter five and gone straight to six. I wrote it because you have to have five to get to six.

—SINBAD IN THE 1995 FILM *HOUSEGUEST*

After the election, things around the West Wing fell into a familiar rhythm. They went back to normal—at least, as normal as the White House allows—and presidential politics gave way to office politics.

Before the White House, it hadn't occurred to me that there were so many ways to read—or write—an email that said the same thing. Consider a quick note of gratitude: "Thank you!" in your in-box is a good thing. "Thanks very much" is a very good thing. "Thank you" is genuine. "Thanks" is fine and likely well intentioned, too. "Ty" and "Thx" are more inscrutable. But around the West Wing, throw a period at the end of the shorter "Thanks," and some introspection is in order. *Thanks.* Maybe you were late getting your coworker what he needed, or the news is not as she'd hoped. Perhaps your colleague isn't feeling well, or the Navy Mess burnt his English muffin. It's also possible that whoever is writing "Thanks" *with a period* just doesn't like you. It's all part of the language—the nuance—of the place.

In that way, I suppose the White House is like any office. Cliques formed. Rivalries developed. People read too much into the meaning of otherwise straightforward emails; we sometimes pawned off work or passed the buck. We dealt with the boss's pets. We tried to raise our profiles at work, speaking up and offering insights in front of the chief of staff or finagling an invite to a senior staff meeting, taking on an additional task or two. But we in the Press Office had the unique opportunity to raise our profiles beyond the office and out in the world as well—to "build our brand."

Playbook, Politico's pervasive morning tip sheet, which was emailed to everybody inside the Beltway before sunrise, was a good way to start. Did your birthday make *Playbook*? If so, was it in the headline or just the body? These were some of the gross questions upon which DC social life, which exists only as a function of DC work life, is built. Somehow, attention from hometown papers seemed of a different, less gross sort. A variation on "Local Kid Hits It Big in the White House" was a common headline written about everybody, from the media monitor to major administration players in papers from Arkansas to Alaska. We all came from somewhere. Everybody had a story to tell. Some were no-brainers; some were a stretch.

Schultz had a knack for the art of the stretch. I remember one day he had been lingering around Upper Press, something clearly on his mind. And I knew that if he wasn't spinning a story in service of the president, he was surely working an angle at self-promotion. So this had to be good, fruitful ground for mocking. Josh was by now the press secretary. Same great hair and clean jokes, just with a bigger office and bit of fame even beyond the Beltway.

"Josh!" Schultz called, sensing an opening as Josh departed his office. "Do you have any flags with me placing Louie in *Doggie Du Jour Magazine*? It's for their Washington Power Player Pets edition."

This gave new meaning to the term "pet project," I thought.

"Would you be in the article, too?" Josh asked.

Schultz gave him a look that indicated the whole point was so that he would be included. He was the power player in this equation, after all. He produced the outlet's metrics, inexplicably had them at the ready: circulation of 230,000 and 3 million online subscribers.

"I definitely think you need to do this. It would be nice for Louie," Josh offered generously.

"Totes," Schultz said with his signature swivel, smile, and quick watch check.*

Self-promotion didn't always run like clockwork, though. In fact, the *Hill*'s infamous "50 Most Beautiful" list could get downright ugly. Nominations poured in anonymously to the *Hill*, one of DC's most popular publications. And each spring, it was time to

* Despite aggressive lobbying by his owner, Louie did not make the cover.

whittle down the fifty best looking people in the city, to be named and profiled in the summer for the *Hill*'s yearly exercise in self-aware superficiality. Staffers began jockeying for position. Feelings could be hurt and egos bruised. It was a nasty process, and I was in charge of it when I wasn't tied up with stories about White House varmints. Although, you could say I was dealing with a different sort of White House fox.*

It was up to me, when the nominations for White House staffers came in, to send each nominee a note that somebody thought they were hot and had submitted them for consideration—the height of awkward. "Are you willing to participate? To get your photo taken? Oh, and by the way, the *Hill* will judge, based on your photos, whether you actually make the cut." They hesitated, but most who were nominated took part.

Still, the process was better than I thought initially. The first time I was put in charge of the story, a coworker and I were under the impression that it was our duty to determine who among our coworkers were the most handsome and most beautiful, and to report back to the *Hill* with options. Now, *that* was an uncomfortable brainstorming session.

Eventually we took our list of comely coworkers to Josh. Somewhat aghast, he said that it wasn't the White House's responsibility to choose who should go on the list. Instead, like the holiday receptions, we just managed those who had been tapped to participate. I recognized immediately the error of our ways, but looking at Josh, I

* I know, I know. I groaned writing that line.

couldn't help noticing his rolling brown locks. *That hair*, I thought. *What an oversight.*

In truth, I didn't need to worry about making nominations, because folks were more than willing to do that themselves. I had to flag for a coworker that he was trending on a popular gossip website because his interns had been misusing official resources, busily sending out solicitations via prominent White House email lists asking hundreds of friends of the administration—many of them quite high profile—to vote for him. It was not a good look, but I was pleased that my intern's Sinbad book report had now been supplanted as the least productive use of a White House intern's time since the Clinton years.

Still, I wasn't innocent in all of this; I did my fair share of self-promotion. I had my wedding announcement in the *New York Times* and looked for my name in *Playbook* many mornings. I even asked—okay, pleaded with—Keith, a regional spokesperson in charge of press in the Northeast, to pitch me to the *Philadelphia Inquirer*. No dice on the *Inquirer*, but I did, in my final year, take part in the "50 Most Beautiful" list. I did not crack the top 10.*

• • •

Like many offices, we obsessed over lunch, wondered how early was too early to start asking about plans or what was on the mess menu. The White House Mess is a West Wing mainstay, a focal point for

* Okay, I may not have cracked the top 40.

countless discussions and rendezvous as well as a source of much aggravation. Staffers called down from their desks and placed an order for pickup one level below. But they didn't do delivery for anyone not named Barack or Joe.

The mess is located in the basement of the West Wing. A quick trip down the stairs at the entrance to Upper Press, past the chief speechwriter's office and the suite of national security offices and cubicles just beyond Pete Souza's nook (which used to be the White House barbershop), you turn down a narrow, nautically themed hallway toward our collective watering hole. There's the formal dining area for special guests and senior staff that I mentioned with regards to the UK State Dinner, but the real mess is the pickup window, flanked by two TVs, one set to ESPN and the other to the news. A line forms down the hall to the small window.

Thursdays served as "Mexican Day," which always prompted a longer-than-usual line, because the reliably wonderful chips and *queso* were a real crowd pleaser. Most Mexican Days, to ensure I got a hot batch of *queso*, I'd monitor the bottom right corner of my computer screen. The earliest you could call for lunch was 11:30. So at 11:28, 11:29, I would ready my hand at the phone, eager to dial the number I knew by heart: 71535.

The mess would occasionally bring in celebrity guest chefs—from José Andrés to Guy Fieri—to cook us some of their favorites. It was a highlight, usually months in the making. Thing is, on the mornings-of, I had a tendency to forget about the guest chef. As I would announce to my coworkers in Upper Press that I was headed to Subway for a crummy sandwich, Velz and Desiree would snicker but fail to save me from myself. "Enjoy your Five Dollar Footlong," they'd crack.

Most of the time, it was just as well. Celebrity guests generated the longest lines of all. Sometimes they meandered up the nautical hall and back down the corner toward Pete's office.

As you slogged closer to the pickup window (about three customers out), if you glanced to your right, you would find—no more than six feet away—an understated brown door with an oval gold placard. This was the entrance to the White House Situation Room.

This was an area of great stress. Options were presented quickly. Like so many decisions at the White House, sometimes the only choices were bad or worse.

And I'm sure it wasn't so easy in the Situation Room either.

It always made me laugh, White House staffers and guests sloshing about the mess with their coffees and Cokes, while on the other side of that door to the Situation Room (really a suite of smaller "situation" rooms), life-and-death decisions were constantly on the docket.

I remember well the morning when Jimmy, breathless, approached the new guy at the mess. "This is the third time I've had eggs this week, and they're always runny, and I asked for hard eggs, and how hard is it to make hard eggs, because I don't like runny eggs, and please just make me some new eggs." By the end, his voice was so high that his words were hitting a register almost imperceptible to the human ear. Velz watched the debacle unfold and asked what was the matter. Jimmy repeated his concerns verbatim, only quicker and now at a pitch only dogs can hear.

"This ain't Chuck E. Cheese's, people," Velz would say. "This is the White House." His familiar refrain was a way of saying that everybody should be at the top of his or her game in the West Wing. Runny eggs simply would not do.

Truth is, the mess, and those who worked in it, helped make the West Wing work. They were a huge part of life at the White House. We shouldn't have complained, but like any office cafeteria, it got to a point where they were an easy target—a punching bag in an extremely stressful environment where it wasn't okay to complain about how hard our jobs were, so moaning about the mess provided momentary relief. Accordingly, Jimmy and Velz weren't wrong. They were speaking for hundreds of staffers, giving voice to those whose frustrations would have gone unspoken. Sometimes it had to be noted that while it was the US Navy that got Osama bin Laden, the navy men and women of the mess couldn't quite seem to get the difference between rye and wheat. Of course, they did plenty of dishes well. I was partial to the chipotle turkey melt, once ordering it five days in a row. Antoinette, keen to take matters into her own hands, joined the mess board to exert influence; I pushed her to make the melt more readily available.

The Navy Mess brought in a new rotation of folks every few weeks or months, and there was—apparently—a very steep learning curve. Toward the end of the administration, a new man started at the window. Let's call him Gary.*

Gary, bless him, was the embodiment of incompetence. Orders

* So named by a coworker after the snail in *SpongeBob SquarePants*.

were wrong or lost. Lines grew longer and longer. The already sinewy grilled chicken became even more stringy, prompting senior staff to file complaints through their assistants. People took to calling Gary the "hot-mess mess guy," not to be confused with the "hot mess guy," who was tall, dark, and handsome—and making waves at the White House, especially within the gay staffer orbit.

Things came to a head, as they so often did, with Peter Velz.

It started with the premature call. The mess was famous for them. "Order ready in the mess for Velz." We always took them at their word. If the professionals behind the counter said it was ready now, it was ready now, we thought. These guys were military, after all. Velz sprinted downstairs, excited for his lunch. He waited in a longer-than-usual line that extended about to the enclosed model of a US Navy ship. He missed emails from his bosses and calls from reporters, only to learn from Gary, standing squat, squarely in the middle of the pickup window, that "No, sorry sir, your order's not yet ready." Velz plodded back to Upper Press, dragging his feet a bit.

"These are the guys with the nuclear codes," he lamented as he leapt back to his desk, answering his always-ringing phone.

It was the mess again. "Order ready in the—"

Down he went—to wait in line yet again. Hungry, Velz looked at the display as he got closer to the window. It was the special of the day: glazed chicken (the good chicken) and yummy-looking fries. The display looked even better than the description in the online menu. Just the midday pick-me-up that he needed. At the window, Gary pushed the cardboard container to Velz, who inspected the contents.

"There's no fries here."

"Yeah, it doesn't come with fries," Gary countered.

"I'm looking at the display right now, and there are fries."

Gary remained stoic as Velz's blood pressure skyrocketed: "Sometimes the display is inaccurate," Gary explained.

"Well, then, it's wrong on the online menu, too!"

"I don't believe that to be true," Gary said, forcing Velz to flee upstairs.

"I'll show them . . ." he muttered to himself, falling back into his seat behind me. Ignoring the ringing phone. The thing about Velz is that he admits when he's wrong. It's what he taught his interns year after year. Mistakes can be corrected, but you need to own them. No lying. Now, the flip side to that very positive trait is that when Velz is accused of being wrong when he knows he's right, well, then—he must set the record straight.

The printer kicked to life. As quick as he had come, he was gone again.

Peter stomped back down to the mess, rushing by the line. Now, Velz is a man who treats the queue with great respect, but he had been scorned. He had tunnel vision aimed at the little opening and the little man who had screwed him out of his fries.

No words were spoken. Velz didn't even need to show the menu, hot as it was off the printer. His look said it all. Teeth clenched, veins exploding through his forehead in frustration, he was met by Gary giving him puppy-dog eyes—his tail between his legs.

Velz's fries were there waiting for him.

The folks in line offered a redeemed Peter congratulations. Head nods, a spot of applause. Smiles and thumbs-up. They would all get fries now if they so desired. Mission accomplished.

I wondered what was going on in the Situation Room then.

• • •

The *Hill*'s "50 Most Beautiful" proved that Washington, DC, really is show business for ugly people, but that didn't keep real celebrities away. And you never knew who you would run into on the way to the mess, or who was waiting for you to exit the restroom. From Drake to the Pope, from Kendrick Lamar to Bibi Netanyahu, we had no shortage of high-profile guests at the White House.

I had moved into messaging when I learned that Pope Francis was stopping by for an official visit, so unfortunately, I had no reason to be in the Oval Office during the president's meeting with His Holiness, which was a bummer for my mom, a churchgoing Catholic all her life.

I was raised Catholic—was even lucky enough to have my beloved Uncle Wally, a priest, live with us for years while I was growing up—but I was never very religious. Praying, when I did it as a kid, was born mostly of superstition, driven by desires: to do well on a test, for instance, or in the hope that He could make Stephanie "like" me in fifth grade. Today my prayers have been reduced to resuscitations, born of superstition and limited to right before takeoffs at the airport. I never felt the need on Air Force One, but get me on a Delta or United flight, and you'd better believe I'm throwing up a Hail Mary and an Our Father as we barrel down the runway. My beliefs more closely mirror my nana's partisan rather than sacred baptism. Still, Pope Francis was to me an important breath of fresh air for the Catholic Church, which helped shape me growing up—a crucial leader on the world's stage. I wanted to meet him. My strategy was simple. I would exit the Upper Press door toward the restroom the moment he was walking the same route to his meeting in the Oval Office.

We did these sorts of laps all the time when somebody famous was in the lobby—Oprah, Bill Gates, Michael Jordan, everybody came through—but I didn't just want to see the Pope, I wanted an interaction with His Holiness. But how to make that happen? It took me a few hours, but I nailed it.

I would fake a sneeze—*Achoo!*—thereby forcing the Pope to bless me.

I ran the plan by friends, coworkers, bosses. I thought it was fool proof. They found it foolish. Most called it absurd. And nobody thought it would work. Desiree found it particularly distasteful and gave me five red-zone points for even mentioning the idea.

The day finally came. The Pope arrived to great fanfare; the faithful flocked to Washington. There was much pomp and circumstance throughout the city and especially at the White House. I realized quickly there would be no opportunity for a run-in in the West Wing: his route would be different. My only chance would be on the South Lawn, where Pope Francis would speak alongside the president. The day was beautiful, marked by clear skies and a summer-like sun—unusual for so late into September. Cheers erupted from down the lawn, like an audible "wave" at a sports stadium, trailing the bishop of Rome as he zipped up the South Lawn in his little black Fiat. He was moving much too quickly to hear a sneeze, so I held back, kept my powder dry. He exited his popemobile and stepped to the dais. I was about fifty feet away; too far, oh well. It was foolish, after all, and, I realized, likely offensive. A sin, maybe.

I looked up at the sun, a little frustrated, but also awed by the proceedings. I had just been at my desk, plugging away at talking points, and now, on a brief break, I popped down to listen to the Pope and the president in the backyard of the White House. The sun caught my eyes again. I felt it coming immediately. *Oh, no.* I heaved back and threw my head forward, releasing a thunderous—very real—sneeze. The Pope didn't notice. My bosses, seated next to me, thought I was being a jerk.

Desiree gave me a glare I hadn't seen since she'd learned I had asked Crystal about *Black-ish*. "Red zone!" she hissed.

• • •

"Thanks."

I received a number of those notes of nonthanks from the Staff Secretary's Office, the department tasked with producing a briefing book every night for the president. The dense book is filled with dozens of tabs: memos, draft remarks, letters from the public, and briefs from offices across the White House, from the Office of Management and Administration, to the National Security Council, to the Communications Office. President Obama stayed up late into the night reading the book. Theirs was a thankless, meticulous task, and the Staff Secretary's Office team is hyperfocused on the details: fonts, spacing, deadlines, and the like.

That's how I knew there was nothing haphazard about the email that Ted, a well-liked, longtime member of the staff secretary's team, had sent me early one morning from his windowless basement office. Communications was regularly late with its memos, and he wondered—and probably worried—if I was responsible for submitting the president's NCAA March Madness memo to be delivered in the afternoon. I was, and I told him so, which meant I was beholden to Ted for the rest of the day. "Thanks." Always ready to set a deadline, Ted lumbered through the halls with a teddy-bear-like affability and an infectious, memorable laugh. All completely at odds with his online persona. His reply to my message, "Thanks."—more of a screw-you than a thank-you—set the tone as I walked into Upper Press.

Jimmy asked about my weekend. Velz gave his standard answer: he mowed the lawn, which was one of his favorite things in the world. Bobby called me Bashar. The usual.

I noticed Jimmy's pencils again and realized something: we had no pencil sharpeners in the office. I wondered if that meant he was sharpening them at home and bringing them in. The pencils were a matter of pure optics, which is where Upper Press thrived. Nowhere was our mandate on more vivid display than a few weeks earlier, when we sought to remind America that the president was taking very seriously his responsibility to nominate a Supreme Court Justice in the wake of Antonin Scalia's sudden death.

It was Denis McDonough's idea. Not to be confused with Mitt

Romney's famous 2012 gaffe about potential female hires being presented to him in "binders full of women," we went about building a massive binder of options. There was a lot of skepticism among senior communications staffers, who thought the whole thing was silly. Denis stopped by Upper Press as folks were grappling with the best way to move forward. Velz and Desiree gave him a bit of crap about the idea. "Really, Denis? A binder?"

Somebody piled on about how it made a whole lot more sense to download the options to the president's iPad, which might as well have been attached to POTUS's hip. You could find him in his rare down-time enthralled, scrolling through that thing—playing the game Words with Friends or reading the *New York Times*.

Denis understood that the idea was a little bit silly, and he was a good sport—taking the ribbing from staffers with a smile. We weren't changing his mind, though. He sensed that his ploy would work. So he pushed back, asserting that we needed the biggest, most official presidential binder for POTUS. And we knew, too, that an iPad did nothing for us. There's no picture there.

It was a "be for what's going to happen" kind of a moment in Upper Press, which had become a West Wing aphorism for when we saw the writing on the wall. Might as well make the process as painless as possible. In this case, we knew the chief of staff had made up his mind: the binder was going to happen. And since our team's reservations were relatively mild, it was best to execute, or at the very least, to get out of the way.

I was in the West Wing for four chiefs of staff: Bill Daley, Pete Rouse (interim), Jack Lew, and Denis McDonough. Among varying levels of effectiveness, Denis seemed most suited for the position. He ran a tight ship. A tall, thin man who looked—appropriately—like he didn't get enough sunlight, Denis had an affable Minnesota twang and remembered everybody's name, from senators to janitors, from Barack to Gary from the mess. He often rode his bike to work. (Crystal and I rode with him once, flanked by Secret Service.) He is an impressive man, as dedicated to the cause as anybody could be, having started with Obama in 2007 and served as chief of staff for the entire second term. To his deputies, he could be intense, and some senior staff referred to his office as the Dragon's Den, but Denis was crucial and as good a chief of staff as a president could have. So when he pitched the binder, we knew we needed to be for what was going to happen.

Binder assembled and in the hands of the president, Velz and Desiree gathered the pool photographers, videographers, and print reporters from the Briefing Room and set them up at the door to the Colonnade (because the Colonnade means serious business). They went to Brian too, reminding him that POTUS needed to make a thing of the binder. "He's not just going to put it in his briefcase, right? We'll see it on camera?" they asked Brian, which was met with a healthy eye roll, given the specific question and the general context of the night.

Brian cued the president to lug his absurd binder from the Oval toward the residence—highlighting for the American people that he was thoroughly weighing his options *and* working after dark into the weekend. The binder, as pointless as Jimmy's pencils, was a little on the nose—even for us—but Denis was right. The press went with it, including the photo in nearly every article on the pending Supreme Court pick. And the video accompanied every story about the deliberations. It's how the message got made.

Nearly a month later, on this Tuesday in March, the president was still mired in that god-awful binder. He had yet to make a decision regarding the high court.

Even so, I needed him to focus on another court and a different pick: his NCAA college basketball brackets weren't going to fill themselves out. POTUS was agonizing over the tiered, webbed printout like it was a piece of landmark legislation. I asked Brian for another update over email: "Has the president made up his mind?"

"No."

"You know I'm talking about the basketball bracket and not the Supreme Court, right?"

He knew.

I typed "Thank you" and then thought better of it.

I held down the Delete key until only a *T* remained. I added the *y*, pondered a moment, and let fly with just "Ty."

My two-letter response was meant to create the sense of harried frenzy on my end. "Sure, I saw your note, but I'm too busy to spell out my response. I've got papers flying around, folders strewn about. Every letter counts to me. I'm stapling and typing, and I've got stuff to do." It was, admittedly, office optics run amok.

Later, as I was about to wash my hands in the restroom across the hall—the one Brian monitored—a thud rocked the door to the bathroom. It felt like an earthquake, which we had actually dealt with years before when I was sitting in the EEOB. Apparently, and probably not surprisingly, when buildings start to shake on the White House complex, the assumption is that a bomb went off and the building is about to implode. But this I knew was different. Maybe Brian was trying to catch the culprit in the act?

No, this was just somebody who had refused the courtesy of a quick double knock before pushing on the door. You see, the politics around the single-stall bathroom on the first floor of the West Wing were fraught. There was one school of thought—which I subscribed to—that said you knock no matter what. There was a second theory that you just pushed on the door. If it was locked, then it wouldn't open. No harm, no foul. Of course, not everyone remembered to lock the door, and I refused the potential for such awkwardness among coworkers. The dueling philosophies drove me nuts. I was so sure that one was correct, but consensus can be hard to come by in DC.

Back in the bathroom, reeling from the thrashing at the door, I felt fortunate to have remembered to lock it. This dude's push was absurdly forceful, like he'd thrown his whole body into it. To spite whichever coworker this was, I washed my hands much longer than usual. I even used soap. *This guy can wait*, I thought.

Hands freshly washed and thoroughly dried, I opened the door and looked up. And then kept looking up. And looked up some more, craning my neck until the forceful attempt on the door made a whole lot more sense.

It was Shaq.

He said something, but I couldn't make it out; his voice was too deep to register. I walked away, stunned. I was ready to recount the run-in as I returned to Upper Press but found a note waiting for me in my in-box from Jimmy. Staff Sec was asking about the NCAA memo again. I was annoyed but knew better than to reply to Jimmy with anything other than a "Thank you!"

Moments later, Brian rushed to my desk. I thought maybe he had the same hunch I did about Shaquille O'Neal, but his visit was about something different: "You know about college basketball, right?"

"Yeah," I said, realizing I hadn't remotely kept up with this season and likely couldn't even name the four top seeds.

"The president needs to see you."

• • •

"Mr. President, Pat knows what's going on."

With that, I was thrust into the Oval Office—the floor creaking as I stepped in. The president was seated—head down—at the Resolute desk across the room, which felt like a mile away with no one else around and no clue what I was doing or why I was approaching the leader of the free world wholly unprepared. Pete Souza, who was always there to catch a photo, wasn't even around. Normally, after you go into the Oval Office, you wait a few days and then sheepishly email the White House Photo Office: "Hey there, any chance Pete snagged a photo when I was in the Oval?" If there were a way over email to purposely bump into someone and then just so happen to ask for a favor, that's what these awkward notes would amount to. Still, it would be worth it. Usually, you would receive a photograph that would make your mom cry. With Pete absent, I wondered if this Oval Office visit even counted.

As I approached, I noticed that there was just one piece of paper on the president's grand desk, occupying his time and energy. President Obama often recounted that if something reached his desk, then it had to be a very difficult decision, because if it were simple, somebody would have solved it long before it made its way to the Oval Office. And his desk, the Resolute Desk—a gift from Queen Victoria to President Rutherford Hayes and used by many subsequent presidents—was worthy of the business that got done on it.

So what was this lone sheet of paper dominating the chief executive's attention in this moment? It was the college basketball bracket we had printed for him. I suppose some of the picks were difficult, but I suspect some of the sixteen-versus-one seeds could have been delegated to a cabinet secretary.

He looked up at me.

"Hey brother, so for this NCAA thing . . ."

Oh shit, he called me "brother." That's cool.

"Last year, did we run through the Sweet Sixteen or the Elite Eight on TV?"

Oh shit, I have no clue. I barely know what you're talking about. I could ask him a follow-up, but this seems a pretty simple either-or proposition that I was evidently brought in specifically to answer. I could tell him I'd double-check, but isn't that what I was supposed to have done already—

"Sixteen."

Oh shit, I just lied to the president.

I said it with total confidence. A bald-faced lie to the president of the United States in his own office. I rationalized that I didn't *know* I was wrong; I just didn't know if I was right, either. And I could check and confirm the moment I got out of there. It's not that I was purposely pushing false information; I was just leaving out that I wasn't actually sure the answer was sixteen and that I had no real evidence for the guess in the first place. It was a lie of omission by commission—if that's a thing. (It's not.)

Jesus, I thought to myself, *considering I was basically baptized a Democrat, a lie to Barack Obama has to be worse than a lie to the Pope!*

The president, oblivious to my internal debate, made a decision: "Got it. Well, I just want to do eight this time—that way we can talk more about the actual teams rather than spend all that time filling the thing out on air."

"That makes total sense, sir," I said, not knowing if this was a problem for ESPN in any way, shape, or form. Out of the corner of my eye, I noticed that Pete had crept in, capturing my presidential lie for posterity. "I'm sure they'll be all for that," I told the president.

As I thanked him and turned to leave, President Obama looked up from his bracket once more:

"Thanks," he said—I suspected with a period.

6

Disaster Casual

Ubuntu is very difficult to render into a Western language. It speaks of the very essence of being human.

—DESMOND TUTU

Put yourself in his shoes. Imagine: you've just arrived in Africa, your own father's homeland. Because this is one of your most meaningful overseas visits, you're traveling with your mother-in-law, one of your daughters, and your wife—herself the descendant of slaves. You are touring Goree Island, the infamous, haunting marker of the transatlantic slave trade off the coast of Dakar, Senegal.

You conclude your visit to the both literally and figuratively dark Maison des Esclaves: the "House of Slaves." You move toward a small doorway bathed in light. You step out of this haunting memorial and are instantly at the vantage point of so many Africans who, for hundreds of years, took in that very view as they were forced to board boats embarking for the New World. Out of this "Door of No Return," your children's ancestors could have been forced to North America to live and die as slaves. Some of those men and women who exited the portal might even have gone on to help build your family's current home.

You are America's first black president.

If ever there was a place to consider the past, the future, and where we stand now, then this place—where humanity took root and racism took hold—is it. Out on this ledge overlooking the Atlantic, you're eyeing the vast blue expanse and contemplating these enslaved men's and women's journeys. Simultaneously, the African continent—indeed, the entire world—considers your own journey. From a community organizer with a funny name to the leader of the free world (still with a funny name). You're hope-and-change incarnate, and this place and time, this moment, captures that—for you and for your family: the First Family. The eyes of the world are upon you; you must be simultaneously feeling the triumph of this important visit for your presidential self, and a private, personal sadness about this dark history.

And then a boat full of reporters floats into your view, snapping, clicking, gawking.

A bunch of White House journalists get into a boat off the coast of Africa: it sounds like the beginning of a bad joke. I wished it were a joke. Instead it was my job: to mind the press pool no matter where it took me, as reporters angled for a view of the president. I was mortified the minute we hopped off the dock and into the boat. It felt intrusive, like a celebrity house tour. To me, we had no business being in the president's frame. But such is life when you're traveling with the leader of the free world. Unfortunately, the White House press corps did not share my concern. Shameless almost by job definition, the members of the president's press pool were adamant that they get the shot. And, of course, we in the White House Press and Communications Office—sometimes equally shameless—wanted to drum up as much positive coverage of the trip as possible. So, sick and sunburned, we piled onto our glorified pontoon boat as the Secret Service, scanning and scoping all the way, screamed by on their intimidating police crafts.

I imagine we looked a bit out of place in our dark suits and dress shoes, the choppy water pitching and pulling us every which way as we zigged and zagged toward our anchor point roughly sixty yards beyond the notorious door through which President Obama and the First Family would peer. Confident that the president was running behind and trying to stave off seasickness, I trained my eyes on the horizon and zoned out. I hoped we wouldn't tarnish the president's visit. As a press wrangler, I had grown accustomed to bringing the press in to take photos or shout questions at the top (beginning) or bottom (end) of a meeting, performance, visit, or otherwise notable event.

Determining when to pull the pool was an acquired skill. It was nearly impossible to please all parties, particularly the press, who wanted to stick around forever, and the president, who usually wished that they would scoot off after just a moment or two so he could get back to business. This pool spray was entirely different. We wouldn't have time to pull up anchor and drift away while the president continued to take it all in alone. No, we would cover his entire time at the door.

As I worried that it was too much, a *ker-plunk* emanated from the other end of the boat, and I heard a kerfuffle among the press. Like the hapless mother in *Home Alone*, I quickly counted heads. Everybody was accounted for. No White House correspondents overboard. Thank God, because that would have been a *thing*. Relieved, I zoned out again until a woman, looking particularly steamed, broke my gaze.

"My adapter went overboard," she said in a tone that suggested she'd had nothing to do with it and, simultaneously, that there was something for me to do about it.

"I'm sorry, what?" I asked.

"My adapter. It fell in the ocean."

I understood her knee-jerk reaction to tell me, the White House staffer—and their minder—what happened. After the 2012 election, the White House press corps and I—as well as the military camera crew that traveled everywhere with us—had become close. But this was also exactly the kind of request, thinly veiled as a declarative comment, that I had a hard time stomaching. Did she think I had a Speedo on beneath my suit? That I'd slip into my flippers and dive into the Atlantic Ocean for her adapter?

Evidently, that's exactly what she thought, because the next thing she said was, "Can you try and get it?"

I laughed, but only so I didn't scream. I was already in a foul mood because our captain had dropped anchor significantly closer to the Door of No Return than I had anticipated. From here, we were certain to be a floating distraction to the president and his family.

As we circled clockwise toward the door, the reporters flooded to the port side of the boat—dipping our dinghy to the point where it seemed we could soon capsize. *I refuse to die this way,* I thought. *So close to my wedding. Stephanie will not be happy.* Just then, the current began to circle us around the anchor, forcing the press pool to adjust and to dart from side to side. You've not seen panic on the high seas until you've witnessed a group of White House photographers, reporters, cameramen, and sound techs scrambling. It turned into a real-life roulette wheel, with reporters staking their shot, gambling with their bodies on which spot would be tops when the president finally exited the door.

After a final spin, President Obama, in dad-khakis and a white button-down shirt with no tie, appeared. He stepped to the bottom ridge of the door.

"Bingo!" one of the veteran photographers proclaimed. Shutters flickered and clicked, a million miles per second.

His eldest daughter, Malia, mother-in-law, Marian, and wife, Michelle, appeared next. The press pool snapped away. I looked to the right side of the island, where I saw Marie on land. During the campaign, she had become one of my closest friends at the White House. That's why she felt the need to warn me before we were wheels up for Africa that this would be her last foreign trip with the president; that she would soon leave the West Wing for a fast-growing tech start-up in San Francisco.* In fact, she planned to depart DC the day after my wedding, which was fast approaching.

* Marie's was one of the earlier moves in what would become a major migration of Obama people from DC to San Francisco.

Stephanie wasn't exactly thrilled when I told her I'd have to travel to Africa with the president for eight days just a few weeks before our wedding, just as the final planning kicked into high gear and as we were closing on our new home in Washington, DC. I looked forward to telling my bride-to-be about the boat and the adapter and the seasickness. I would reiterate to her that it wasn't all fun, this whole traveling with the president thing.

Marie was following another pack of photographers and journalists as they worked to get an additional angle from land. For bigger trips or more newsworthy events, the press sometimes requested that two press pools be assembled, allowing for greater coverage. This was the case throughout much of our Africa trip. One by one, the photographers who were following Marie skidded down a rock-strewn slope—a small cliff, really. It reminded me of our trip to Petra, Jordan, where Marie, dedicated as ever to the job, set up a line of rocks to mark where the photographers could stand. That prompted a stern talking to from a very official-looking Petra staff member for altering a UNESCO World Heritage Site.

Jesus, I thought as some of the photographers fully tumbled to the ground for the second angle, scraping their arms and knees. Marie nearly did the same. It wouldn't have been the first time she'd been injured as a wrangler. A few months before, on our trip to Jerusalem and the West Bank, Marie managed the pool during the president's visit to the birthplace of Jesus while I hung with the charter. As President Obama quickly—and unexpectedly—rounded a corner, Marie turned to clear a path for him, yelling at the pool to run, and rose before—bang!—smacking her head on the low ceilings. Concussed at Jesus's birthplace. The memory of that was funny to me, and I laughed as the sound of the rocks rolling down the ledge carried over the water to our boat. While the photographers with Marie neglected to protect their legs, shoulders, and heads, they cradled their cameras like children. And at the bottom of the rocky ridge, they put them to use.

I turned back to the reporters on my boat. Each was laser focused on the First Family, shooting photos, videos, and capturing sound. The print reporters tapped out their dispatches to editors back in the United States without even looking down at their phones or laptops, which were perched perilously along the edge of the boat.

I was wrong. None of this was shameless. They weren't in the president's way. The members of the press were doing their jobs. They were there to tell his story. A couple centuries ago, a person who looked like Barack Obama wouldn't have exited that door as a free man, let alone as the leader of the free world. So this was more than a nice family moment; it was bigger than this larger-than-life American family. It was for the people of Senegal, who said that the trip signified that their small country "matters." It was for the children who lined the streets as our motorcade twisted and turned through Dakar. And it was a moment for kids back home, too—from Detroit to Des Moines—who might be inspired by this glimpse at history to think beyond the boundaries that might have been drawn around them. This was a story worth telling. At least, that's how I justified the awkward, floating troop of Beltway reporters I was responsible for traipsing through Africa.

The First Family disappeared, and the reporters rushed to file their photos and footage. I looked over to Marie, giving her a weary wave and a thumbs-up. The day nearly done, I gazed over the side of the boat to the water below and caught a quick glimpse of a shimmering object on the ocean floor. Another day traveling with the president.

• • •

During my time at the White House, I did countless domestic trips and nearly twenty foreign visits with President Obama.

Traveling with the president was thrilling, as he was received by folks from every walk of life and from every country you can imagine with exhilaration and delight. It was like tagging along on tour with your favorite band—except we were traveling with the world's biggest superstar. Our front man just so happened to triple, in the view of much of the world, as a brilliant politician, trailblazing leader, and one of the marvelous minds of our time—unless you asked the talking heads on Fox News, who were usually busy blasting him for using Dijon mustard, playing golf, or wasting taxpayer funds on Air Force One.

But not even Fox News could get you down when walking up the stairs to the president's plane. As everyone knows, the commander in chief travels in style—and Air Force One does not disappoint.

The plane underscores America's manufacturing strength and highlights our technological prowess, but it does something more.

It provides an aura. It represents our country's greatness, American majesty on display every time the 747 labors to a landing around the world, which is no accident. The Kennedys, well versed in the importance of style, teamed up with a noted commercial designer, Raymond Loewy, to produce the legendary aesthetic down to the font that exists to this day. President and Mrs. Kennedy understood better than most the importance of branding, and on Air Force One, they succeeded. Greater than the sum of its parts, the plane is ethereal. In the correct context, with the right president aboard, the plane is the globe's single most potent symbol of democracy.

Well, technically, there are two planes that we identify today as Air Force One, used roughly equally often to ferry the president and his team across the country and around the world. These Boeing VC-25 aircrafts were built specifically to safely move the president through the sky. There are only two, with tail numbers 28000 and 29000—they are identical twins. So much so that it was impossible for me to tell from my normal spot—the very last seat on both planes—which was which. I looked for a thread loose on the plush leather seat or a scratch on the small desk next to me, but there were typically no discernible differences. One of the planes did have an issue with the back bathroom, the one next to my seat. The lock would get stuck somewhere between Occupied and Unoccupied—not ideal—which generated an awkward encounter or two. Other than that, the planes were the same, the layouts unchanged.

In the very back of the plane, just in front of the last galley, is where the press pool sat—confined to the smallest corner of the plane—with me. There was no Wi-Fi,* so aboard the most technologically advanced plane in the sky, we kicked it old school. Literally. *Old School,* with Will Ferrell, Luke Wilson, and Vince Vaughn, was one of the popular movies we watched, along with *Dodgeball,* starring Ben Stiller and (again) Vince Vaughn, which, for a time, was played on almost every leg of travel. There were magazines covered in plastic binders, like the ones in your dentist's office. They were just below overflowing bowls of candy, like the ones you'd never find in your dentist's office. The food on board was wonderful, and we were fed every leg, no matter how short the flight. While we were often feted with fancy dishes and the alcohol of our choice, there was always a persnickety photographer or two who insisted on a peanut butter and jelly—no crust. Still, the food and drinks as well as the entertainment helped keep the press contented, because they were stuck in their cabin, not allowed to roam the rest of the plane.

Fortunately, I was granted more freedom.

As I exited the press confines, I'd find a separate, similarly small, cabin that housed the traveling Secret Service agents. This is about as casual as you will see the professionals of the United States Secret Service. Their jackets, for once, off. Their gun holsters often slung over the seat in front of them—a vivid reminder that this ain't Delta.

To the left of the press cabin sit the members of the US Air

* A particularly slow excuse for Wi-Fi was added late in Obama's second term.

Force, all impeccably—and uniformly—dressed in their blue AF1 bomber jackets. Ahead, the plane opens up into the guest cabin, which extends the full width of the behemoth 747. Eight reclining leather chairs—plush and brown—corner two wooden tables. Congressmen and congresswomen hitching a ride to their home districts settle into this area for the flights, as do other distinguished guests. Extremely distinguished guests, on the other hand—from the Bushes and Clintons to Bruce Springsteen—usually hobnob farther up front.

Ahead of the guest cabin is a small office with two of the slowest computers on or off Earth, as well as the staff cabin, similar in size and look to the guest cabin.

Then things get presidential. Walking forward on the right is the conference room, where Obama spent much of his time playing spades with trusted aides.

President Obama, presumably the busiest person on the plane, was never much for taking the opportunity to sleep. If he wasn't reading briefing books, he was usually game to play cards. For hours. Sleep-deprived aides sometimes struggled to keep up. Jay was a frequent partner, which was a problem for me. You see, I often needed to talk to Jay about a reporter question or press issue, which necessitated me entering the Air Force One conference room and putting the game on hold as I chatted with Jay. I did not like interrupting the president's card games. As he rose through the ranks, Schultz made his spades debut, too. Trouble is, he didn't know how to shuffle, so for a few weeks, he kept a deck in his office and practiced behind closed doors.

In the front by the staff cabin is the doctor's office, where we were free to drop in with whatever mundane maladies we faced. The president's doctor, Ronny Jackson, as well as a nurse or two, were always nearby. I usually stopped by with a headache or a cold, but they were an ever-present reminder—along with the operating table and armed men on board—of the risks the president faces. The flight deck was on the second level, leaving the front portion of the plane available for the president's office, his custom Air Force One jacket waiting for him on his deep-brown leather chair. And at the very front, the president's private quarters, complete with a bed and an impressive bathroom.

But beyond the bedroom and bathroom, and forgetting about the fantastic food, which we passengers were charged for whether or not we ate (good government at its best . . .), the greatest part of flying on Air Force One is the atmosphere. The rules are loose. Tray table down for takeoff? Sure. Want to change into pajamas and sleep on the floor? No problem. Folks who are typically spread across the White House's eighteen-acre campus, and sometimes across Washington, DC, itself, are put together in one confined space.

There was a long-running prank pulled against the newest wrangler on Air Force One, whereby we were made to believe that we were responsible for the parachutes to be handed out to the press in the event of an emergency. I fell for it momentarily—but having read chapter 1, that shouldn't shock you. More surprisingly, when it was my turn to pass the prank on to a newer wrangler—Velz—he fell for it too.

When I came clean, he offered an interesting perspective on how someone as innately skeptical as he is could fall for such a ludicrous lie. "Well, if you told me two years ago when I graduated college that I'd be taking my first trip aboard Air Force One, I wouldn't have believed you," he said. "Because it's completely insane. But I am, so I mean, yeah, if you tell me there are parachutes, why wouldn't I believe you."

We were already at 99 percent unbelievable—in rarefied air—so parachutes seemed plausible.

And each journey took on a surreal, adult field trip feel. You came back knowing just a little bit more about the people you work with. After all, there's no better way to get to know folks than to travel with them. Or fall asleep next to them, as I once did with Brian Williams. I thought it best not to tell him that his photo hung over my desk alongside David Cameron's.

And Air Force One is where I got to know President Obama a little bit better. From his casual wear to his habits to kill time, Air Force One was the perfect place to get a sense of Barack Obama off the clock. Up in the air, this plane, filled with the most powerful people on Earth, is momentarily disconnected from Earth, deaf to the drone of cable news. Alienated.

But as we descended, our disconnection slowly evaporated. BlackBerrys began to ping as we returned to Earth and picked up television reception again. We sometimes turned to CNN or the local news, which often covered the president's arrival live. Watching Air Force One descend on television while aboard is trippy. It's a slap-yourself moment. Hard to comprehend. Seeing the plane touch down, like you've seen in movies and countless clips from the news, it's hard to conceptualize—hard to believe—every time.

I remember one trip, as we closed in on the runway and CNN kicked to life, airing our landing live, I turned to one of the grizzled photographers. He'd done thousands of flights. He just smiled.

"It never gets old."

"I'm still trying to wrap my head around it," I said. But there's never any time to do that. Because the moment the wheels halt and the familiar arrival bell tolls, the men and women of the air force—just one cabin over—jump to their feet, the Secret Service secure their weapons, and the men and women of the press ready their cameras. The president is wheels down, and the trip's about to begin.

• • •

We got our money's worth out of that plane. We had to. After all, the president needs to be in a lot of places for various reasons, from domestic travel and foreign trips, to vacations and campaigning, to disaster visits and funerals.

DOMESTIC TRAVEL

Official domestic and campaign trips were, not surprisingly, the most prevalent form of presidential travel. From rallies and factory visits to diner drop-ins and hikes through national parks, we criss-crossed the country in service of the president and his vision for America. But when things hit close to home, many staffers—myself included—tried to kill two birds with one stone. Hometown visits are a good opportunity to introduce the president to your family, which is exactly what I planned to do when I heard we would hold an official event just outside Philly, not far from where I grew up.

I'll never forget spotting my in-laws' house from the window of a helicopter trailing Marine One through the air as we flew to the event. I'll also never forget the way the president looked at me that day.

Like I was a moron.

Stephanie hadn't yet met my boss. And because I knew the Africa trip I mentioned earlier was on the horizon—and dangerously close to our wedding—I thought POTUS's visit to the suburbs of Philadelphia early in 2013 was the win-win moment to make the meeting happen. She and my mom had waited backstage all morning. Marie, who arrived at the event site early with the press charter, got them situated. I was traveling with the president and the smaller White House press pool, which always arrived a few hours behind the charter. Eventually the rumble of our helicopters overtook the venue. The folks in line bounced back to life and out of the haze of a long wait as our helicopter came in for a landing. With additional helicopters touching down all around us—rotors vibrating, blades ratcheting off, and our engine freshly cut—I disembarked our helicopter, Nighthawk 4, and darted toward the warehouse. Let's be real: getting off of a helicopter in a suit—it's a good look. So, I was confident; ready to make a good impression on the president and my fiancée and to smooth the way for the Africa announcement.

The line kicked into gear, moving in fits and starts. After greeting my mom and Stephanie as well as a few other familiar faces in line—one more excited than the next—I jumped ahead to the front of the line and checked in on the president. He seemed to be in a great mood. Just what I needed. Smiling and laughing. Glad-handing, in the best sense of the word. Perfect for an introduction. I returned to my mom and fiancée as they inched closer to POTUS.

"What should I say to him?" Stephanie asked anxiously.

"Anything. Just be cool."

"Not exactly helpful, Pat," my mom interjected.

After a bit more nervous small talk, we were ushered closer, his laugh was more booming, and his unmistakable voice became clear. The president was just beyond the dark blue drapery, which the White House advance team piped throughout the warehouse. We slipped into the slit in the drape. He greeted us warmly, exuding his cool, comfortable vibe. Like they'd all been friends for ages. Stephanie—who had been a wreck—was immediately at ease. After making introductions, I stepped off to the side.

My mom had recently been elected to the Pennsylvania State Legislature as Madeleine Dean, her maiden name. Turns out "Cunnane" doesn't fit as well on a lawn sign. She told the president of her priorities for the state. He listened graciously, and—as if everyone in the building didn't know his entire personal history—he offered, "The state legislature is how I got my start in politics."

My mom smiled wryly. "You know, I heard that somewhere . . ."

Next, the president pulled Stephanie in and put his arm around her. Pete was about to take the picture, when the president waved me over: "Jump in."

I demurred. "Oh, that's all right."

Photo courtesy of Doug Mills

Me, mildly confused, in front of Air Force One during the 2012 campaign.
Surely in a swing state.

Photo by Pete Souza courtesy of White House

Pretty clear in hindsight that he can tell I don't know what I'm talking about.
Note the paper on the Resolute desk: the NCAA basketball tournament bracket.

RIGHT: A final photo of the Upper Press crew in Josh's office on the day before JPalm left to help run Hillary Clinton's campaign. From left to right: Howli, me, Desiree, Peter, Jennifer Palmieri, Crystal, Antoinette, and Josh Earnest.

Photo courtesy of Lawrence Jackson

Photo courtesy of author

ABOVE: Part of the later-term Upper Press crew at Camp David. From left to right: Liz Allen, me, Peter, Jen Psaki, Courtney, and Sarah.

Photo courtesy of White House

RIGHT: Playing with Obama the day after Thanksgiving 2016 at Joint Base Andrews.

Photo by Pete Souza courtesy of White House

Prepping President Obama for his episode with Jerry Seinfeld for *Comedians in Cars Getting Coffee*.

Photo courtesy of Doug Mills

Trailing Marine One through the air in Nighthawk 4.

RIGHT: From left to right: Peter, me, Desiree, Bill Murray, Liz Allen, and Josh Earnest.

Photo courtesy of author

Photo courtesy of author

LEFT: Drake stopped by and took over my desk. Nowadays, you can call him on his cell phone.

Photo courtesy of Pablo Martinez Monsivais

My memory of this was that I made Conan laugh. My memory was very wrong.

RIGHT: Bugged Russian teddy bear given to me at the G20 in St. Petersburg. His eyes kind of give away that he's hiding something.

Photo courtesy of author

Photo courtesy of author

ABOVE: The infamous horse photo. No comment.

Photo courtesy of author

RIGHT: Bo rummaging through Upper Press for food. Also, my desk in a familiar state: a mess.

Photo courtesy of Evan Vucci

LEFT: Proposing to Stephanie in the Rose Garden (she said yes).

Photo courtesy of Stephanie Cunnane

RIGHT: My nana and me just after finishing my time in the Obama White House. She'd just relayed one of her favorite mottos to me: "Take no prisoners; have no mercy."

Photo courtesy of White House

LEFT: My niece Aubrey going in for a hug just after saying, "I love you, Barack Obama."

Photo courtesy of Peter Velz

ABOVE: Obama cruising by the Oval Office.

Photo courtesy of Peter Velz

RIGHT: Obama steps out of "The Beast" after showing Jerry his ride.

Photo by Pete Souza courtesy of White House

The president looks at me quizzically as I explain the surprise Mother's Day calls. Also, my wife tells me you're not supposed to wear black shoes with a blue suit.

Photo courtesy of White House

The president provides perspective—and hope—the morning after the 2016 election. You can see me above the vice president's head.

Photo courtesy of White House

My family stands with Obama in the Oval Office for a departure photo near the end of the second term. From left to right: dad, Stephanie, me, 44, mom, Harry, Alex. Lots of buttoned blue suits.

The president's beloved "body man," a six-foot-nine-inch all-around good guy named Marv, piped up.* "C'mon, you gotta be in it." I politely declined once more, but POTUS waved me over yet again, and I made my way to them.

Looking at Stephanie, I tried to explain myself.

"I thought you should get your own . . ."

I should have shut up then. Enough said. The president and Stephanie sort of glanced at each other. My mom gave a puzzled look from the other corner. I finished the explanation.

"You know, just in case things don't work out."

FOREIGN TRAVEL

President Obama was remarkably popular around the world. Despite arguments to the contrary, the data—from both Pew Research Center and Gallup—show that America enjoyed a steep upward shift in the way the world regarded us with President Obama at the helm. Pew's spring 2016 "Global Attitudes & Trends" survey is striking. Confidence in the US president to do the right thing regarding world affairs bottomed out around 10 percent to 20 percent among our close allies in Western Europe and skyrocketed almost overnight into the 70 percent, 80 percent, and 90 percent range as Obama took over.

I saw it firsthand, from South Africa to Saudi Arabia. It sometimes felt like folks around the world were even more excited to

* Marv took over after Reggie Love left.

catch a glimpse of America's president than so many of the citizens we interacted with across our own country.

Once in a while, in the very last seat of the president's plane, my empty mind would flash back to my 2009 voyage around the world on Semester at Sea; the trip felt like a strange underlayer, like worn flannel, beneath my trips around the world with Barack Obama. The theme for our semester had been the South African word *ubuntu*. It was an abstraction back then as we crossed the Atlantic and didn't impress me much as we set sail—sort of kitschy—meaning the "oneness of humanity," but its imprint came into clearer focus as we arrived in port after port, starting with Marrakesh, Morocco.

To my young self, the city seemed in a constant state of motion. A cosmopolitan town made up of people with modern places to be. But just through a narrow passage and around a tight corner or two, Stephanie and I entered the souks. It was like stepping back three centuries: utter pandemonium. Men with monkeys tried to collect our money. A black cobra stared me down from his mat in the middle of the market. There was welding and weaving, hawking and bartering. Not much English, but one man did offer a few camels in exchange for Stephanie, who was by my side. I thanked him but politely declined. Stephanie punched me in the shoulder. Hard.

The man with the camel offer then asked if we were American. We nodded reluctantly. His eyes lit up: "Obama!" he yelled. A local passerby chimed in without breaking stride: "Obama!" It was the same exclamation we received as we made our way down and around the continent. In Namibia, men and women honked their horns and chanted "Oh-Ba-Mahhh!" and "welcome to Africa!" You would have thought I was already traveling with Obama. Instead, we were Americans benefiting from his global glow. *Ubuntu* was beginning to dawn on me.

Foreign trips with Obama were grueling. The days were jam-packed, the hours were mad, and the flights were long, which made for some laxer-than-usual encounters on Air Force One. Since leaving the White House, it's hard not to notice how stylish President Obama has become. As he gets farther from the buttoned-up demands of the presidency, more and more of his shirt buttons go undone, and, clearly, it works for him.

But he wasn't always so fashionable. On overnight flights, he frequently changed into his flight-casual gear. Athletic zip-up sweatshirt (okay), unusually tight sweatpants (not okay), and, of course, sandals—with white socks (really not okay). Had America seen this version of Obama, the infamous tan suit would have seemed a step in the right direction. It was a disconcerting vision of our very cool POTUS. But it seemed to keep him loose, because he kept it real on those flights.

Late in the administration, as news was leaking of Trump's plans, or lack thereof, to adequately address cybersecurity in the wake of the 2016 elections, Obama, aboard Air Force One, disposed of his measured rhetoric and let fly with a more concise than typical appraisal of the situation: "That shit cray," he said, strolling out of the conference room.

Speaking of cybersecurity and shit being cray, Russia proved one of my more memorable foreign trips with the president. The G-20, an international economic summit made up of nineteen countries and the European Union, was in Saint Petersburg. It was a long day and a half. Vladimir Putin played host on the immaculate, massive grounds of the Konstantin Palace, across a small sliver of the Gulf of Finland, where staffers and the press were staying in a local hotel.

We took advantage of a high-speed ferry to usher us across the gulf, where we took part in some more heated than usual pool sprays and spent a good deal of the day waiting around in a series of large tents the Russians had set up for us. We were each given a goody bag, which included a teddy bear and a zip drive (the zip drive went immediately into the trash for fear of spying). During the day, wandering around the G-20, I was struck by how familiar such a heightened international gathering could feel. It wasn't so dissimilar from the bicycle trade shows I had attended as a kid with my dad, who's been in the bicycle business since he started sweeping floors at a local shop when he was twelve—shuttling in and out of booths, reconnecting with folks you haven't seen in a year.

At night, the stakes became clearer as we trailed Obama's motorcade to Peterhof, once the Russian emperors' country residence, where now the globe's leaders debated what to do in the wake of a chemical attack in Syria, presumably undertaken by my supposed doppelgänger, Bashar al-Assad.

We waited in our parked pool van for more than five hours as the leaders failed to come to an agreement on a way forward in Syria, with Putin a major obstacle to progress. Then suddenly we heard a series of booms, and our car rumbled and shook. "A light and music show," our press lead assuaged me. It was *Hunger Games*–esque. I always found it odd—and somewhat comforting—that the world's leaders, having argued vehemently over dinner, would come together to watch a bizarre performance. It was like a cooling-off period, and it turns out they may have needed one. I learned that President Putin, after Obama had made his strong case, said to our president: "You've got some big balls."

So the cultural celebration was a reminder that, for these men and women in power, whatever your agreements or disagreements, having just manifested themselves in personal interactions, what mattered was your representation of country, not yourself or who had the biggest balls. Best not to let anyone storm off angry.

And so we didn't get back to the ferry dock until around two in the morning. We sprinted to catch the last boat. I slumped in my seat, ready to sneak in a nap, when my BlackBerry lit up. Who would call at this time of night? A reporter would. A pool TV producer was losing his mind, lighting into me. He had stayed behind to do stand-up shots, and there were no more ferries. How dare I let that Russian ferry depart? I think I would have had a better chance of diving overboard in Africa after that fallen adapter than I would have had stopping the Russian authorities from letting the ferry leave. Turns out the press pool and boats don't jive.

It wasn't the best way to end the trip, but at least I got a teddy bear out of it.

VACATION TRAVEL

Despite what the opposition party—Democrat or Republican—cries out, and in spite of the barrage of negative stories from the other side about taxpayer waste, every president needs a vacation, every president deserves a vacation, and every president takes a vacation. And notwithstanding what Fox News would have you believe, President Obama took significantly fewer vacation days than his predecessor or, it appears, his successor. Still, he took two primary vacations each year: one to Hawaii during the holidays and the other in August to Martha's Vineyard. After the 2012 election, I tagged along on both; the press needed to hang around, even on Obama's break—because the presidency never truly takes a day off.

Vacation travel was the exact opposite of foreign travel. Whereas foreign travel was high-stakes and filled with staffers and reporters who were ready to work around the clock, vacation travel was filled with reporters and staffers looking to do as little as possible. Me, foremost among them.

My first such trip—to Hawaii for the holidays after his 2012 reelection—was a stark reminder that on most presidential working vacations, the emphasis is on *working*. As the stress of the campaign evaporated, and we began to look to a fresh start approaching a new year, Washington managed to manufacture a new crisis just in time for the holidays. Turns out we were careening toward the "fiscal cliff," which was a frightening DC term that basically meant a bunch of laws were set to come into effect—the right mix of increased taxes and decreased spending; a sequestration of sorts—that put the country in a panic and placed a newly resurgent economy in peril. Turns out the debt-ceiling impasse that I couldn't understand while at the EEOB a year and a half earlier—the one that had tethered me to my computer for fifteen-hour days in the summer of 2011—had helped push us toward the cliff. Its 2011 "solution" was set to smack 2013 in the face, jeopardizing the holiday plans of a whole lot of Washingtonians.

I had been secretly emailing with Marie's boyfriend, Andrew, a former Joe Biden staffer, because he was planning to surprise Marie in Hawaii. Just one problem, I had to tell him: we might not be going. Stephanie had already purchased her tickets to join me in Hawaii as well. But as the departure date approached, it looked more and more likely that Andrew and Stephanie (who were strangers at this point) would be enjoying the holiday in Honolulu without Marie or me. Stephanie eventually canceled her flights, while Andrew rolled the dice. And it paid off.

With only an hour or so notice, Marie and I jumped in a White House vehicle and raced to Joint Base Andrews. I called my nana as I bounded up the steps to the plane next to Bo. Turns out I wouldn't be home for the holidays this year. Or so I thought.

Obama World decamped each Christmas to the Moana Surfrider Hotel on a particularly touristy stretch of Waikiki Beach complete with striking views of the piercing-blue Pacific. Of course, as a wrangler on duty, you were typically up and out with the press pool before dawn and back at the hotel long after the sun had gone down. But days off more than made up for the long days stuck in a van with the pooled press. From snorkeling with Schultz to hanging off duty with reporters in Hawaiian shirts at an actual pool, the whole thing seemed a bit like a TV special. You know how when a sitcom becomes tiresome, they set it in a fresh location for an episode? I felt like I was living one of those episodes.

But our special seemed to be getting canceled. The fiscal cliff was getting nearer, and we were no closer to a solution. Washington, frigid and deadlocked, was calling. So it was important to make the most of our potentially limited time in Honolulu. That meant hitting a local bar with the off-duty Secret Service. Going out with the Secret Service was like hanging with the cool kids, so I wanted to make a good impression.

I failed. A couple of the guys came up to me at the bar and offered to buy me a drink. Of course, I couldn't say no, but I didn't know what to order. I sheepishly asked for a mai tai, which I regretted immediately, especially since Marie ordered a "bourbon-rocks" in that impressively quick way some people do; no pause between "bourbon" and "rocks." The bartender, a stout middle-aged woman, asked to see my ID. Right in front of my new agent buddies. With an embarrassed huff, I handed it over. She eyed my Pennsylvania license with suspicion before retreating into the backroom, telling the other bartender to "hold that mai tai."

I tried to laugh it off with the Secret Service until she returned waving my license. "This is expired," she said. "I can't serve you. I should cut this up!" And so, I was denied a mai tai in front of the Secret Service. One of the burlier agents came up to me after the bartender reluctantly returned my license, and, under his breath, offered to "find another way to get you your mai tai." I was mortified. I wanted to get as far away from there as I could. Fortunately, I was in luck.

Word came down that the president was needed in Washington, so we were quickly back on Air Force One headed for winter. A midvacation break. For the president, it was an opportunity to avert financial catastrophe. On my end, it allowed me to spend New Year's

Eve with Stephanie. I made the mistake of complaining about having to endure the long flight back. "On Air Force One," Stephanie said drily. "That comment reminds me of Paris," she said. "Remember?"

I did. Shortly after my Semester at Sea, my dad's bicycle company, Fuji Bikes, sponsored a team in the Tour de France, so my family, Stephanie, and I went to Paris to watch the final stage. At the conclusion of the race, my dad hosted a party for the team and riders. Stephanie and I had walked all over Paris that day, and I was tired by the time the party started, so I took a seat as the dancing began. A thin young man about my age approached me at the table and sat beside me. "Why are you seated?" he asked.

"Ugh, I'm exhausted. My legs are on fire," I said.

"Oh, I didn't see you out there—what team were you on?" Turns out, I was complaining about my sore legs to a man who had completed one of the most grueling physical tasks known to man, the Tour de France, just hours earlier.

It was that lack of awareness that I displayed at dinner with Stephanie. It could be easy to lose context, existing in the bubble. But sometimes my problem was just the opposite. I could focus too much on the context; get inside my own head to the point of inaction. Nowhere was this clearer than on my second vacation trip.

• • •

The basketball was flying right for his face.

As my team hurried the ball up court, I trailed behind. "Lollygagging," my eighth-grade coach would have called it. In truth, I was merely conserving energy, so I could best help my team. And the president was on my team—so *my* team was really more *his* team.

Semantics aside, that basketball was still whizzing right for *his* unsuspecting dome. And because I was conserving all that energy chugging slowly up court, I was in the best position to see it. You could also make the case that I was in the best position to stop it.

I leapt into thought: *What do I call him here?* "What do you call the president?" It's a question I was asked often during my time at the White House, but the truth is, I'm no good with names, and titles are worse.

Now, depending on your lot in life, there are a number of acceptable ways to address the commander in chief. "Sir," for instance, or "Mr. President." "Boss" works too. Bolder folks have also used "Barack," "POTUS," or "Forty-four." His children even called him *Dad*.

Again, I'm not the best with names. I don't remember them. I don't feel comfortable using them. I avoid them at all costs. I construct sentences—even entire stories—so as not to back myself into the corner of calling my in-laws, known to the rest of the world as Jim and Debbie, anything more than "you," "he," or "she."

So I'm definitely not about to call the president "Forty-four." Or "Dad."

But I need to get his attention fast. After all, the Secret Service isn't exactly springing into action. Most of the agents are stationed outside the small gym, patrolling the deserted grade school parking lot. But considering we were on Martha's Vineyard, where it seemed the residents' wealth was matched only by their liberal leanings, the biggest threat to the president was undoubtedly on court with us.

Recognizing Dr. Martin Luther King Jr.'s fierce urgency of now, I quickly narrow my choices. Even though he had called me Pat when he'd chosen me recess-style for his team, I knew "Barack" wouldn't work. That whittled it down to "Sir," "Mr. President," "POTUS," or "P.," which was catching on around the White House as the new *in* term. Similar POTUS-like acronyms are used for the other principals as well: the First Lady is FLOTUS; the vice president is VPOTUS; and, most unfortunately, the Second Lady is—

Thwack! I'm too late. As the ball strikes Barack Obama's face, I cry out, conflating "Sir!" and "POTUS!" into what most closely approximates the awkward acronym for "Second Lady of the United States."

The other eight players go comatose. Is he mad? Have we done serious damage? Did somebody just say "SLOTUS"? Is the game over? I desperately hope not. It was my day off. And my shooting was on point.

Plus, it was a whole *thing* for me to get there.

As in Hawaii, I worked one day on and one day off. Desiree was currently on duty, so the emphasis that day was on *off.**

Earlier that day, I met the president's bubble of protective cars and personnel in the afternoon at his first stop of the day. We call these unscheduled visits OTRs, which, depending on who you ask,

* Desiree continues to assert that it was more like "one day on, two days off" for me.

means "on the run" or "off the record." Come to think of it, OTR could just as easily stand for "on the record," and that could really cause some trouble in this business.

Regardless, I went and advanced the OTR at a local restaurant on the water in Oak Bluffs. The president knew the owner and thought a dreary-day drop-by might be fun, generating a bit of positive press on a rainy day. Of course, in the world of right-wing blogs and Fox News, it would more likely degenerate into headlines such as "Obama Dines Out as Americans Starve for Leadership" or "In Case You Forgot, Obama Still on Vacation."

Walking toward the restaurant, I noticed two broad-shouldered men sitting silently on a bench scoping their surroundings: mostly boats and khaki-clad kids. The two dudes were draped in dull Hawaiian shirts and cargo pants. On closer inspection, they also wore earpieces, Kevlar undergarments, and packed standard-issue Sig Sauer pistols. Secret Service chic, their outfits and outlook said, "Yeah, I'm prepared to give my life for the president, but I'm also on vacation."

While looking out for a decent perch for the protective press pool to get a shot of the president entering and exiting the restaurant, I neglected to look out for oncoming traffic and was nearly hit by a slow-moving RAV4-ish blue junker driven by a gangly goofball who, on closer inspection, turned out to be Larry David.

My personal hero's beady eyes bored a hole through the windshield of his mom-mobile. It was the first time I'd seen him in person. I was very much in his way, and he let me know it. It was the ideal Larry moment; the perfect first impression: mix-up, minutiae, magnificent. I could almost hear the *Curb Your Enthusiasm* theme music, my ringtone, play us off.

The interaction propelled me the rest of the day—and it loosened me up on the basketball court, where I had drained three three-pointers in as many offensive possessions. I'm a decent-at-best basketball player, but things were going better than expected. That is, before the headshot heard around the gymnasium. One of the other players, a Chicago doctor, had even awarded me a "permanent green light" to shoot. But I took it more as a look-both-ways-and-if-the-President-isn't-open-then-feel-free-to-launch-it kind of yellow light.

I assumed that my chances of continuing my rare hot streak in the gym, my chance to keep playing with the chief executive, were shot, but POTUS shook off the hit and kept things going. We lost all three games we played that day, blowing significant leads in each. That was the last time I was asked to play basketball with the president.

I should mention that he wears pants when he plays basketball. And he tucks in his shirt. Other than that, he's quite a solid player, better than me. But whenever he trails the team up court, rather than "lollygagging," he's "leading from behind."

DISASTER TRAVEL

In every presidency, there are a handful of poignant moments. These are often born of what we called "disaster travel": quick-turn presidential trips meant to respond to natural or man-made disasters. These proved some of the most meaningful, wrenching, and yet oddly uplifting trips President Obama made. Before every trip, foreign and domestic, we received an email from the trip coordinator with details for the day. Normally, the note advised us to wear business attire. Sometimes, more ominously, it would call for "disaster casual."

I did two natural-disaster trips that called for boots rather than suits, to New Orleans in the wake of a hurricane, and to New Jersey following 2012's Superstorm Sandy. Accommodating a presidential visit necessarily funnels resources from emergency responders and cleanup crews, something the White House takes into account when determining if and at what point to tour damage and meet with survivors. It's a tricky balancing act: refrain from going, and you look like you're ignoring the problem; go, and risk being seen as taking advantage of wreckage and heartbreak for a photo op.

But those photos were important; a way for the world to empathize. So our advance teams would hit the ground a few days before us and determine the best route for the president to walk, drive, or fly to get a sense of the destruction. It could feel staged as we prepared for the visit, but once on the ground, it was clear: the president needed to see the damage. The rest of the country needed to see it, too. Like the rest of the world needed to see the president and his family at the Door of No Return. Natural disasters often made for odd bedfellows. I remember watching in the cold as New Jersey's Republican governor, Chris Christie, put his arm around President Obama—these two fierce rivals—putting politics aside to do the right thing for an American community.

Mother Nature's wreckage could be hard to stomach, but there was nothing more gut wrenching than man-made disaster visits.

There is also no better opportunity for a president to step up to the plate and do his job. And there are few things more stirring than a commander in chief, regardless of politics, rising to the occasion and meeting the moment.

It is a calling. For President Clinton, it was the Oklahoma City bombing in 1995. For President George W. Bush, it was standing atop the rubble three days after 9/11, finding his voice in a bullhorn.

It's hard to know how important these visuals and speeches are; how crucial it is for the commander in chief to unify the country—in sorrow, common decency, and resolve—until you come across a president who doesn't know how to do it or, worst of all, chooses not to.

President Obama knew to do it and how to do it.

I'll never forget the morning of December 14, 2012. It started off quiet. Bobby and I bantered about lunch. Matt probably called me Bashar. Reporters inquired about their Christmas photos with the president. But then news started to break about a shooting in Connecticut. Not much was known as the cable news channels began to break to helicopter footage and local news reports. Maybe a few casualties. Then Clark, an assistant press secretary who had been coordinating with the Department of Homeland Security, quickly entered Upper Press, looking for our bosses. He couldn't say what he knew, but he seemed shaken, glancing quickly at the television by my desk. "It's really bad," he said.

Not long after Clark's visit, the full extent of the horror at Sandy Hook Elementary School in Newtown was exposed. Twenty-six dead. Twenty of them five- and six-year-olds. It was the single most somber day I experienced at the White House. The joy of the season—a West Wing decorated for Christmas; the verve of staffers energized after reelection—was sucked away as the president wiped tears from his eyes in the Briefing Room.

It was hardly the first mass shooting that President Obama needed to respond to publicly (in fact, it was his fourth), and it wasn't even the first I was around for. In 2011, Arizona representative Gabby Giffords and eighteen others were shot in the few weeks I was off between ending my internship and starting as a staffer; and on the 2012 campaign, I woke up at a hotel in Florida to news of a lone gunman opening fire in a crowded movie theater in Aurora, Colorado, killing twelve and injuring seventy. We would cancel the rally and head back to DC that day.

But everything about Sandy Hook was different.

We arrived in Newtown three days later. The days are short in Connecticut in December, and night had long since fallen by the time we made our way toward the event space for the interfaith prayer vigil. A high school theater, like so many I'd been in before. A quiet town. I waited as the president met backstage, for hours, with the families of those who'd been murdered. I kept looking to the front row, where I imagined the families of the fallen would be seated, until it hit me: the sheer number of those killed meant that everyone in the room was directly impacted. There was no *front row.* I had never been in a room like that, and I hope never to be again. The sense of loss was all-encompassing; the sadness incomprehensible. I mean that literally. I felt pangs of despair, but my brain couldn't compute the gravity of that place and time. So I would experience a few moments of clarity about the horror that had happened, but my mind would then bounce back protectively into nothingness.

The grief draped over everyone in the hall like a funeral pall. Even members of the Secret Service were brought to tears.

That night, Barack Obama carefully balanced honoring the victims with a call to action; a refusal to let this happen again. By this point, the president had been deemed the "consoler in chief," and he rightly thought that this would finally push Congress, with the overwhelming support of Americans, in the direction of commonsense gun legislation.

He was wrong. He called Congress's failure to act to help curb these kinds of shootings the most frustrating part of his presidency.

The president would be asked to address the nation in the wake of many more mass shootings. He would respond to nearly twenty before he left office, including the most deadly mass shooting in United States history in Orlando, Florida,* a bigoted terrorist attack on the LGBTQ community, and the particularly appalling racist attack at the Emanuel African Methodist Episcopal Church in Charleston, South Carolina, in June 2015. "I am very mind-

* As of this writing, the 2017 attack on Las Vegas has eclipsed Orlando in terms of carnage. And, if this book lasts in print very long at all, Vegas too will surely and sadly be surpassed.

ful that mere words cannot match the depths of your sorrow, nor can they heal your wounded hearts," Obama told those assembled, heartbroken in Newtown.

But the president's words—any president's words—are crucial and can begin the healing. Obama's light-in-dark moments came from reacting not just as a president, but as a person and a parent. He knew that Americans' eyes are often opened only in the wake of these horrible events, and the window to keep them opened is short. In Charleston, he asked that we not allow "ourselves to slip into a comfortable silence again."

He was more than our consoler in chief. Obama pushed the conversation forward. He reminded us that though our politics are often small, these moments can lay bare the best in us, displaying our better angels and our big hearts. But his speeches weren't fairy tales, either. He forced us to remember, his words were haunting, and he did his best to stir us to action—so that these speeches might become less common.

President Obama often turned to Scripture to begin and end these kinds of remarks, most notably in Charleston, when he discussed the idea of unearned grace. Ephesians 2:8–9 tells us "Grace is the gift of God, not a result of works, so that no one may boast." Sure, Obama is an elegant, graceful man, a man of warmth and charisma. The final, essential ingredient, though, is a humility that leads to an open heart. Obama's humility is real—not put on like a false cloak—and that left the door open for grace to slip in. Grace, not earned, as he said that day, but grace as a free and benevolent gift of God. And grace for the benefit of those around him. To console. To inspire.

He famously finished his eulogy to Rev. Clementa Pinckney, the senior pastor at A.M.E. church and a South Carolina state senator, that June day, singing:

Amazing grace, how sweet the sound
That saved a wretch like me.
I once was lost, but now am found
T'was blind, but now I see.

Going in, Obama had thought about singing but wasn't certain. The moment needed to be right. He was humble enough to leave his heart open, to see if that bit of grace might slip in. Sure enough, it did. To good effect. The crowd came quickly to its feet and embraced him in song.

• • •

It was Obama's confidence wedded to his genuine humility that I witnessed connect in place after place, person after person, of every geography and station in life. Nowhere was that more evident than when we flew back, last minute, to South Africa for the funeral of Nelson Mandela.

We had only a few days to plan. Typically, we'd hold a series of meetings, a week or more, in the Situation Room. There we would take part in a SVTC (secure video teleconference), pronounced "civ-vitz," with the advance staff who were already on the ground. They'd do much of the heavy lifting; the face-to-face meetings needed to pull off a presidential visit. Many countries provided little resistance to the way we needed to do things to move the president across a foreign country. Sending helicopters, the Beast (the president's heavily-armored limousine), even weapons ahead of time on cargo planes. Allowing our press into events. Gift-exchange protocol. But other countries were more set in their ways. "You're in South Africa now," our staffers heard over and over from their counterparts in the lead-up to Mandela's funeral. Still, nothing compared with China or Russia, both of which showed little to no desire to work with us on anything. Flexibility, not their forte.

While we sat around the mahogany tables of the Situation Room, the advance staffers halfway around the world crammed into a tent in a hotel room.

The president's advance team was made up of men and women from across the country, many of them just out of college, who were ready to jump into action on a moment's notice. Often, they were away from home for weeks or months at a time. Truth is, they laid the groundwork, did the grunt work—the hardest work—so that when we touched down on Air Force One, there wasn't much to worry about. Their dedication to the job—and their importance to the White House—can't be overstated. Neither can the logistical complexity of a foreign trip, right down to the tented hotel rooms.

The tents were in response to security and eavesdropping concerns. And to further obscure conversations, they blared pop music, sometimes Britney Spears hits, outside the tent to deter anybody who might try to listen in. Occasionally, I'd catch a "Hit me, baby, one more time" and suppress a laugh.

"It's gonna be a shit-show," somebody said of the world's leaders coming together for the Mandela affair, flying in last minute, jamming the streets with motorcades and crowding the hotels. (Our delegation alone often took up three or more floors of rooms.) I continued to stifle my laughter at the absurdity of it all; the idea that we were the ones in the room—or, more precisely, that I was somehow allowed in this room as those more important than I pulled together a global event in short order.

The United States government did save a bit on air fare, as President and Mrs. Obama offered to plane-pool with George W. and Laura Bush and former Secretary of State Hillary Clinton. We all flew down together. A few hours into the flight, President and Mrs. Bush popped back into the press cabin. He brushed by me when he recognized a sleeping reporter. Bush tried to jolt him awake and scare him a bit, which prompted that famous Bush laughter: "*he-he-he,*" with the signature shoulder shake. The former president and his wife chatted with us for nearly two hours, yukking it up with the reporters he knew during his administration—talking mostly about mountain biking and painting. He seemed to cherish being back on the plane, and it was infectious. This was a leader I had felt such animosity toward, and yet here in the back of his old plane, it was impossible not to like him. He had charisma, and, more than that, he seemed like a good guy.

We landed in Johannesburg and rolled immediately to a Radisson Blu Hotel on the outskirts of the city. It was the same hotel we had stayed in six months prior, just after our trip to Senegal and the Door of No Return. Only this time, we didn't have hotel rooms—just a conference center and access to the gym and showers to refresh before the funeral. One unfortunate younger reporter was doing just that when the president walked in on him, nearly nude, in the locker room.

I couldn't stop laughing at the thought as I waited in the motorcade. This was such a different trip than my first time to South Africa on Semester at Sea, when Stephanie and I traveled by ferry to Robben Island to view Mandela's cell where he had spent the majority of his twenty-seven unjust years in prison. It was distinct, too, from my second trip just a few months before, when I watched the president view Mandela's cell. This third trip would be a somber occasion. Or so I thought.

Then, we were off. Winding our way among a sea of never-ending motorcades to the ninety-five-thousand-seat FNB Stadium on the outskirts of Johannesburg.

Turns out, it wasn't so somber. It was a four-hour celebration. We waited on a mezzanine level as the crowd danced, cheered, and sang. The weather didn't look like it was going to hold out in this open-air stadium. The president took a selfie with the British and Danish prime ministers. I remember spotting NBC journalist and anchorman Lester Holt and walking over to him, but then stopping as I neared him, turning away. *I'm not going to be the guy that tells Lester Holt I love what he's doing on* Dateline *at Nelson Mandela's funeral,* I thought.

Speaking of focusing on the wrong things, Google "Nelson Mandela Funeral Obama," and you need to scroll through a page and a half of snarky "selfie-scandal" stories regarding the picture taken of Obama, Prime Minister David Cameron, and Prime Minister Helle Thorning-Schmidt of Denmark—before you can find the text of the president's speech. Now, getting in trouble for taking a selfie at a funeral is just the kind of nonsense that might make for a solid spec script of a modern-day *Seinfeld*, but the amount of time and energy spent on this pseudoscandal was astounding. And the reflections on what it meant for our society—that we were a boorish, impolite bunch; that civility was on the decline—were overwrought. Those who were in the building knew that it wasn't an altogether out-of-place action at what was really a joyous occasion. And those of us who've lived through the past few years recognize that this wouldn't even register on today's skewed scale of civility among public officials.

Even so, it's all the press wanted to focus on in the wake of the service, along with speculation about Obama's handshake with Cuban president Raul Castro, as well as the bogus sign language interpreter who stood a few feet from Obama during his speech colorfully inventing signs from whole cloth. It's not entirely surprising that such distractions would occur. Those international events were a little like Thanksgiving dinner: getting family, often from far-flung corners, under one roof. Things will go awry; stuff will be blown out of proportion. Still, Josh put it correctly when asked yet again about the nonsense: "It's a shame that you had a service that was dedicated to honoring the life and celebrating the legacy of one of the great leaders of the twentieth century that has gotten distracted by this and a couple of other issues that are far less important than the legacy of Nelson Mandela."

Josh was right. And what Obama said about Mandela mattered.

I waited with the pool at the edge of the tunnel to the field as it began to pour. A mounted police officer was nearly thrown off his horse as the huge animal reared onto its hind legs. Whether Sandy Hook, or Charleston, or the Mandela funeral, I used to worry how any man's words could meet the gravity of these moments. Surely, he worried too, I thought, looking at the packed FNB Stadium, a stage so grand and imposing. A moment later, President Obama and a sea of Secret Service rolled by. We trailed him to the stage, where the sign language interpreter was waiting.

President Obama began, "It is hard to eulogize any man—to capture in words not just the facts and the dates that make a life, but the essential truth of a person . . . How much harder to do so for a giant of history . . ."

And after comparing Mandela to Gandhi, and King, and Lincoln, Obama said: "Given the sweep of his life, it's tempting, I think, to remember Nelson Mandela as an icon, smiling and serene, detached from the tawdry affairs of lesser men. But Madiba himself strongly resisted such a lifeless portrait. Instead, Madiba insisted on sharing with us his doubts and his fears; his miscalculations along with his victories. 'I am not a saint,' he said, 'unless you think of a saint as a sinner who keeps on trying.' "

Continuing, Obama argued, "It was precisely because he could admit to imperfection . . . that we loved him so. He was not a bust made of marble; he was a man of flesh and blood—a son and a husband, a father and a friend . . ."

There, in the pouring rain, surrounded by thousands of people whose journeys I did not know, I was struck that in the language Obama used to describe Mandela, he could have been describing himself. And that the arc of history ties together men and women, whether giants like Obama and Mandela or ordinary people like me and the stranger huddled next to me by the stage.

"And finally, Mandela understood the ties that bind the human spirit. There is a word in South Africa—*ubuntu*—a word that captures Mandela's greatest gift: his recognition that we are all bound together in ways that are invisible to the eye; that there is a oneness to humanity; that we achieve ourselves by sharing ourselves with others, and caring for those around us."

Where had I heard that word before? On a boat floating in the middle of the Atlantic in January 2009, the dawn of the Obama presidency.

"He not only embodied *ubuntu*, he taught millions to find that truth within themselves . . . It woke me up to my responsibilities to others and to myself, and it set me on an improbable journey that finds me here today. And while I will always fall short of Madiba's example, he makes me want to be a better man."

It was dawning on me, against my will: *ubuntu*. And in the pouring rain, Obama's confidence, ability, and openhearted humility met the moment, and in rained grace.

7

The Normals

The only normal people are the ones you don't know very well.

—ALFRED ADLER

My first dream job was trashman. I'd hang off the banister of my nana's bottom staircase like I was clutching the back of a hulking garbage truck rolling down Roberts Avenue, vaulting quickly on and off, grabbing neighbors' cans. Next, I did a stint as a professional baseball player, before landing on something that stuck. Writing. Screenplays, specifically, which to my eight-year-old mind were two or three pages scribbled on one of my mom's yellow legal pads. Yet as school kicked into high gear, I never gave my future career—writing, baseball, or trashman—much thought. I just sort of assumed it would work out. From the warehouse to the White House, I was very lucky.

But even after a few years in the West Wing, in my mind lingered that yellow legal pad.

Following the 2012 campaign and a few final foreign trips, I remember sitting back at my desk in Upper Press, having largely been on the road for a year, wondering, *What now*? There were to be a number of staff changes, and I didn't know where I would land.

I thought maybe it was time to go. After the excitement of the campaign, how could a desk job possibly compare? My parents knocked some sense into me. "Stay and turn out the lights," they insisted. They didn't have to say it more than once.

Dan Pfeiffer was promoted to senior advisor, moving down the hall, across from the Roosevelt Room; Jen Palmieri, onetime Clinton White House staffer (and future Hillary Clinton campaign communications director), was bumped up from deputy to take over Dan's position; Katie Beirne Fallon, who would soon go on to lead Legislative Affairs, came in as deputy comms director, followed by Amy Brundage, previously a deputy press secretary. Eventually, Jen Psaki would come on as comms director, and Liz Allen would take over as deputy. That's not to say there was an unusual staff churn in the second term. It's just the way it worked in many of those high-level jobs: do a couple years and then move on to the next challenge.

I had nine direct bosses during the second term, seven of them women. All of them wonderful. All mocked me mercilessly, but I owe each of them a great deal of thanks. They helped me grow from wrangling to writing and expand to message planning and development.

Now, in the second term, I fell into my dream job. Even more remarkable to me than tagging along on Air Force One. I was one of the White House staffers tasked with telling the president's story.

There are many ways to narrate, to message: speeches, interviews, trips. But the goal is always the same: to take what the president's been working on behind the bulletproof glass of the Oval Office to the people. Distill it. Explain it. Promote it. Connect with Americans. And the best way to do that was to talk directly with them. That's what I got to do.

• • •

In *Veep*, characters sometimes refer to them as "normals," but in the real West Wing—often dozens of times each day—we referred to them as "real people" or "RPs." They are the elusive living, breathing Americans we depend upon to make a point—tell a story—or push a message. Whether it's a cute kid, an adult who overcame the odds, or, best of all, a Republican who has had a change of heart, the right real person is worth his or her weight in gold. To find them, we often turned to OPC: the Office of Presidential Correspondence.

"It's one of the most optimistic things you can do."

That's how Cody Keenan, the president's chief speechwriter for the second term, would describe the act of writing a letter to the president. To sit down, often alone at the end of a long day, the weight of your world—kids, mortgages, illnesses, heartbreaks—on your mind, and start writing "Dear Mr. President . . ." With the hope that maybe, just maybe, somehow, your note will find its way to the most powerful man on Earth. More often than you'd think, it did.

I've written a lot about what it is to be inside the presidential bubble. It's a remarkable experience, but it is disconnecting, and it's important to guard against that detachment—to resist a clouding of perspective on the country you're working to serve.

So it was even more important for Obama to understand the mood of America, the struggles of everyday people. He needed a lens beyond the bubble. He wisely decided early on that letters would be that lens: ten letters from across the country every night, selected from among thousands that poured in every day, for him to read late into the evening in the Treaty Room, his personal office in the residence.

Put on like a pair of reading glasses every night to help him focus, the letters were called the 10LADs, for ten letters a day.

The Office of Presidential Correspondence was composed of fifty staffers, dozens of interns, and hundreds of volunteers—sorting through letters and emails. When my Uncle Bob read mail as a volunteer almost twenty years earlier, there wasn't much in the way of email or texts. It was all hard mail. All letters get read, coded, and initialed. In Uncle Bob's day, P-150 was the code for a letter that required a generic "Thanks for your note" reply. There were hundreds of codes back then, from abortion to Middle East peace—everything had a category. Skills from his days as a US Navy radioman likely served him as he coded. Well, maybe. Turns out, women would often send their panties. "We've got another pair!" somebody would call out. "The amount of sexual stuff that came in for Bill Clinton cannot be overstated," Uncle Bob told me.

Obama's OPC saw its fair share of lunacy, too. But we were the first modern White House, thanks largely to Howli and OPC Director Fiona Reeves, to lift up the oft-forgotten letter-writing tradition housed in the lonely fifth floor of the EEOB, as a cornerstone of our second-term messaging. A window onto the world, the letters were vehicles for empathy—a way to understand what mattered to folks across the country, to hear from the people who put the president in office (and many who didn't). It would become our deepest well for finding real people to meet the president.

The gush of letters provided a conversation with the American people that led to a fascinating dialectic—unemployed; underemployed; thanks, Obama; screw you, Obama—about what was really going on in their country. Fiona's team would send around a word cloud at the end of each day culling the most common words from the daily correspondence. Every time I clicked open those emails, America's fragmented identity came into clearer focus.

One word was always largest—centered—surrounded by a rotating set of buzzwords signifying specific issues. *Guns, police, abortion*, for instance. But the recurring, centered word, every day, was *Help*.

It's the same thing I called out to Velz almost daily: "Help, Peter, please." I was terrible with technology. Peter was proficient. An Excel genius. I was attempting to copy and paste two photos and place them side by side for comparison. It wasn't going well. It was SOTU season, and stress was high.

Every year, the three weeks leading up to the president's State of the Union address were madness. The chief speechwriter was buried under stacks of research and policy papers, fending off edits from everybody with a pet project to push—from the State Department to the Environmental Protection Agency—while Communications was busy preparing a slew of policy rollouts, travel, and events. During those frenzied few weeks, I focused first with Howli and later Liz Allen on populating the First Lady's State of the Union guest box, inviting folks from across the country to sit with Mrs. Obama.

President Reagan began the custom in 1982. He invited Lenny Skutnik, a previously unknown federal employee who had leapt into action a few months before when an Air Florida jet crashed into the 14th Street Bridge in Washington, DC, shortly after takeoff, saving a passenger from the icy Potomac River. Skutnik would serve as an example of American heroism—of everyday citizens displaying the spirit that makes America great.

Reagan called Skutnik out by name in his address, thus beginning a White House tradition that was expanded upon over the years: filling the House Gallery with folks the president could reference in his annual speech. Pulling heartstrings, pushing his message.

We took it very seriously. There were categories to lift up, from the original—"American hero"—to "small business owner," to "cute kid," and even "corporate titans." We were careful to reflect America's diversity. There were groups to hit, from Native American, Hispanic, and LGBTQ, to white, black, and Asian American, as well as members of the disabled community. It wasn't to check boxes, though the process necessitated that; it was to appropriately represent the people who make up the United States of America, the people the president would address.

"Diversity doesn't just happen," Howli would say.

Some people hit multiple categories: small business owner from Alaska who is a veteran? Jackpot.

Sometimes my box suggestions strayed, like when I pushed for the Pope or Sinbad, or Larry David, whom I insisted would need to leave early for it to be funny. There's a West Wing maxim, which I first heard from second-term communications director Jennifer Palmieri, that you wanted to hear when you threw out an off-the-wall pitch, four little words: "The idea has merit." Of course, none of these ideas of mine garnered those golden words. But there was always plenty of merit for inviting buzzy guests to the box, and back when the reelection campaign was looming, Dan knew how to generate good buzz and push our messaging.

Debbie Bosanek: not exactly a household name. Fortunately, her boss is. For months, Obama had been pushing for a fairer tax code: "Warren Buffett's secretary shouldn't pay a higher tax rate than Warren Buffett," he would say. We called it the "Buffett rule." It was an appeal to common sense. So, ten months out from an election that would turn on the economy, Dan invited Buffett's secretary to sit with the First Lady. Debbie's presence made the point.

In subsequent State of the Union guest boxes—with the reelection campaign a worry of the past, and the confidence of a second term—we focused less on swing states and more on stories worth telling: Americans, known and unknown, in the tradition of Lenny Skutnik.

I was debating between two such candidates, both older white men, for the hero category, when I called out to Velz for tech help.

Both men were approved by multiple policy counsels and our exacting research department. One a police chief and the other a fire chief; each an American hero in his own right! With a quick eye roll and some magician-like moves on my keyboard, Velz had them side by side. Once the photos were aligned, a crucial difference between them became clear. The police chief was clean-shaven, while the fire chief wore a bushy mustache. Straight out of central casting.

I picked the fireman with the hero 'stache.

Sometimes I didn't want to choose. Sometimes choosing was impossible. Often, there was no mustache to make things clear. I came to another photo, this one of American heroism in action. It was of a man, Carlos Arredondo, wearing a cowboy hat and rushing a bleeding, badly injured man to safety in the wake of the 2013 Boston Marathon terrorist bombing. Jeff Bauman, the man being rushed to safety, would go on to lose both of his legs and play a crucial role in identifying the bombers. He and Carlos became friends. I hemmed and hawed. So I suggested, let's bring them both. Howli thought a minute before saying: "The idea has merit."

"Didn't even need your help this time," I told Velz as Ned walked in. Ned was tall, thin, and quite smart—and, like everybody else, a bit quirky. He was a detailee from the Central Intelligence Agency (meaning he was technically an employee of the CIA, though he was working at the White House) who served as the National Security Council's spokesman and a top deputy to National Security Advisor Susan Rice. I liked giving him a hard time when I could. So I tried to bring up a recent fact I had learned about him, but my punch line was punctured by fits of early laughter about something else.

"Giddy-up!" I heard Josh yell out of our sight line from his office. I knew what it was about instantly. My heart sank, and I checked my email to find a familiar photo. It was me, shirtless, riding on a horse in the ocean. An absurd shot pilfered from my unprotected Facebook page that Velz or Desiree or Antoinette would send around to loosen up the office or cut the tension. Or just to put me in my place.

"Guys, guys." I tried to regain the room. "You know Ned showers with his dog?"

No reaction. They focused on the photo, and Ned filled me in on how widely the horse picture got around: "You know Susan's on this email chain, right?"

I was felled again. And then it got worse.

Two agents approached my desk. One looked vaguely familiar. I worried. Did I remember him from a while back at the bar in Hawaii? Had he finally come to let me have it? *Who orders a mai tai? Who forgets valid ID when traveling with the president?* Nope, he had a different question: "Did you travel with the president to Russia?"

"Yes."

"Were you given a teddy bear?"

"Yes."

"We're going to need that. Turns out, it was bugged."

Unfortunately, I had no idea where it was—still don't—and am very curious as to what nonsense the Russians heard me say. Of course, they could have just waited a few years for the Presidential Records Act (PRA) to take effect and comb through our emails. The PRA mandated that all presidential records, including staff emails, be preserved. So we knew that eventually our emails—our private tiffs and petty spats—would become public. The act loomed over most White House staffers like a drunk buddy who knew a secret. Now, with the exception of a few period-for-subject-line emails, I tried to keep my more moronic comments verbal and therefore off the record.* Unfortunately, Velz liked to follow not only the letter but also the spirit of the PRA law—and he took to preserving the more colorful quotes as heard in Upper Press, sending them around for posterity via email.

I was too often the one offering the quotable (read: mockable) lines. For instance, in the warped blear of a late afternoon at the height of a stressful stretch of policy rollouts regarding criminal justice reform, I looked quizzically at a link somebody sent to me. I rubbed my eyes and reasoned out loud that "the longer the link the newer the link." Quickly, I realized this didn't make an iota of sense. I heard the typing behind me, and quickly a blast email brought the starkness of my stupidity to the fore.

"'Good Lord, this hyperlink is so long! Is it the most recent hyperlink of all time?'—P. Cunnane, with a bit of tech wisdom."

That prompted a familiar chortle that made its way around the room, from Liz and Bobby to Desiree and Jimmy, who was lighter with the knowledge of an impending, well-deserved promotion—away from scheduling and toward substance in the EEOB. Then, loudest, Velz's maniacal laugh, which helped cut the tension of a taxing afternoon.

* The shirtless horse photo is in the PRA many times over.

Criminal justice reform meant a great deal to Obama; it was an important policy plank of the president's second term. He wanted to combat the exploding prison population, especially for non-violent, often low-level drug offenders who were unduly punished, frequently along racial lines. Sure, he delivered speeches, gave interviews, and wrote op-eds, but there was one way to gin up extra attention; to focus the United States on the issue. Why not do something that's never been done before?

We needed to send the president to prison.

Early on, a smart, sardonic woman named Lauren held the role of director of message planning. When somebody—usually a policy person with little understanding of vetting, event logistics, or optics—offered an out-there suggestion, she would politely turn them down with what became her catchphrase. "That's a bridge too far," she would say. As we prepared to send Obama on the first trip of a sitting president to a federal prison, I couldn't help thinking back to Lauren, who sat in Upper Press for years—before Howli, Liz, and Courtney eventually took over—and the difference a few years (and second terms) could make.

Still, second terms weren't free passes, and some of the vetting reports we received from the research department on real people we wanted to engage with the president were a little too real. As I reviewed a few vetting reports, I remember shouting to Liz:

"Not sure about you, but I'm good with the dude who shot a guy, but I don't think we should have POTUS meeting with a hooker!"

I could hear Velz start typing even before I finished with that thought.

• • •

Throughout his terms, the president was introduced at most of his events by an RP, somebody with a compelling, relevant story to tell. Part of my job was selecting these folks and helping them craft their introductions. Often, we turned to OPC to send us batches of germane letters.

Sometimes they were kids, like the thirteen-year-old girl Ayla, who wrote to POTUS and FLOTUS from Massachusetts about the Women's World Cup. She was upset with her brother for having claimed, "Boys are so much better at soccer than girls." "Whoever is reading this should know that I hate the fact that boys sports always get the most attention," she wrote. So, when the US Women's World Cup came by to be honored by the president, we asked Ayla to introduce Obama in front of the team in the East Room. She read her spunky letter to the world, going viral in no time, garnering more attention than many of the men's teams that came by. And, for a news cycle, she helped solve the very problem that spurred her to sit down and write to "whoever is reading this."

As one of the people on the inside reading the notes, scouting for real people, it was hard not to develop a *type*. Whereas Howli had a penchant for chubby babies and old men who wore their hats high atop their heads, I had a thing for grandmas and people who had changed their mind about the president. Perhaps that's why I'll never forget Brent Brown's letter.

To my President,

I sincerely hope that this reaches you, as far too often praise is hard to come by. Apologies to people who deserve it perhaps even less so.

I did not vote for you. Either time. I have voted Republican for the entirety of my life.

I proudly wore pins and planted banners displaying my Republican loyalty. I was very vocal in my opposition to you—particularly the ACA.

Before I briefly explain my story, allow me to first say this: I am so very sorry. I understand written content cannot convey emotions very well—but my level of conviction has me in tears as I write this. I was so very wrong. So very, very wrong.

You saved my life. I want that to sink into your ears and mind. My President, you saved my life, and I am eternally grateful.

I have a "preexisting condition," and so could never purchase health insurance. Only after the ACA came into being could I be covered. Put simply, to not take up too much of your time if you are in fact taking the time to read this: I would not be alive without access to care I received due to your law.

So thank you from a dumb young man who thought he knew it all and who said things about you that he now regrets. Thank you for serving me even when I didn't vote for you.

Thank you for being my President.

Honored to have lived under your leadership and guidance,

Brent Nathan Brown

As soon as I got to "I did not vote for you," I knew that OPC had a potential gem. And the note only got better. Like any good story, it had a turn—"I was so very wrong."—and a gripping twist: "You saved my life." I got Brent on the phone as soon as I could.

Calling RPs was part of my job. I used to listen as Howli and Lauren before her did the same. "Hi, I'm calling from the White House in Washington, DC," they'd say. I used to laugh at the last part. "Everybody knows the White House is in DC," I'd mock. But when I started making the calls, I got it. Overexplaining was a means to delay the initial response of the RP on the other end of the line, giving cushion for the sentence to sink in, for reality to register: *the White House is calling.*

A favorite party trick among first-time fliers on Air Force One was calling family and friends from the plane. The onboard operator would dial out. Your mom or dad would pick up and hear: "This is Air Force One, please hold for Pat." There was power in those words, even if I was calling for no reason at all. But my parents already knew where I worked, where I was that day. I imagined that a letter writer receiving an out-of-the-blue call from the White House was more meaningful.

With Brian in mind, I tried to uphold the decorum of it all. "This is Pat Cunnane, and I'm calling from the White House in

Washington, DC." There's nothing like surprising folks with a phone call from the White House. It's a remarkable experience, calling people, sometimes as they are really struggling, and letting them know that their president cares. That their optimism in sitting down to write has been rewarded. They have been heard. And, that the president would like to meet them.

I once called a man whose husband had recently been killed in the 2015 San Bernardino, California, terrorist attack. His strength was extraordinary. I had no idea what to say to him. As much as I thought about the impression my words, purely as a vehicle of expression from the White House, made on him, he made a far greater impression on me.

My first interaction with Brent Brown wasn't so eye-opening. My impression was mixed.

"Now *that's* a bridge too far!" I murmured to myself as I read Brent's first-draft introduction of President Obama for his upcoming speech on the Affordable Care Act. I swiveled my chair 180 degrees to Velz, gave him a you'll-want-to-capture-this look, and circled another 90 degrees toward one of my bosses. "Liz!" I shouted.

"Yes, Pat!" she shouted back.

"We can't have our introducer reference testicles, right?"

I could hear Velz typing.

"That's correct, Pat."

I entered Liz's office, thinking that we might be getting pranked, and closed the door behind me.

"All of our RPs get ARP'd, right?" I asked Liz, referring to the "arms-reach-of-the-president" background check the Secret Service did for those coming within close proximity to POTUS.

"Yes . . ." she said, which made me feel a little bit better.

With the exception of his line thanking the president for his "testicular fortitude," Brent's initial introduction was powerful. Too long, but powerful. I went back and forth with him over email. His notes were unusually long and spiritually deep. Now, I sometimes had a tendency to skim things throughout the day; it wasn't easy keeping up with many hundreds of emails daily. So, at first, Brent's notes didn't seem coherent. Suddenly I worried that it was all too good to be true. Had I been blinded by my thing for people who changed their minds about the president? Could his note have been a ploy? Had we fallen for the perfect fake letter? After all, if I were to mock up a note that I thought was sure to get a response from the White House, it would look like Brent's.

We decided to move forward with Brent as the introducer and a member of the president's lunch. If anything appeared amiss at lunch, we could pull him as the introducer. I desperately hoped the lunch would go okay, because telling the president's story required telling the stories of those who he's helped. America needed to hear Brent.

The Office of Digital Strategy (ODS) would have agreed. In the second term, Jason Goldman, who was part of the founding teams at Twitter and Medium, came aboard as the chief digital officer for the White House. Digging into the analytics, he and his team found that engagement based on personal narrative and experience worked best.

In short, story mattered.

"So whether that's Alex, the 6-year-old kid talking about refugees, or Brent, the GOP Wisconsin letter-writer talking about ACA, or Virginia McLaurin, the 106-year-old woman who danced with POTUS and FLOTUS at the Black History Month reception, they are all personal, emotional stories that convey American themes and values (and values represented by Obama) in powerful ways," Jason explained. His findings on what broke through validated what we had been trying to do for years with RPs and tracked with Americans' ability to see themselves in President Obama; to see their family in the First Family.

So I was optimistic when Brent stepped to the podium. My worries were misplaced. Brent's correspondence with the president and then with me wasn't rambling or illogical, as I had feared, it was of a piece, sincere—and deeply moving. His words, passionately placed one after the other, email after email, were in communion with his experience.

We've stayed in touch, become something of pen pals, and every time I finish reading one of his long and winding notes, I am rejuvenated, invigorated by his story and therefore by the president's story. Brent always states explicitly what he told the world when he stepped behind the presidential podium:

The president saved his life.

After recounting that he had never voted for Obama and the ways he had cursed the president's name, Brent humbled himself before the crowd and the cameras, relaying that due to a serious disease, he was driven to bankruptcy, unable to receive care. "I was literally a dead man walking," he told me. His hope was gone. But then, in front of the world, he said something changed. "But then this guy signs this bill . . . thanks to his fortitude, thanks to his unwavering visions of mercy even toward me, this chump gets a second shot at life . . . I was worth saving. *We* are worth saving."

Brent's introduction was viewed something like fifty million times. He lost many of his conservative family and friends as a result. But, as he's told me, he gained some new ones, too—including a former president named Barack.

• • •

Obama rightly considers himself a writer. It sometimes seemed like that's what he knew, at a base level, was his thing, his primary talent. Before professor, before politician, before president. Writer. Author. Speechwriter.

He is also an insatiable reader. Beyond his onerous nightly briefing book, which I was partially responsible for helping to fill to bulging proportions with event memos, draft statements, and op-eds, as well as decision memos and—most time-consuming of all—interview prep materials. To say nothing of the far more important sensitive or classified documents in his massive binder—more than enough reading for a week, let alone a night.

Still, he found time to read widely. From Marilynne Robinson, to Maurice Sendak, to Abraham Lincoln, to Gillian Flynn, the president became a sort of reader in chief. We even took to releasing his vacation reading lists and set up a number of conversations with authors and interviews specifically about his reading habits.

The press seemed to sometimes perceive an aloofness to the president, but I think that was born of his unique take on his job. Beyond political machinations, he seemed more interested in what motivated human behavior. Standing in countless Oval Office pool sprays, minding the press, I could almost see him studying the moment even as he was the center of it.

His reading fed into that. He used books the same way most of us do: to learn, to get out of our own bubble. Like hearing from letter writers, escaping into a book helped to put him in the place of others. To empathize. Earlier in his life, they provided a foundation of knowledge, an undercurrent of information that he would draw on as senator, president, and parent. As he has said, during his final two years of college, Obama sequestered himself, studying the texts of the world's great philosophers. He has admitted that he may have gone overboard in those years and taken himself too seriously. But those readings no doubt contributed to his vast perspective, helping to contextualize his time in the Oval Office.

My favorite book, as I might have mentioned, was *Sinbad's Guide to Life*, so safe to say I was out of my league. But the president did like to write first drafts of speeches on yellow legal pads, so we had that in common. I looked up to his prose, was awed by his rhetoric, and shared his love for writing.

My mom, a professor of writing and rhetoric before she entered politics, ensured that my brothers and I could write, and write well. She mentioned Strunk and White (William Strunk Jr. and E. B. White, authors of the writers' bible *The Elements of Style*) so often around our house that you could be forgiven for thinking they were relatives.

The first piece of writing I did that garnered a bit of attention was in fourth grade. We had been asked to write about our hero, an assignment my teacher, Mrs. Montgomery, was eager to review during parent-teacher conferences.

I began the essay by lauding my dad. He rode his bike across the country, I noted, adding that now he had his own bicycle company. And did you know he saved my uncle's life, leaping in front of a falling wall?! It was a one-page paper; I spent the first four-fifths on my dad's heroics and business acumen before turning to my mom, a remarkably impressive person in her own right, for one sentence: "My mom likes fine hotels and happy hour."

"Just coming from happy hour?" my dad cracked as my mom entered the classroom a few minutes late. Mrs. Montgomery nearly fell out of her seat.

It's the same reaction Desiree gave me when I showed her something I was proud of: my first peer-reviewed and accepted piece of writing. For the online Urban Dictionary.

You see, for much of President Obama's second term, I had been trying to make a saying that I came up with—"Got that sun in your eyes"—catch on around the West Wing. I define "Got that sun in your eyes" as "behaving differently due to proximity to someone or something deemed cool," something that tended to occur when celebrities stopped by, which happened more than I could have ever imagined.

Truth is, the White House is practically Hollywood East. Major stars came through constantly. Sometimes to be honored. Other times to meet with the president. And frequently just to check things out and get a tour from a staffer.

I remember one Sunday morning when I entered the White House and regretted momentarily that I hadn't showered. *Oh well, it's Sunday,* I thought. *Who cares if I look god-awful? No one will see me.* No sooner did I take my seat than the door creaked open, and in walked a bevy of beauties. Only these weren't just any beautiful people. These were three Hollywood A-listers: Kate Hudson, Reese Witherspoon, and Kate Upton, just checking things out. I really regretted not showering.

Speaking of showers, another particularly memorable drop-by was Bill Murray, who hung around the West Wing for the better part of an afternoon when his beloved Chicago Cubs were playing the Washington Nationals in the 2016 National League baseball playoffs. He came into Upper Press to our shock, just sort of ready to hang. Desiree, who was not shy and rarely had the sun in her eyes, prompted a discussion of golf—a mutual passion between Bill and me—which led to an uncomfortable conversation about the showers at a course we had both played recently. We chatted about water pressure, heat, and the awkward fact that there were no doors to the showers.

Eventually Desiree grabbed my phone and showed Bill videos of my golf swing. As he began to critique my form, I snapped out of the moment and thought about the insanity of the White House, this place where anybody in the world was just a call away. A surreal beehive of bizarre activity. Visits from folks like Bill Murray and Bruce Springsteen, George Clooney and Leonardo DiCaprio, added to the lore of the place and the sense that I'd had from my earliest days across the street: that the West Wing was some Hollywood set. But this was real, and as Bill Murray exited our office, he turned back to me with a piece of advice: "You should thrust your hips more. You'd hit it farther."

"Thanks."

"Plus, you'd be a hit on the dating scene."

• • •

Gradually, I improved my own writing, mechanically and substantively. My mom would teach her students that the best of writing is the intersection of strong writing skills, experience, expertise, and humanity. The first three I got: mechanics matter; life experience matters; and knowledge matters.

It was the last element that mystified me. What's the *humanity* notion? How does that fit? My mom would tell me and her students that good writing leaves an impression most when we feel the warmth of the writer behind the words, when we sense her uniqueness—his humanity. That's when words "sing," she would say.

You knew it when you heard it. And I heard it in 2004 when I was just sixteen, and a little-known senator with a name I couldn't at first pronounce burst onto the scene, reading the words he wrote about the country he believed in. Even twelve years later, it remained true. The greatest story Obama told was America's. In place after place, in small towns and on the biggest of stages, he was an advocate for America with a writer's touch and a storyteller's grace.

I wanted to be a part of it. After I'd had "writer" tacked onto my title in 2013 by Katie Beirne Fallon, I tried to play it like a benign bump in position, no big deal—an excuse to pay me slightly more than the White House minimum. Truth is, on the inside, I was beaming. *Writer.* At the *White House.* I couldn't believe the way things were falling into place. Maybe I'd get to write something that mattered.

Of course, most of what I began with was bottom-of-the-barrel writing. I started with dry memos to the president, glorified logistical documents, before adding guidance memos, in which I helped guess what questions the president would be asked and suggested what he should say in interviews or press conferences. I became a choke point between staff sec and the communications department, which prompted countless calls from Ted.

Upper Press proved a challenging place to concentrate on writing. The area was chaotic, frenzied; to help me concentrate, I'd blast music into my headphones—usually 1990s pop music; sometimes the Canadian band Soul Decision—to cover up the conversations around me.

The president once popped into Upper Press unannounced while my headphones were in. I half stood and anticipated his "How ya doing?" answering with a fervent "Excellent!" Only, that's not what he asked. As he turned away from me, a little faster than usual, I realized he had actually inquired how my golf swing was. Mine was the antithesis of the right answer to the question. Golfers are perennially in the process of tweaking this or tuning that; only goons think their golf swings are "excellent." Golfing is a language, and

I had duffed my answer. The president left without a word, and I was confident that I wouldn't be invited into his foursome anytime soon—and also that I wasn't always so good at predicting what he planned to say.

I certainly couldn't have predicted that I would indeed get one more invite to the golf course. Previously, I had played in the group behind him a number of times on his annual vacations to Martha's Vineyard and Hawaii. But this time, I was asked to play in his group. It was late fall, the day after Thanksgiving, and it was cold; I hadn't swung a club in months. But I jumped at the chance—*I'm going to play golf with the president of the United States!*—departing before dawn from Cape May, New Jersey, where I was celebrating Thanksgiving. I drove to JBA in Prince George's County, Maryland. I was so eager that I arrived hours early and posted up at a McDonald's just off the base, taking a few practice swings in the parking lot.

Joint Base Andrews didn't have the best courses in the world, but it was convenient for the Secret Service, so the president played there often. As I approached the first tee, I was met by a former staffer a couple years older than me, who was a frequent presidential golf partner, and a man in his fifties who worked at JBA and would be joining our group. We heard the roar of the motorcade and then the softer growl of dozens of golf carts—including one that was armored—parading down to us. "Let's do old guys versus young guys," the president announced as he arrived on the tee box.

Most of the round went off without a hitch. I played better than expected—even got a lucky bounce off a Secret Service golf cart flanking the fairway and back into play. After about the fourth hole, you begin to forget you're playing with the president. You loosen up and ignore the scores of armed men and women watching your every putt. That's because there's a ritual to golf; an honor system and an unspoken tradition. The president doesn't putt first just because he's the president. Whoever is "away" (farthest from the hole) putts first. The president's no less immune from shanked shots than the rest of us. So we joked and talked about sports. The game seemed in some ways to serve as an equalizer—that is, until the match got tight.

By the seventeenth hole, the president's team had the chance to put us away and win our friendly wager. To my shock, I sank a twenty-foot putt and kept our team alive. I was feeling pretty good, basically strutting my way to the eighteenth tee, where the match would be decided. As I stood over the ball, the president said:

"Fairway's pretty narrow out there, isn't it?"

Oh my God. The president's trash-talking me.

But I felt emboldened by his taunt, telling myself I was going to stripe it down the middle as I took the club back like I'd done so many times before. I felt good at the top of the swing before snapping my hips forward, like Bill Murray suggested, whipping the club through the ball and right down the midd—Nah, I hooked it into the woods.

I navigated my way through bushes and beneath massive trees to find my ball, perched hopelessly under a thorny bush. I was surprised to find the president right behind me. "Make sure you play it as it lies," he said good-naturedly before heading back to the fairway, where he was in the line of my next shot.

I debated hitting it backward to avoid asking the president to move, but the match was on the line, so I yelled from the bushes. "I'm coming right toward ya, sir!" And he hopped in his cart and moved out of the way. I dribbled the ball out toward him and had an approach shot that needed to be on point to have any chance at squaring the match. Instead, I launched the ball well over the green.

As we approached the eighteenth green, the president continued over to where my ball sat. A Secret Service agent chimed in, "Sir, your ball is on the green."

"I know," the president responded. "Just wanted to see how rough of shape Pat is in."

I ended up triple-bogeying the last hole.

We lost.

But at least I made an impression.

I remember at the very end of President Obama's second term, he graciously took photos with staffers and their families in the Oval Office; each night, he would sign a bunch of the photos upstairs after work with a one-line message, usually thanking the staffer for his or her great work and service. I was looking forward to mine. A piece for the mantel. I'd pass it down to my grandchildren one day. Then I heard the laughter.

Velz got word from the Outer Oval that something was up with my photo. I thought maybe they'd pranked me and had the president sign the horse photo or something. Velz delivered the photo to my desk with a smirk. Apparently, a bunch of people had seen it already. I opened to find the photo of me and my family—so far, so good—and the note below in Sharpie: "Pat—Thanks for the great work . . . and the foursome!"

". . . and the foursome!"

That was not the language of golf. Just like you never say your swing is "excellent," you don't say "thanks for the foursome." "Thanks for the round" would have been the more likely wording. But the president's awkward phraseology was a fitting way to end my time in the West Wing, given how it began with Sean and the taxicab. Most of all, it was another reminder that I couldn't predict what the president was going to write.

Still, like I was saying, in the second term, I tried. I started with presidential quotes. Somebody just got nominated as the railroad administrator? Somebody needed to compose the generic sentence of support from the president. With Strunk and White dancing in my head, I set out to make every bland statement purr. Before I knew it, I was writing a few statements each week, usually with little notice and even less time to pull something together. The topics ranged widely, from members of Congress retiring, to one of my specialties: death statements.

When celebrities, politicians, or other notable people passed away, the president often wanted to pay his respects in writing, and I was always happy to jump in.

The process, though quick and frenzied, usually took shape the same way: swift information gathering on my end: What's the president already said on the topic? Do we have a policy paper on the issue? Sometimes I needed to hop over to Wikipedia for a quick lesson in whomever or whatever I was just tasked to write about. Then I'd whip something up as rapidly as possible—sometimes I had a day; other times, an hour—and I'd get it around for review from the appropriate policy council, the lawyers, the chief speechwriter, and, most importantly, our much-admired research department. Ask anybody from the Obama White House, and they'll tell you that the research department was the hardest working. The staffers there logged longer hours than anybody and rarely enjoyed a free weekend. They were on call in times of crisis, but they were also tasked 24/7 with helping us to avoid the crises in the first place—an almost unbearable pressure that they bore with good humor. They checked facts and kept us honest, and no statement was ready to go until they signed off.

Sometimes my statements and jokes, op-eds and quotes, didn't need clearance from the Oval Office. It wasn't exactly the State of the Union, after all. But, to me—the memory of my mom's yellow legal pad and my first glimpse of Obama at the 2004 convention on my mind—it might as well have been.

For the more important statements, there was one last person outside of the research department who needed to lay eyes on the thing—and he was the best writer in the building. I remember in early 2016, I was asked to craft a statement from the president about Aretha Franklin for the *New Yorker*.

"Should you really be the one to write about Aretha Franklin?" Desiree asked.

"You could say that about everything they send me," I retorted.

Still, she was right. I struggled with it more than most assignments; probably wasn't the best person to opine on the Queen of Soul. (I've always had trouble describing music.) I got it into decent shape before a senior speechwriter with a background in music and a wonderful, lyrical way with words took a pass and improved it immensely. I thought it couldn't get better. But then we received the president's version. I expected he would barely glance at the draft, given the far more important items on his never-ending to-do list, but Obama, the writer, couldn't resist. He took what we thought was a polished "statement from the president" and turned it into a potent declaration on the power of music—he made it sing.

"Aretha's one of a handful of artists I believe are truly essential to the American story," he wrote. "American history wells up when Aretha sings. That's why, when she sits down at a piano and sings 'A Natural Woman,' she can move me to tears—the same way that Ray Charles's version of 'America the Beautiful' will always be in my view the most patriotic piece of music ever performed—because it captures the fullness of the American experience, the view from the bottom as well as the top, the good and the bad, and the possibility of synthesis, reconciliation, transcendence."

All in all, I wrote hundreds of pages in his voice. It was the honor of my life.

Sometimes, as with the Aretha statement, I felt little ownership over the words. Other times, I received no edits, and I'd bask in my own small glory: my words had become his, etched somewhere in the far corner of history, just behind that speech nobody remembered or the death statement everyone forgot. Still, it was there. And it could not have meant more to me.

Obama excelled in each of the four categories that my mom theorized combined to create great writing. He mastered the mechanics and the rhetoric. He had the humanity. He lived the experiences. And he had the knowledge. In fact, his understanding of history provided him the ability to contextualize our generation's current state; a fleeting chapter in America's long, snaking saga. It's why he rarely felt the need to lash out at the media, and why he seldom seemed flustered when heckled or when things went wrong in the Briefing Room. That's not to say he wasn't tested. And, sometimes, it was kind of my fault.

• • •

Desiree burst out laughing, turning to Velz. A mild-mannered, somewhat new reporter named Phil had just called from the Briefing Room. "The room is pretty crowded today," he'd told her. He thought the president should know. For whatever reason, this struck Desiree, Velz, and me as a bizarre, hilarious report. Of course the Briefing Room was crowded. The president was about to speak.

I had finished his presser memo, the last of 2016, the night before. The process had been relatively smooth. We anticipated that the news would be largely about the election and Russia's interference. We also prepared for questions regarding the tragedy unfolding in Syria, centered on the president's response—or lack thereof, according to his critics. He was ready for those questions; the folks in the Staff Secretary's Office barely had to bug me to get the thing in on time.

The day was off to a quiet, decent start, so we couldn't help having a little fun. Desiree and Velz asked me to prank call Phil. I hadn't been a wrangler since he'd started coming around full-time, and he likely wouldn't recognize my voice.

"Hello, sir. This is the White House fire chief," I intoned, having no clue if there even was such a position. "I hear you're concerned with the number of folks in the Briefing Room."

"Oh, no, I, uh . . ." he waffled.

"Sir, could you please count the number of people in the Briefing Room?"

"Uh, I'm not sure how many—"

"I'm going to need an exact number," I said, stifling a laugh.

"I'll have to get back to you," Phil said, hanging up. Immediately, he emailed Desiree, freaked out. I started to get nervous. Though countless pranks had been pulled on me, I always worried about trying my hand at one. My mind went instantly to the worst possible scenario. For example, remember Sean's trick on me years earlier? Had our positions been reversed, I would have been too afraid to pretend to pick up a prostitute. What if the cab driver was an undercover cop?

Fortunately, with this simple joke, I couldn't see any dire consequences a step or two down the road, and we were in the clear as the president took to the podium.

"Good afternoon," he started. "This is the most wonderful press conference of the year. I've got a list of who's been naughty and nice to call on." He got a laugh out of them; the briefing was off and running. After Obama parried questions about Russia and the election, Mike Dorning of Bloomberg asked the president a two-part question on Syria, including: "Do you, as president of the United States, leader of the free world, feel any personal moral responsibility now at the end of your presidency for the carnage that we're all watching in Aleppo, which I'm sure disturbs you—which you said disturbs you?"

"Mike, I always feel responsible," he started, continuing with a thoughtful, thorough accounting of the process by which the US government assessed options for Syria. Suddenly a commotion took hold in the back of the Briefing Room.

"I'm sorry, what's going on?" the president asked, concerned.

The room was indeed crowded, and hot. Somebody had passed out. What followed was two minutes and twenty seconds of dead air. The president—live on television—was standing behind the podium waiting, calling for somebody to help, repeatedly asking that we grab the White House doctor and then offering directions to the doctor's office as the sick woman exited the Briefing Room doors. "Just go through the Palm doors; it's right next to the Map Room." It was the waiting, though, that was excruciating. Two minutes and twenty seconds feels like an eternity on live television. He was left hanging. This scenario was definitely not covered in my memo.

As reporters and pundits on TV and Twitter rushed to coin stretched, snarky metaphors, drawing parallels between the president's supposed failure to help those in Syria with his inaction from behind the podium as he called on others to help the reporter in need, I knew we should have taken Phil's weird note more seriously. The room was, in fact, too crowded, and somebody passed out. I was dumbstruck—or maybe just dumb—wondering how the one time I try to pull a prank—the only time I didn't overanalyze the potential ramifications and failed to consider a worst possible scenario—it came to pass. On live TV. At the expense of the president. I realized a couple of things then. First, maybe my next memo to POTUS should be about the need for a White House fire chief. (He would need a mustache.) Second, I knew pranks weren't one of my skills. I would never live up to Sean's example. Better to stick with what I knew.

• • •

I knew real people. And I knew we had something in Sharon, whom we pulled directly from one of my preferred categories: grandma. Sharon Belkofer is a sweet and spunky grandma, great-grandma, and Gold Star mother. I didn't have to ask Liz about ARP checks; Sharon had already come within an arm's reach of the president. In fact, she had hugged him—more than once—proud moments she liked to retell.

We were looking for a special introducer. This would be the most high-profile introduction of the president in his eight years in office. There were no introducers for State of the Union addresses, just the sergeant at arms who shouts the president's entrance to the floor. No real people cuing the president before his somber addresses to the nation, just a silent nod from the wrangler in the corner signifying it's time. But for his speech at the 2016 Democratic National Convention in Philadelphia, supporting Hillary Clinton, we had to find someone with spark.

Fortunately, Desiree had an idea. She called over to Joe, one of the president's close aides and common golf buddies, to stop by from the Outer Oval and tell us about his "pen pal." Turns out, he'd become friends over the Obama years with a woman who'd had a series of quiet moments with the president. The minute he started telling us about this woman named Sharon, it clicked. We had to get her on the phone right away. Sharon's voice was pitch-perfect, earnest, and excited—she had the spark—so we made the ask, and she gladly accepted.

I got word from the lawyers that Sharon's speech would be classified as political, meaning that, as a White House staffer, I couldn't legally work on Sharon's speech. Now, the lawyers could be overly cautious, but that's because they took their responsibilities so seriously—and they kept us out of trouble. So if I wanted to help with the speech, I'd need to take a day off from the White House and work from home, which I did. Sharon and I had a series of warm, endearing conversations batting around language that I will always remember. It was clear to me why Joe had become pen pals with this woman who could be his grandmother.

I remember watching Sharon, in her shimmering black outfit, walk out onto stage in front of the world. I was terrified for her. Anxious at the boisterous Philly room. Would they calm down and listen to her story? My nerves calmed the moment she stepped to the podium. She didn't seem nervous. She basked in it all, and as she started in, she called out her home state of Ohio. A little crowd work from a little old lady went a long way.

The arena quieted as she began: "I know President Obama has meant so much to millions of Americans across the country. I'd like to tell you what he means to me," she said. Sharon told her story through the lens of a series of presidential hugs. One of her three boys—all of whom served their country—made the ultimate sacrifice six years before. Tom, a lieutenant colonel, was killed in Afghanistan. That tragedy prompted hug one. An embrace of support and consolation. "I cried all over his suit," she said. "Tom would have been so embarrassed."

Next, a couple of years later, she crowded toward a rope line at an Obama event in Ohio, just hoping to get a picture signed. Then she heard from an aide that the president wanted to see *her*. "And I got my *second* presidential hug!" she said. This time she didn't cry so much; instead, something ignited inside of her. "I was inspired," she said. "Maybe this sweet old lady could still make a difference."

This was why we chose Sharon. As the Obama presidency drew closer to its conclusion, we wanted to lift up what it all meant. What this president meant to America. Sharon Belkofer summed it up: "Some people in this world make big differences. My son Tom made big differences. The president continues to make big differences—and smaller ones, too, like the inspiration he poured into me so that I might make a difference of my own."

Sharon knew that her community's schools needed more resources—and at the age of seventy-three, she decided to do something about it. She ran for her local school board, knocking on doors in the cold, bad back and all.

And before her speech in Philadelphia, she told Obama, "I won big!" That's when Sharon got her third presidential hug.

President Obama has always had a unique ability to speak to what America stands for, to tell our nation's story. And for eight years, he helped write it. Yet as the Obama chapters closed, we found that real people were better equipped to write the real legacy of the Obama presidency—to tell his story as it became our own.

8

Interviews About Nothing

Just tell him you're the president.

—JERRY SEINFELD TO BARACK OBAMA

President Obama's joyride around the South Lawn of the White House in a classic Corvette almost never happened.

I called my youngest brother as soon as it looked like it was on. Alex is a huge car nut and *Seinfeld* buff. I told him the news and swore him to secrecy. He asked a series of questions.

"So he's going on *Comedians in Cars Getting Coffee*?"

"Yeah, can you believe it?" I said.

"No, because Obama's not really a comedian, is he?"

"No," I said.

"Does he drive?"

"Not really."

"Does he drink coffee?"

"He's more of a tea guy."

"What could go wrong?" he asked.

On December 6, 2015, just two days before our scheduled shoot with Jerry Seinfeld's *Comedians in Cars Getting Coffee*, the president delivered an address to the nation—our most formal, serious, and rare form of speech—to reassure America that we would defeat ISIS, and to comfort a country on edge, reeling from yet another terror attack, in San Bernardino. The massacre at a party took the lives of fourteen of our neighbors, friends, and family as they came together to celebrate the beginning of the holiday season.

"My fellow Americans, these are the steps we can take to defeat terrorism," he stated somberly from his podium in front of the Resolute desk.

Needless to say, the American media and political environment weren't exactly ripe for comedy, and my bosses were rightly worried that the United States might not be ready to watch their president be funny with Jerry while the nation's flags flew at half-staff. It seemed very likely that months of work, and my chance to collaborate with a hero of mine, were stalled.

• • •

When it comes to politics, comedy doesn't get enough credit. Similarly, Sinbad gets short shrift when it comes to his role helping to elect the first black president of the United States.

It started when Obama's chief rival in the fierce 2008 primary, Hillary Clinton, recounted a story: she said that when she was First

Lady on a goodwill mission, she landed in Bosnia under sniper fire. Fortunately, Sinbad, who played Secret Service Agent Sam Simms in the 1996 blockbuster *First Kid*, was also on board and set the record straight years later as the claim came under scrutiny. "I think the only 'red phone' moment was 'Do we eat here or at the next place?' " Sinbad said shortly after Hillary's mischaracterization, prompting a great deal of blowback against Hillary and propelling Obama to the presidency. (Okay, it's possible there was more to his history-making election than that.) Clearly, the role of comedy in politics is no laughing matter.

But seriously, silly stuff counts. Comedy can do two things in politics: it can help you or it can hurt you. Consider that there are talented people paid big money to mock the president every night. It's no different than a school cafeteria: better to be in on the joke.

That's why the president was always the first to make fun of his graying hair, comment on his perceived aloofness, crack wise about his days getting high, or even joke around about the birther nonsense. Because he knew what many of us learn in grade school.

There's no quicker way to disarm an antagonist than with a little self-deprecation and a lot of laughter.

• • •

The *Comedians in Cars Getting Coffee* idea had first come about years before in a "blue sky" creative meeting where staffers were encouraged to throw out imaginative ways to use the president's time. I believe the first person to mention *Comedians in Cars Getting Coffee*—Seinfeld's burgeoning online series in which he drives about in classic cars, stops for coffee, and talks with comic friends about anything, everything, and nothing—was advisor Brian Deese, who, incidentally, was also the man largely credited with putting together the measures that saved the American auto industry. The pitch didn't quite go anywhere then, but I thought the idea had merit.

A couple of years later, I repitched the concept, tethering it to the White House Correspondents' Dinner (WHCD), DC's annual "nerd prom," where politicians, White House staffers, journalists, and celebrities pack themselves into the cavernous basement of the Washington Hilton to gawk and guffaw, and—most importantly—to hear POTUS do a little stand-up. Along with the White House Christmas parties, the WHCD is the hottest invite in the city. And every spring, the holiday party dynamic I described in chapter 3 was flipped. The reporters, in charge of the dinner; invitations up to them. White House staffers left scrambling for tickets and favors from the press.

In a transactional town, tickets were worth a great deal more than face value, and bartering for them could leave you with a bad taste in your mouth. In fact, to a lot of people in DC and across the country, the whole weekend represents what's wrong with Washington: glad-handing, backslapping, celebrity gazing. Preparty brunches. Preparties. After-parties. After-party brunches.

The truth is, it's also a lot of fun. And in its own small way, I think the dinner is important, too. The Correspondents' Association recognizes the year's best reporters and rewards young aspiring journalists with scholarships to hone their craft. It's also an opportunity for the most important person on Earth to let off some steam, get roasted by the headliner, and—more to the point—poke fun at himself. If the president didn't attend these dinners, it would be a sign that he was no longer willing to laugh at himself. Of course, not attending was inconceivable to President Obama.

One of my earliest goals at the White House was to write a joke for the president's speech, but I was too timid at first to try my hand at submitting any one-liners. The speech was primarily written by speechwriters Jon Lovett and, later, David Litt, with input from other top speechwriters, senior staffers, and some of Hollywood's funniest folks, from David Letterman to, yes, Larry David. Prior to the 2014 dinner, I re-upped the Seinfeld pitch. We should have Jerry come by the Oval Office and give POTUS pointers for the big night, I suggested. A joke coach. Then Jerry would drive a nervous Obama to the Hilton, providing more tips along the way. It would play as a video introduction for Obama's speech. The key, as I saw it, was that Obama needed to be eager but terrible in the video, with a stilted delivery and unrelatable content, like lamentations about the food on Air Force One. He needed to bomb for it to be funny. Unfortunately, the only thing that bombed was my pitch, which went nowhere—but it kept the notion alive and Jerry on "the list."

The list was made up of ideas, some quite "out there" and probably a bridge too far, that remained presidential possibilities. I added one titled "Bike to Work Day": I suggested that POTUS grab his bicycle and ride down Pennsylvania Avenue to the Capitol on National Bike to Work Day to deliver a speech about the *work* that Congress needed to do. That one landed flat, as did a bit that many staffers suggested about sending Obama to a classroom as a substitute teacher, blackboard and all, to embrace his tendency to slip into "professor mode."

Velz and I worked very hard to get Howard Stern into the mix. We wrote a detailed memo to our bosses outlining the many pros to a sit-down with the "King of *All* Media," an unusually thoughtful interviewer with a vast audience that we would do well to connect with. Now, the reason we weren't risking our jobs submitting a memo that called for the commander in chief to get chummy with a formerly infamous shock jock dates back to 2014.

It's the same reason a lazy drive for coffee wasn't a nonstarter and why it seemed to "have merit." For opening up these new avenues, we owed a debt of thanks to an irreverent, derisive man named Zach Galifianakis. The playing field that presidents use to engage the public was changed in March 2014 when Obama famously appeared on the rumpled comic's *Between Two Ferns*—a popular web series that thrived on discomfiture—to promote the Affordable Care Act.

Part of the conceit of the show is that it's amateur hour, which would contrast perfectly with the professionalism of the White House. So, in late February 2014, the crew brought dinky Ikea end tables, which Velz helped to set up before the shoot. Following the taping, he approached Upper Press with the famous ferns in hand. After giving one to Schultz to help spruce up his sparse office, Velz recounted the interview through fits of laughter. We were all a bit nervous, given that this was a unique format that involved line reading and acting, as well as improvisation on the part of the president.

The tone was set early when the audio guy haphazardly miked POTUS at the door to the Dip Room. He applied a large piece of white tape to the outside of the president's navy lapel and let the cord hang loose. Amateur hour. On purpose.

The point of the show is that Zach is super annoying. And POTUS was to play the annoyed, mildly offended counterpart. Problem is, the room couldn't tell on first run-through whether the president was just a solid actor or genuinely pissed off. After all, Zach did ask what it felt like to be the last black president and called POTUS a "nerd." Velz and Valerie Jarrett, as well as Jay and Cody, held their breath. Then a wide grin gave it away.

POTUS was in on the gag. And he crushed his performance. Velz said he and the other staffers standing off to the side of the Dip Room could barely hold it together—that it was nearly impossible not to burst out laughing. Velz, who spent a good deal of his days opining with unusual sophistication on the latest television shows and movies, was spot-on in his review. He predicted it would be a hit, and America agreed with him.

The results were remarkable. We reached the young audience that we needed to sign up for health care through the as-of-then much-maligned website HealthCare.gov, which had a very bumpy rollout. Enrollment for the president's signature legislative achievement was lagging behind expectations. We needed a jolt. Six minutes on a campy video series provided just that. Visits to HealthCare.gov skyrocketed 40 percent, enrollment was up, and the fake interview has been viewed more than fifty million times. It got us back on track—well, at least until one month later, when the White House red fox story pushed it off the evening news.

We knew we had something. We'd proven the concept.

The second term allowed us to take more chances than the first. We didn't mind if the Right ripped us for the Galifianakis interview, which they did. (Bill O'Reilly helpfully reminded his viewers that Lincoln wouldn't have done it.) The truth is, right from the start of the administration, the president pushed the envelope. It seems commonplace now, but he became the first sitting president to do a late-night interview (with Jay Leno for *The Tonight Show*), adeptly mixing moments of comedy with policies of consequence.

Around the same time of the *Between Two Ferns* interview, we pulled out all the stops, pressing the issue of ACA enrollment. It was a stretch of time, under the determined leadership of Denis McDonough, fully focused on salvaging Obamacare—of transforming the term from punch line to triumph.

I remember writing a memo to the president the night of February 6, 2014: "You will take part in an interview with Mista Madd for the *Madd Hatta Morning Show*." There was a space at the top of each memo labeled "From." I was so embarrassed to be explaining Mista Madd's clout in the Houston urban and rap establishment that I tried to keep my name off it. I thought back to one of my bosses relating a story from the last time Obama had given such an interview. "Oh, the indignities of this office," he'd said with a sigh from the Resolute desk.

This was sure to be another indignity, I thought. Still, it wasn't up to me. We needed to promote enrollment, so I continued with the memo—putting in the usual talking points, tough questions and answers, and relevant statistics. And the next day, as we got a call from the Outer Oval that *he* was ready, I quickly printed a copy for Jennifer Palmieri and handed it off, fingers crossed.

A few minutes later, she was back, her face red with what I hoped was laughter and not anger.

"JPalm . . ." I said tentatively.

Turns out after she told the president that he should address the Madd Hatta as "Mista Madd," the president flipped to one of the last pages of the memo, pointed, and said, "Here's what Mista Madd is not going to ask me about: the CBO report." Jennifer and another staffer, Tara, burst into laughter, which Pete Souza caught at just the right moment. It could be hard to know what to include in the president's memos—what mattered and what didn't. He was probably right in this instance, but there were times when things left out of the memo came back to bite us.

My colleague Jeff and I had been pushing our bosses for months to send Obama to Chipotle. We both loved the place, and at the time, America did too. Finally, they relented, sent Obama on an OTR to Chipotle. Couple things: like so many middle-aged men and women, he needlessly added the possessive—Chipotle*'s*—which is a particular pet peeve of mine. I've found that the most common version of this invented possessive is Nordstrom*'s*.* It's almost impossible for me not to correct that one. My dad gets particularly frustrated when I correct him on his invented possessives, but then I remind him that he once thought human babies don't open their eyes for months.

Still, most didn't notice the president's minor gaffe, because he made a major gaffe the same day. You see, I didn't think it necessary to include in the memo that one does not reach one's arms over the sneeze guard to point to what one would like to order. Turns out,

* I once heard "Burger King*'s*," which was so beyond the pale, all I could do was laugh.

I should have. Obama was captured on camera hulking over the protective glass. As *New York* magazine put it: "Obama Leans over Chipotle Sneeze Guard, Infuriates Nation." It was his Swiss-cheese-on-a-cheesesteak moment, John Kerry's famous faux pas at Pat's King of Steaks in Philly.* This was a few months after Mista Madd, and I had learned my lesson—that regardless of what the president thinks, best to include. Better safe than out of touch at "Chipotle's."

For a long time, Souza's jumbo of JPalm hung in Upper Press, a constant reminder that we'd once put the president on the phone with Mista Madd. And, more importantly, that the world didn't end. Maybe it was "unpresidential," but if it got an additional person to sign up for health insurance, it was worth it.

We were as comfortable as we were with any of this, because Obama had proven from his first correspondents' dinner performance that he could deliver a joke. In fact, that's the only reason Jerry was interested to begin with. He wouldn't invite just any president onto his "little show," as he described it. According to the comedian, Obama had landed just enough one-liners to qualify.

• • •

I've talked about how he could be self-deprecating, but Obama saved many of his best barbs for others. It was hard to predict how the president's foils—from Trump in 2011 to journalists in 2016—

* I think the only thing worse would have been if he called the place "Patrick's."

would respond, but Jen Psaki knew when she saw the first draft of the 2016 speech that one of the targeted reporters would be offended. Even though the joke was lighthearted, she pushed for its removal but was eventually outvoted.

I assumed that any reporter who was mocked by the president from the podium would take it as a badge of honor: a sign of grudging respect; that you'd risen to such heights that the president would care to knock you down a peg by poking fun.

I assumed wrong. Jen was right, and for her foresight, she was rewarded with upset emails from the butt of the president's punch line. The reporter had taken the hit to heart, assuming there was some sort of personal animus behind the barb.

The shot got a good laugh in the room. Probably not worth the headache it caused Jen, but a solid laugh nonetheless. I was crowded into a table in the corner of the massive ballroom. Hadn't heard back from Tyler, the speechwriter in charge of the last speech, on whether any of my jokes made the final cut, so I knew to assume that none did. That is, until I heard the president start down a familiar setup and then land *my* punch line! I almost fell out of my chair. I was overjoyed. And then a few minutes later, it happened again. I was stunned.

Tyler came up to me at one of the after-parties—he was genuinely excited. "I wanted it to be a surprise!" he said. "You got two in—same as Larry David."

And with that sentence, I felt my time at the White House had reached its peak. Obama ended his speech by raising his microphone and bellowing "Obama, out!" As he dropped the mike to the floor, and the crowd rose, I couldn't help thinking about how well it was all working out. Sure, I was sad things were ending, but he was going out on a high, Hillary was just a few months from election, and I had gotten jokes into what was "perhaps the last" White House Correspondents' Dinner.*

Months later, in the immediate lead-up to the election, we were preparing for a visit to Jimmy Kimmel's late-night show. We received what I thought was a genius idea. Jimmy's team had asked to have the president perform iconic speeches from famous presidential TV shows and movies. *Independence Day*, for instance, when Bill Pullman delivers a soaring call to action in the face of an alien invasion. Or the one we suggested back to them, when Michael Douglas's President Shepherd beats back his rival in a stirring defense of his girlfriend at the climax of *The American President*: "This is a time for serious people, Bob, and your fifteen minutes are up. My name is Andrew Shepherd, and I *am* the president."

But when the president received our memo, though he thought it funny, he decided no. We went with a proven winner, another segment of "Mean Tweets," in which the president read mean tweets about himself. Helping to cull through the real mean tweets in contention for reading on the air was a trip. We navigated them well, I thought, choosing the correct mix of random, mean, and funny. Turns out, we screwed up the last one.

For the big finale, he read a tweet from @realDonaldTrump:

* POTUS joked that 2016 could mark "the last" WHCD, a reference to Donald Trump's devastating effects on the country in the unlikely event he became president.

"President Obama will go down as perhaps the worst president in the history of the United States!" Then Obama looked at the camera and said, "Well, @-real-Donald-Trump, at least I will go down as a *president*." Then he dropped the phone.

• • •

It was always about more than being funny. We made a concerted effort to meet Americans where they were—and where they were was changing. Nobody understood that better than Jason Goldman. He, more than most, recognized that "during the Obama presidency, there was this dramatic shift in how people consumed information." As he put it to me recently, "People forget that in 2008, we were on the second iPhone, that the mobile revolution hadn't fully happened, that while Facebook existed, mobile video didn't. And while Twitter existed, it was in its infancy."

So as these now-ubiquitous mediums matured, our strategy for communicating with the world needed to grow up too. We were a bunch of Millennials trying to keep up. That's not to say that *Comedians in Cars Getting Coffee* would replace *Meet the Press* or that YouTube video gags would replace conventional press briefings. In fact, throughout our second term, traditional journalistic outlets continued to represent the most meaningful channel to communicate the president's message. But we would have been negligent not to adapt. "We had to embrace a strategy where you didn't try to reach everyone at once but instead were very specific about who you were trying to reach and why," Jason said.

Yet social platforms have their benefits and their drawbacks. They allowed us to connect in a deep and meaningful way with a niche—granted, sometimes still very large—audience. But as Jason cautioned, it can be a difficult platform for persuasion: often we were connecting with folks predisposed to agree with what we were selling. And we were wary about devolving into an echo chamber. We already saw that beginning to take root on the Right, and Jason was well aware of the "robust marketplace for dark conspiracy on the web."

That's why it was so important to me that the Seinfeld conversation be content free. An interview about nothing. I wanted it to exist in a sort of media vacuum—even as, all around us, things were changing.

During some downtime in the office, I read an article in *Wired* about a crazy-looking bird called the crossbill, named for its peculiar bill, which crosses awkwardly over itself. It evolved that way to do battle with a type of pine tree that's developed sturdier cones specifically to try to keep the crossbill out. They're locked in what's called coevolution: two distinct species evolving in response to each other. It reminds me a great deal of the mutuality between the president and the press that I described in chapter 3, and it informs what my position toward the end of the administration was all about.

By the time I became deputy director of messaging, the coevolution (or devolution) of the press corps and the White House communications strategy was well under way. Things had changed in just a few years. Think about it: at the beginning of 2015, President Obama's voice didn't exist on Twitter. "Despite having tens of millions of followers," Jason recently told me, "the @barackobama account was considered a campaign asset, and most of the content there was not in his voice; only those signed '-bo' were from him." So in 2015 the White House created @potus, and, Jason said, "The president directed that all of the content on that channel would be in his voice, and he would be involved personally in the creation of it."

Of course, the creation of his official account didn't mean POTUS was up early tweeting out his frustrations with the media or musing online late at night in the residence about policy. For the most part, according to Jason, "Our stance with @potus was not to use the channel to break news, because we both felt an obligation to the traditional media covering the White House and felt that policy announcements—in particular—were more appropriately rolled out through traditional means so that the implications could be understood by the public." Our presence on Twitter didn't take the place of structured rollouts with the *Wall Street Journal*; it didn't supplant discussions with the *New York Times* editorial board; Twitter was an additional tool in our arsenal at a time when the media environment demanded it.

The Bush messaging people certainly didn't need to contend with Twitter. Things were different. Back then, Facebook practically still had a "the" in front of it. For us, Facebook was *the* way people communicated. Back then, memes were confined to funny cat things on weird websites. For us, memes were a political force. And, to me, they were fascinating.

Political memes seemed to grow out of our ever-tightening time frames, our diminished attention spans, and Americans' collective desire to be in on the political debate. Think about it. Few people read full articles these days—"Who has the time?" we say—but we inhale headlines and spout opinions. So political memes became a kind of headline in a picture. Like emojis, they're a quick, compelling way to communicate. Often, they convey comedic commentary on a specific person. The first time I really grasped the power of political memes was the legendary shot of a cool-looking, sunglasses-clad Hillary Clinton checking her BlackBerry. That image, captured by frequent pool photographer Kevin Lamarque, was worth a thousand memes. And it embedded this sense of calm, unflappability, and even a dash of panache in the image of Secretary Clinton. It was a permission structure to see Hillary as a little bit cool. It wasn't entirely unlike the famous Obama *Hope* posters plastered around the country in 2008 (an analog meme). A tight image and defining word or phrase below, memes are essentially digital advertisements.

Now, of course, memes can be negative, too. And some of the most viral memes were downright cruel—or played on an undercurrent of racism or misogyny. They were used to fan the flames of conspiracies or to push misinformation. Memes became so omnipresent and so influential that they were actually cited by Defense Secretary Robert Gates as a reason not to release the photos of a deceased Osama bin Laden: for fear that the images would immediately be turned into memes that could provoke a response.

None of this is a surprise, given that memes are simply a way we communicate online. They weren't ideal for a debate, though. That's because memes fell into the category of social media discourse that, as Jason explained, was less likely to change minds than it was to shore up support or bolster beliefs. Still, they are an important part of the recipe for deepening sentiments and fueling enthusiasm, which is crucial when it comes to voter turnout.

Shortly after almost seventy million Americans turned out to vote for Obama in 2008, he was faced with multiple inherited crises, and for a couple years, he was focused on combatting those and passing the Affordable Care Act. When I came aboard, things were stabilizing, but Americans didn't seem to be noticing, and Democrats got wiped out in the 2010 midterms. Shortly after, the president made a comment about how one of his administration's biggest failures was that we didn't tell our story well enough, as we were too focused on policy and bogged down in crisis. Each department had an email distribution list that looked something like this: DL-WHO-Legal or DL-WHO-Research. After the president's comment, I remember one of the speechwriters joking that they should change theirs to DL-WHO-BiggestDisappointment.

Now, if you're a communications staffer—regardless of party—you know that *all* problems are communications problems. And the president's comment was not surprising (or, by the way, wrong). After all, we would never knowingly push bad policy, so if the polling was off, then people must not be getting the message. At least, that's what every noncommunications staffer could be forgiven for thinking.

In the second term, we worked especially hard to be sure people got the message. And as I moved into writing and messaging, it was time to start looking at legacy, which brings me back to memes. As we were winding down the second term, a particular vein of memes took hold: the Obama-Biden friendship memes. The most potent memes, like the best jokes, were built on a kernel of truth and then taken to a level of absurdity. The Obama-Biden memes did that well. They were the perfect antidote to the rancor of the 2016 campaign, and as we prepared to depart the White House, they predicted the nostalgia America would soon feel.

To capitalize on the memes at the height of their popularity, I pitched that we compile the three most popular memes and film Obama and Biden acting them out, word for word. A little departing gift to America from Barack and Joe. That pitch died quickly; went nowhere. With hindsight, I'm glad it did.

Memes seem still to be in that category of media best not co-opted by candidates or presidents. Sometimes it's just better to let the internet do its own thing. With Seinfeld though, I thought we could pull it off.

• • •

But the question loomed: Could we stomach the drive around the South Lawn so soon after the San Bernardino attack?

We had been working on it for months. To get anything out of the ordinary done around the West Wing, you need buy-in from the right folks. And putting the president behind the wheel qualified as out of the ordinary. Aside from the shortest of drives in a politically correct, American-made, environmentally friendly Chevy Volt, Obama had driven just once during his two terms: at a Secret Service training facility outside Washington, DC. I'm told he got the vehicle going pretty good, even tried a J-turn or two, and, from what I saw at the training facility—agents driving with skilled recklessness—that doesn't surprise me.

Toward the end of the term, in 2015 and 2016, Jen Psaki made it a point to take advantage of what working at the White House had to offer; to reward the staffers who chose to stick it out to the end. That meant taking the occasional field trip—to the Secret Service training facility or Camp David, for instance. The training facility included a trip to the gun room, where we could handle every type of confiscated gun under the sun, from a bazooka, to a Beretta, to a gold-plated .50 caliber. It was an interesting dynamic, us Obama Democrats wielding these weapons. Later, they let us shoot, too. There was something unsettling about looking to my right, as the gunshots rang out, and watching the high-strung Jimmy unload a gargantuan gun over and over, blasting the target.

We looked on as titanium-toothed Secret Service dogs followed commands and took down a "threat." Velz volunteered to get into the padded suit and get mauled by a dog, but the agents ultimately said no. I don't think our waiver covered it.

We took in a live-action combat sequence—a practice drill for what the motorcade would do in the event of attacks from the side of the road, complete with smoke bombs.

We watched as a knife-wielding attacker lunged over the bicycle rack of the rope line at the "president" as he exited a mock Air Force One.

At first, it felt like a movie set—a carefully choreographed play—but as the armored Suburbans screamed around the corner and out of harm's way, something more sobering set in. We were looking at the reality that the Secret Service guards against 24/7. While we staffers sometimes joke around with them, even take them for granted, their mission was always so much more important than ours. I felt stupid for worrying whether they remembered my mai tai incident.

Still, around the same time, as I sat down with an agent in the East Reception Room—a formal sitting room just off the entrance to the East Wing, filled with fine art and antiques—I worried he wouldn't take me seriously. It was just a couple of weeks before the potential Seinfeld filming. My opening line was a bit bold: "So we want to have POTUS drive around the South Lawn."

He smirked, gave a quick "*Mhmm.*"

"In a Corvette."

"*Mhmm.*"

"With Jerry Seinfeld."

"*Okayyy . . .*"

"So . . . can we make this safe?"

It's the Secret Service's job to make things work. Truth is, some of my biggest fights were with members of the Secret Service on behalf of the press' access. But I always found that as long as I didn't spring things on them at the last second, the agents I dealt with were extraordinarily accommodating. My Seinfeld request was not last minute. Plus, and most importantly, I had buy-in from the right folks. Anita Decker Breckenridge was the president's former personal aide and then deputy chief of staff for operations, a powerful role that's essentially defined as "Gets shit done."

Anita was the right person to have in my corner. Initially intimidated by her, I found common ground with Anita around nineties nostalgia and quickly became impressed by her refreshing candor. She was on board with the White House working with Seinfeld (one of the kings of the 1990s), and with her nod to the Secret Service, so were they.

The final hurdle was determining exactly what vehicle the president would drive. The only time I'd seen him behind the wheel was on the golf course where he took real joy in operating his own golf cart, basking in a simple freedom he was so often denied. Similarly, the staff at Camp David, the ultimate gated community, told me that Obama drove a special cart that had the speed restrictor removed, allowing him to breeze about the impenetrable compound.

I was lucky to travel to Camp David three times during my time at the White House. I staffed the G-8 summit, where I got my first taste of the unique security measures while battling over press access with the navy and marine personnel who run the Camp. The restrictions for filming were tight, and the press pool's cameras needed always to be pointed very narrowly at a precleared location. The wrong angle of a tree could potentially give up too much information on the location of the compound, which is shrouded by remarkable tree cover.

By my third visit—a memorable staff retreat organized by Psaki—things seemed looser without press or eight world leaders to worry about. The professionals stationed at Camp David are particularly protective and proud of the place, though they are not tour guides by trade. And they regaled our communications staff mainly with stories about where Beyoncé and Jay-Z had stayed a few weeks before. They did, however, relate the story of FDR, who was known to drive himself—some say quite aggressively—to Camp David, which was then known as Shangri-La, from the White House in an open-top convertible.

My ambitions for Obama's drive weren't so grand. Jerry wanted to pick the right car for the chief executive, and we wanted to leave it up to him—with just a few parameters. It had to be American made. And, crucially, it couldn't be a manual transmission. Nobody wanted to ask the president if he knew how to drive stick, and, most importantly, we didn't want to see him try to remember how while being filmed.

Jerry came through, selecting a powder-blue 1963 Corvette Stingray. According to Jerry, there is no cooler, or more confident, or more American Corvette, which is why he chose it for the commander in chief.

But would it ever see the light of day?

Anita, Liz, Psaki, and I huddled the day before the shoot. I was a wreck that morning. Jerry and his entire team were en route, and I still couldn't confirm whether it was all for naught. After mild hemming and hawing, and a bit of convincing, we made a decision. With a belief in America's ability to switch gears—if not the president's literal ability to do the same—we went for it.

• • •

The fun part was keeping it a secret.

Working in the White House Communications Office requires you to keep many secrets, which can be awkward, given that reporters are allowed to breeze in and out of your office as they please.

To combat prying eyes, we haphazardly taped screen protectors to our computers, but they helped only from an angle. Get right behind your subject, and they were of no use, which allowed Velz, who sat directly behind me, to call out when I was "less than working." So I sometimes resorted to jamming in as much nonwork as possible when Upper Press was empty.

During one early-afternoon lull, I looked back, realized everyone was gone, and quickly pulled up Amazon. I was in desperate need of new boxer briefs and wanted to seize the moment. I pulled up a promising pair and started clicking through for size and fit. They were a particularly extreme shade of orange, and as I zoomed in to get a sense for the seams, the door swung open and Denis, the chief of staff, walked in. Just as I was eyeing the bulging orange crotch.

I had no excuses ready, no cover story prepared, so I took a different tactic: unbridled honesty.

"Hey, Denis, just doing some quick online shopping. Really need new boxer briefs." *I could have just said boxers,* I thought immediately. *Shouldn't have said anything at all.*

"Let your freak flag fly," he said drily before departing quickly.

That is to say, privacy doesn't exist in the West Wing. And after six years at the White House, it's hard to believe in conspiracy theories, at least those that involve the federal government. They're just too hard to pull off. People talk. People write books.* Secrets don't stay secrets for long—like online underwear orders. Fortunately, in the communications department, our confidences rarely

* The nerve.

needed to last. Our plans and ideas were ultimately intended to be announced, plus we had to hide plans, not the president.

There were important exceptions to that rule.

Moving the president in secret was entirely different. I came to suspect when covert trips were in the offing when the right mix of personnel was acting cagey or behind closed doors. When I was new, and a more senior press wrangler, Jesse, was spotted entering the Situation Room—with no foreign trips currently on the upcoming docket—I knew something was up. And when the trip director and deputy chief of staff entered the press secretary's office for a closed-door meeting without an apparent purpose, I thought—but never asked or wondered aloud—if the president was planning a secret trip to a war zone.

Back when lying didn't come so easily to a White House, these trips created a bit of a conundrum in the form of the "White House Daily Guidance," a schedule that we blast out each night detailing the president's activities for the following day.

For a long time, I was responsible for writing and sending it out to the seven thousand journalists on the White House's media list. The schedule noted what the president was doing, when he was doing it, and, crucially, *where*. This was the only instance where we had to actively mislead the press and public—for obvious reasons of national security and presidential safety.

A few years after I first knew to look for the signs and suspected such a trip was in the works, I got an odd call to visit the director of press advance in her large, elegant EEOB office. Without a word, she ushered me in and closed the door securely behind us. As I sat down, she said:

"The president's going to Afghanistan in a couple days. Can you go?"

The correct answer was "yes," but I hesitated, a conflicting, long-planned family trip bouncing through my mind. To add to the mix, I wouldn't have been allowed to tell anyone—family, friends, wife—that I was leaving or why I couldn't make the family trip. I hesitated too long, and before I could turn her down or ask more questions, she said she had another option and that she'd go with that person: a more experienced hand at secret, foreign travel and a close friend of mine at the White House.

I deeply regretted not handling that situation better. I'd just given up an important, once-in-a-lifetime opportunity.* But just a few days later, with the president away, I began to regret things slightly less while sitting on the beach. Not because of the palm trees or the piña colada, but because my BlackBerry was blowing up.

The wrangler who took my place—through absolutely no fault of his own—had technically outed the CIA station chief in Afghanistan. The National Security Council inadvertently left his name on a list that the wrangler was to distribute to the pool for a very wide press distribution. There is no doubt in my mind that I would have done the exact same thing, and been subject to the same legal questions and public fallout. Suddenly, missing the trip felt a little more okay.

For the Seinfeld taping, even though we weren't secretly shut-

* The first television episode I ever wrote that was produced (for ABC's *Designated Survivor* starring Kiefer Sutherland) involved a president's secret trip to Afghanistan and a missing CIA station chief. Clearly, I'm not over missing this trip.

tling the president into an active war zone, we did need to worry about him bombing—and we did need to keep the taping a secret. We wouldn't be flying to Afghanistan, but the president would be driving, outside, in a powder-blue Corvette with Jerry Seinfeld. While we knew America would eat this up around the holidays, it remained a risk to tape so soon after the attack in San Bernardino and the president's remarks in the Oval on terrorism. We wanted to control the rollout.

So I asked that we schedule the driving portion of the taping during the press briefing. You see, the sliding door to Lower Press, where Marie and Antoinette sat, opened onto a double door out to the Colonnade, with its view of the South Lawn. The only time that doorway was impassable to reporters was during the daily press briefing, so those sixty minutes were our best bet for pulling off the drive portion of the taping without reporters catching wind. The POTUS scheduling team came through.

The next hurdle was getting a powder-blue classic Corvette onto White House grounds without stirring up suspicion from the omnipresent press and camera-wielding tourists who begin lining up for the White House tour shortly after seven in the morning. Velz took one for the team and came in extra early to help shuttle the car through a side entrance and clear security. It was a scene: the bomb-sniffing dogs scrutinizing the Corvette, and the usually skeptical Secret Service impressed by the cool car. Velz and some of the producers stashed the vehicle in a shaded shed by the basketball court, protected from prying eyes by lush tree cover akin to that of Camp David.

That's where I met Jerry. He hopped out of a Suburban and ambled up to me in his signature look: jeans and sneakers, which squeaked as he approached. I wanted to make a comment, get into a back-and-forth on "squeaky sneaks," but thought it better to get down to business than try to beat Jerry Seinfeld at shtick.

"We need to talk about the ending," he began. *Oh-uh,* I thought. My bosses had already killed the pitch that Jerry and his producer Tammy had sent in the day before, which called for the president to be blocked by the Secret Service as he tries to drive off campus. We planned for Jerry to quarrel with the agent (an actual agent, not an actor) when he was driving, but thought it was a bridge too far to have the president driving, acting, *and* arguing with an agent—who, after all, was one of the people there to protect him.

Beyond that one disagreement, my bosses provided us a great deal of latitude. Things were loose on the South Lawn as we prepared for the shoot. Brian, who knew Tammy, was uncharacteristically open to decidedly nondecorous ideas. He even came up with some great ideas of his own, like having Jerry trudge through the bushes. To the delight of Jerry and Tammy, we were willing to completely upend the norms of Oval Office behavior. We set out to plan an awkward encounter to start and then a fun, minutiae-filled interview, including, of course, a drive around the South Lawn.

Still, Jerry thought his version of the ending would kill and that it was the only way to conclude the episode. He really wanted permission to do it. I said I'd check with the "powers that be."

A bit later, a woman approached, eyeing my ID badge. "Wait a minute, what is your name?" she asked. She looked familiar.

"Pat Cunnane," I told her. She was stunned.

"When I was a kid, I had a crush on a guy at camp with the exact same name!" she said.

I hadn't met anyone with my same name other than my dad, so without thinking, I responded, "Maybe it was my dad."

"Just how old do you think I am?" she asked politely. In a rare stroke of common sense, I decided it was best not to guess and instead pivoted the conversation. "I'm sorry, what was your name?" I asked. "Jessica," she answered. Just then it hit me. She was an author, a philanthropist—and Jerry's wife.

As I worried over how badly I had offended Jessica Seinfeld, Jerry circled back. He pressed me on the ending bit, still arguing that the president should get into a pretend fight with the Secret Service. I was stuck between my childhood idol and my obligation to the White House.

It was clear: *I had that sun in my eyes.*

There was only one thing to do: abdicate all responsibility.

"Look, Jerry"—*Oh cool, I just called him Jerry*—"once you're in the car with the president, it's just the two of you. You know what I'm saying? You can suggest whatever you want . . ."

"Okay, I got it," he said.

"But I didn't tell you this. And if I get fired, you have to hire me."

All that was left for me to do was to describe to the president the madness that we had gotten him into.

• • •

I received a note from the Outer Oval on my BlackBerry, probably with a red exclamation point. "He's ready!" But I was down on the South Lawn. My heart leapt into my throat as I sprinted up the driveway and down the Colonnade. It had taken so much to get to this point: I couldn't be late to the Oval Office.

Any of my Upper Press colleagues will tell you that I despise hearing about other people's dreams. It's the worst: "I was in my house, *but* it wasn't *really* my house." We get it. It was a dream. Enough. Still, this is my book, and I get to decide what's in it. There was a dream I often had. I was running, *but* I wasn't really running—making no progress. That's how I felt. The Colonnade seemed longer, just seconds to spare, as I burst past the Uniformed Division officer stationed between Lower Press and the Oval Office and rushed to the Outer Oval doorway, where I was saved by Hillary Clinton.

I wasn't late. Secretary Clinton, on a quick break from her presidential campaign, had been meeting in the Oval with Obama while we prepped the Corvette and the Beast on the South Lawn.

It was one of countless reminders that, while we were sitting in the White House, there was a rampant race among those vying to replace us beyond the gates. There were two watershed moments during the primary campaign, when the race directly impacted our work at the White House.

The first came in October 2015 when closed doors and hushed meetings meant something was going on. I just didn't know what. It was what we sometimes called a "secret squirrel operation." When I gleaned that Liz, who got her start at the White House working for the vice president, was involved—and given the context of growing questions about Biden's 2016 intentions—I assumed he had made up his mind.

Suddenly the press assistants were called into action: told to gather the press in the Rose Garden for an announcement. I didn't know it then, but the vice president was in with Obama. No one knew what his decision was; the president helped him edit his remarks at the Resolute desk. And then we all watched from the Rose Garden as he elected not to run. I was sad for Biden—he would have made a fantastic president—but I was touched by the bond that Obama and Biden so clearly shared, standing side by side in the Rose Garden. Ultimately, I was happy for the clarity. HRC, PIW* as I called her, would be the nominee.

I continued to believe that to be the case even as Senator Bernie Sanders made impressive inroads across the country. Still, Secretary Clinton had secured millions of more votes than he had, and to me, it seemed like a formality that she would eventually clinch the nomination. It became even more of a formality during the second watershed moment, when the primary seeped beyond the gates of the White House, and Bernie Sanders came for a chaotic visit. To put it mildly, the Bernie camp was not prepared for the stop. We didn't know at which airport they were arriving or which entrance to the White House they would use. Our press people were run-

* President-in-waiting, for those of you who didn't read the prologue. (Also, you should really read the prologue.)

ning around like crazy; their press was not in our security system, so Velz had to scramble to be sure they could be swept in time.

As their one-on-one meeting, which lasted roughly an hour, was wrapping up, Bernie's campaign manager came into Upper Press. The senator was going to make a statement at the stakeout location, which was about fifteen feet beyond the windows into Upper Press. We could see hordes of press gathering; the cable networks were beginning to take the feed live. Turns out, the Sanders camp didn't have a binder for remarks, so I found an old one that I had used years before above my desk. Next, they wanted a stand, so Velz rummaged through the chair room (that's where we keep all the chairs) for a music stand, which looked a little ridiculous—but it was the best we could do. Finally, as Bernie was ready, Velz walked the stand out to the mass of reporters, and we all watched from beyond the window as the primary began to wind down.

But back to the Seinfeld taping. Clinton's and Obama's meeting had ended. I was about to head in, but I stopped just short of the Outer Oval Office. Clinton was showing Obama photos of her grandchild on her cell phone. As I struggled to catch my breath, I listened in as she explained what was happening in each photo, the perfect doting grandmother. I couldn't help thinking that if America saw—or eavesdropped on—the literal behind-closed-doors Hillary, their character concerns might be allayed. But, also, that's total bullshit. It wasn't the case that America never had the chance to see Hillary in this homespun light. It's just that they chose not to.

No time to dwell on that because—before I could fully catch my breath—I was ushered inside. As I set foot in the Oval Office, the rush of anticipation was overcome by a very sudden realization: they really only ever sent me in to brief the president for the weird stuff. As I creaked onto the zigzag pattern of the hardwood floors, I remembered just six months earlier, the previous Mother's Day, and the last awkward encounter I had in the Oval.

• • •

For Mother's Day 2015, we decided to shock some moms who had written to the president about relevant issues. It was a peculiar assignment, so it should have been no surprise to me that I was put in charge. I approached the president as he studied his briefing book at the Resolute desk. Jason was standing off to the side. "So you're going to surprise some moms today," I told the president. He seemed to be into the idea of calling some moms around the country on their special day, and I thought, *Okay, maybe this won't be the weirdest thing ever.*

But then the first mom didn't pick up. I had precalled them, made sure they weren't nuts, and told them a White House official wanted to follow-up to ask a few specific questions. I was frustrated, but we moved on to the next mom, Stephanie from Minnesota, who—thankfully—answered her phone. Only problem: she didn't believe it was actually the president on the other end of the line.

"It's really me," he said.

The bulk of the call was Obama convincing her that it was, in fact, him on the phone. He even offered to have her test him with some policy questions: "You want to ask me about Syria?"

Next, we connected with Dawn from Arizona, who had written to the president thanking him for Obamacare. Her son had been bitten by a rattlesnake and—had it not been for the ACA—the medical bills would have cost $170,000. Under the new law, they paid only a $150 copay at the hospital and a $15 copay for each additional visit. Perfect little story, I thought. Just one hitch: I should have known that the president would want to dig in on the rattlesnake at the bottom of it all: How did her son get bitten? Why was he not paying attention? Turns out he was zoned out into his headphones, pounding Kendrick Lamar, which the president approved of from the Resolute desk.

"He's a fine young rapper," he affirmed, as I stifled a laugh, worried we were veering off-course. I was right. Dawn is a corrections officer and it was "CO Appreciation Day" at the prison where she worked, which meant she was in the middle of a luncheon with dozens of other COs. She asked to put Obama on speaker so he could say hi to all of the other folks at prison. He, of course, agreed. And as she struggled to figure out the speakerphone, I knew we had taken a turn. With the president on speakerphone to a bunch of ladies at prison, we had jumped the shark. Or the snake.

As the president politely wrapped up his conversations with the prison corrections officers, he said, absentmindedly, "I'll see you all soon!"

To which Dawn replied something along the lines of: "Well, I hope not. We work in a prison!"

We edited the video heavily.

• • •

The *Comedians in Cars Getting Coffee* video edit would be out of our hands. That's why I needed to get the president's preparation right. "So, you're going to take a drive with Jerry Seinfeld," I said, approaching his desk.

I expected him to be more excited, but after a quick smile, he asked about my memo. "Says this is scheduled for ninety minutes." I understood immediately what he was going to say but had no solution to offer as he continued, "Seems a little long, doesn't it?"

"Yes, sir," I said, adding, "I'm sure it won't actually take that long," which may have well been my second Oval Office fib. It seemed to work, though, as we flew through the rest of the briefing. He had read my memo, which included the rundown, some possible topics, and a few suggested jokes I had written. I could tell he read it because he marked up some of the jokes. I tried to make sure he understood the opening, because that was the only semiscripted part. "The point is that Jerry is being a nuisance," I said. "Pretend like you don't like him. The key is to make him feel very uncomfortable."

"I got it," he said calmly. I worried his confidence might be misplaced, but I certainly wasn't going to ask him if he was sure he "got it," reminded as I was of the viral memes he spawned in 2008 when the race with Senator McCain tightened. "Relax, I got this" was superimposed over a photo of Obama looking cool.

He looked pretty cool now at the desk, so I gave the high sign to the crew, took to the corner of the Oval Office, and waited for Jerry to trample through the bushes and knock on the wavy ballistic glass behind the president's desk.

As usual, I was wrong. My worries were misplaced. The president played the dry, annoyed role perfectly. Never broke character even as Jerry squeaked in, flopped down on the couch in the Oval, and grabbed an apple from the modern-chic coffee table, chomping down obnoxiously. I bit my lip to keep from laughing. It was hard to get a grip on the moment—and before it could sink in, it was over.

They nailed the scene in one take. From there, the real fun began—and one question lingered in my mind. Was I about to get fired for the advice I had given Jerry?

Fortunately, or maybe unfortunately, Jerry never had to hire me. Turns out he did end up convincing the president to play along while in the car. "Just tell him you're the president," he said. His gambit killed.

The episode smashed all viewership records for the show and helped send *Comedians in Cars* into a new category of Emmy nomination. For us, it further humanized the president around the holidays. I'll never forget the picture-perfect responses I saw pour in on Facebook the night it aired, like the random Republican who posted: "I've never been an Obama supporter, but he seems cool. I could get a beer with him." This was particularly thrilling because the person who comes out on the correct end of the "Which dude would you rather get a beer with?" question is usually in good shape. Just ask Al Gore. Or Walter Mondale. Or Stephen A. Douglas.

The week his episode of *Comedians in Cars Getting Coffee* aired, the president's Gallup weekly approval rating was at 45 percent. It would never be that low again, rising steadily over the next fifty-five weeks, up to 59 percent on the day he left office.

That's not to say the president's appearance on Jerry's show directly swayed his approval ratings. It's not causal, but it was part of a concerted effort, with the clock winding down, to show another side of the president. The lighthearted, minutiae-minded, human Obama, revealing both his humor and humanity. And people, regardless of politics, responded.

Best of all, Obama responded too. He didn't seem to mind my fib in the Oval Office. In the end, the shoot had taken even longer than the president worried. "Why don't you let me do fun stuff like that more often?" he asked Denis after the taping.

Maybe we should have. Because it turns out interviews about nothing can really get you something.

9

Friday the Thirteenth

No matter where you go, there you are.

—WHO KNOWS?

I lived about a mile from the office, so, rain or shine, oppressive heat or crippling cold, I walked to work. Typically, it was a treat—a nice way to worry about what the day might bring. The first twelve minutes offer few surprises and are littered with the usual perils of Washington waking up: the guy who refuses to look up from his phone; the gentleman who grabs his Uber in the worst possible spot; the homeless person whose lot in life lingers with me for a block.

It's in the last minute, at the edge of Lafayette Square, as I pass the ramshackle tent manned for decades by a small woman protesting for peace, and cross Pennsylvania Avenue, approaching the gate, when something new is stirred in me each day.

Most White House staffers say it is "humbling." It is not. They are lying.

Sure, the view knocks you back, but it also pumps you up. Yes, the building amplifies your anxiety, but it also fortifies your focus and lifts your purpose—whether your purpose is rebuilding the economy or, like me, refilling your morning Mountain Dew.

So walking into the White House is a lot of things, but it is not humbling. There is no bigger ego boost than strolling through security, past the press, and toward the West Wing, feeling like maybe you belong.

The late White House press secretary Tony Snow once said that it's the people on the outside looking in with the real perspective on the place: "They know what you're likely to forget. You're blessed . . . Leave no room for regrets, for someday, in the not-so-distant future, you will be back where you started: on the sidewalk with the other folks, gawking at that grand, glorious, mysterious place where Lincoln walks at night; and our highest hopes and dreams reside."

If only those passersby knew.

I wondered what they might think if they could peek in; if they learned, God forbid, about my failed Pope sneeze, or the never-caught West Wing pooper, or the broad range of Millennial minutiae that filled our days, beyond the grand walls and behind the bulletproof glass of the building. Those countless moments of nonsense didn't replace the glorious mystery of the place, I would tell them—they resided alongside their and my "highest hopes and dreams."

No day at the White House was the same as any other, but many of the rhythms of the day were more constant, the mix of the minutiae and the momentous consistent. I don't remember many single days from beginning to end, but I'd like to take you through one that stands out.

On Friday, November 13, 2015, I was in Upper Press at my desk scrambling to prepare for the morning senior staff meeting with the twenty most important people in the building, save the vice president and the president, who did not attend these meetings. The morning gathering helped set the stage for the day, and Friday's meeting teed up the next week's activities. The goal was to get everybody on the same page; keep departments apprised of opportunities or flag potential problems down the pike. Typically, it would not be my job to detail our planned messaging, but Liz was out, and the duty of presenting the president's communications activities for the following week fell to me.

I enjoyed when I could sneak into that meeting. You heard weird shit. One time, I remember, the nation's chief scientist was explaining that a civilization-ending meteor had passed unusually close to Earth, which we didn't learn about until two days prior. "So we gotta get better at that," he understated.

Because the meeting was just a few paces from my desk—in the Roosevelt Room across the hall—I crammed until the last possible minute, figuring out the quickest way to get through everything POTUS had coming up next week. You see, the emphasis in these meetings was on speed. Denis ran them efficiently and with zip. On a typical Friday, this would have been easy enough, but the president was going out of town the next week—with six jam-packed days in the Philippines and Malaysia. A mouthful.

As the door closed, Denis turned to me: "Take us through next week, Pat."

After a deep breath, I did my best to speed-read. "On Sunday the president will arrive in Turkey, where he will take part in a bilat with President Erdoğan. There will be a pool spray with statements at the bottom." Inhale. "Then he'll do a working lunch that will include a pool spray, but no statements from the leaders." Exhale. It went on like this for a while, and I knew I was losing the room.

I was wrapping up Tuesday's schedule when the door on the opposite end of the Roosevelt Room swung open.

Fortunately, I was already standing, so when Barack Obama swaggered in, I didn't have to worry about the awkward internal debate about whether to get up when he enters. They used to do it on *The West Wing*, but that was TV. And it seems so . . . formal. No matter: he put the room to ease at once. "I hear this is where you guys do all the planning," he joked, interrupting my soliloquy.

I shut up, and he dug in: "You know, a year ago they said we were dead." He let that settle for a moment. This was definitely *not* on the agenda.

"And ever since, we've just kicked ass."

Safe to say a swear word counts for double, maybe triple, when it's uttered by a sitting president. Next, he launched into a recap of a remarkable year, highlighting a few of the biggest accomplishments from the previous 365 days: the Supreme Court's rulings that the Affordable Care Act was here to stay and that, in America—no matter where you live or who you love—you can get married. A fifty-years-in-the-making shift away from a failed policy in Cuba toward a new course.* A historic nuclear agreement with Iran. Plummeting unemployment and a growing economy. Not bad.

"This was one of the most consequential years in presidential history," said this president. But he was quick to offer credit—this wasn't a victory lap.

Looking around, he said, "Collectively, the folks in this room are responsible for billions of people."

I'm just here to speed-read a slide, I thought.

He kept going: "The actions you take affect *billions* of people."

He may or may not have looked at me prior to this next part, but he definitely said, "Now, if you look around the room, that may be disturbing."

After a bit of laughter and a lot of if-you-only-knew looks, he finished: "But I don't mean that to intimidate you."

Too late, man.

"I mean it to inspire you."

With that, the room erupted into applause, and the president was gone. As the ovation died down—and inspired as I was to get on with the week ahead—I tried to take back the room. I cleared my throat: "So . . . On Wednesday—" But Denis piped up immediately, mercifully: "Let's call it there. Thanks, Pat."

Back at my desk, I was still buzzing from a pep talk I had no

* On this day, my parents were in Cuba. They would call me that night, trying to get information on the news that was still to come.

business getting—and now wondering how many people were affected by my current course of action, I clicked halfheartedly through an article delineating "37 Times You Just Couldn't Even Anymore."

I watched as Pete Souza slipped past my desk and into the press secretary's office. He didn't seem himself. After a few minutes, Josh called me in, and Pete—uncharacteristically shaken—informed me that Rick McKay, a beloved member of the White House photography team, had passed away the previous night. I was to take the first crack at a statement from the president on his passing. Then Cody and the president would take their own pass on it.

I wrote my fair share of these kinds of statements at the White House. Typically, they honored deceased public servants: members of Congress, governors, and the like. Other times, we highlighted the life of a civil rights icon from a bygone era or a notable entertainer or athlete who passed in an untimely manner. My favorite death statement (that sounds horrible) I'd done was for Arnold Palmer:

> *With his homemade swing and homespun charm, Arnold Palmer had swagger before we had a name for it. From a humble start working at the local club in his beloved Latrobe, Pennsylvania, to superstardom as the face of golf around the globe, Arnold was the American Dream come to life.*
>
> *Along the way he racked up win after win—but it wasn't his success that made him King. Arnold's freewheeling, fearless approach to the game inspired a generation of golfers and, for*

the first time on TV, enthralled an audience across the world. Sure, we liked that he won seven majors, but we loved that he went for it when he probably should have laid up.

That spirit extended beyond the links where he gave freely of himself and poured everything he had into everything he did: from building hospitals to personally responding to countless letters from his fans. And he did it all with a grin that hinted maybe he had one more shot up his sleeve.

Today Michelle and I stand with Arnie's Army in saluting the King.

I liked the challenge of death statements. It's not always easy to succinctly eulogize someone in the voice of the most powerful man in the world. These statements needed to be broad enough for lay people to appreciate, but more importantly, they needed to be threaded with specifics—inside jokes, even—so that the tribute meant something to those closest to the deceased.

I remember when I'd gotten word about the death of the woman whom I passed by each morning in Lafayette Park: an elderly lady who for decades had been protesting for peace. I tried to convince folks to do a POTUS statement for her. Her name was Concepcion Picciotto. I had jotted down some notes, stray phrases in what would ultimately remain an unpresidential statement: "Concepcion was my neighbor. There is no more worthy way to spend a life than to fight for peace."

I was voted down, but one of my bosses came up to me a few days later and said they had been mistaken; it would have been a nice thing to do, to lift her up from her humble position in the park across the way.

There was, of course, no question about the statement for Pete's friend. He was a part of the Obama family. That's why everything felt so different—finding material for the first draft of an appropriate tribute. Usually, I mined Google and Wikipedia for facts and memories worth recounting; now I was sourcing material from grieving friends. I didn't know Rick well, but my coworkers did; they put plugs in for a favorite pet, a beloved pastime, or a small quirk. I sent in my draft, confident that Cody and the president would improve it, and yet still unsure whether the statement would do him justice. Like a snapshot grabbed at just the right moment, it just needed to capture him, I thought.

• • •

"Larry David?" Antoinette's disdain was evident as she reacted to my email.

"Yeah, Larry David," I replied, miffed.

"I don't think so. I want this to be taken seriously." A close colleague and friend, Antoinette used a standing desk in our cramped office.* I'd never given the standing much mind, but in this moment—as she cut down my suggestion—her adjustable Varidesk really pissed me off.

"How does that make sense?" she added.

* Antoinette had moved from Lower Press to Upper Press.

I was incredulous. "The exact reason I wrote: 'For lifting up the little things and bringing the country together around a show about nothing.' "

She was baffled: "For the Presidential Medal of Freedom?"

At this point, Desiree turned to me. "Red zone!"

Each year, the president awards the medal—the nation's highest civilian honor—to individuals who, according to the White House, "have made especially meritorious contributions to the security or national interests of the United States, to world peace, or to cultural or other significant public or private endeavors." Simple enough.

White House staff members were given the opportunity to weigh in on the list of selections. We could offer up individuals we deemed worthy of the honor to then be whittled down and eventually selected by the president. To me, the "cultural . . . endeavors" and especially the "other" language is broad and open to interpretation, as evidenced by former honorees Lucille Ball and Stevie Wonder. That's why I put forward the *Seinfeld* and *Curb Your Enthusiasm* star. But others took a different route.

"You mean to tell me that Larry David deserves the Medal of Freedom more than Malala Yousafzai (a young Pakistani woman who stood up to the Taliban and earned a Nobel Peace Prize)?" somebody asked.

"Or Rosa Parks?" somebody else added.

My desk mate picked up her red pen as I readied my response.

"Can't he deserve it as much?" I joked.

Tally mark.

"And so close to Black History Month!" Desiree chimed in as she took pen to Post-it.

Double tally mark.

"Dude, we're way clear of Black History Month," I protested jokingly, consulting the calendar.

Another tally mark—this made five in one morning. That long, assertive strike across the previous four meant that Larry's hopes for a medal were slipping away. So were my hopes of reconnecting with Larry, whom I hadn't seen since he'd nearly run me over on Martha's Vineyard two summers before.

Truth is, I had recently written a pilot for a political comedy about America's first First Man, inventively titled *First Man*. The script had gotten a bit of attention in Hollywood, but no offers. So it's possible my Larry nomination was clouded by personal admiration of what he's achieved. Still, I genuinely felt it appropriate to honor America's favorite misanthrope—and a brilliant storyteller.

On the afternoon of the thirteenth, a couple of film producers—Tim White and Matt George—dropped by the White House for what we called a "rogue tour": a quick, nonsanctioned look around the West Wing. They were producing Rob Reiner's film *LBJ*; we had met months earlier as they scouted the White House. Tim, who would quickly go on to major success in Hollywood with Steven Spielberg's *The Post*, was working with me on *First Man*, and even more interested in politics than I was.

We offered official West Wing tours in the evenings after seven thirty, but they were a whole thing to organize and—of course—meant staying well after seven thirty. So the better option for folks who had offices or desks in the West Wing was to simply bring in guests to visit "where we work" and then in a just-so-happen kind of way to pass by the Oval Office, the Cabinet Room, the Roosevelt Room, and the Briefing Room.

That was my plan for the producers, but things were off to a rocky start when "ROTUS" (receptionist of the United States) called me into the West Wing lobby and reminded me that I needed to wait with them because Matt, who is originally from Australia, had a pink badge. The Secret Service provides color-coordinated badges to guests, press, and staff. Those born outside of the United States are given pink badges and require an escort at all times when moving around the campus. Matt wondered why he was adorned with a pink badge, and because I think the whole foreign national thing is rude, I told him it was because he was wearing jeans.

There is a similar hierarchy of badges among White House staff. You wear either a blue or a green badge. (Interns get light-blue and press wear red.) I was given a blue badge when I made the move from media monitor to the West Wing. Green grants you access to the EEOB, while blue means you can go wherever you want, West Wing included. It's a silly split, and many people much more important than I was sat across the street wearing green.

On this afternoon, the president was running behind and had not yet left the Oval Office for an event on the State Floor of the mansion, so we waited in the main West Wing lobby, which is the formal entrance and exit point for White House visitors whose appointments are not meant to be kept a secret. As soon as the president left his desk, with the help of one of the president's body men, I was going to sneak both producers into the Oval for a quick peek around. But before we could, the door to the Roosevelt Room opened and out walked the vice president and former secretary of state James Baker.

Have I mentioned that the vice president is a close talker? A very close talker. It was hard to tell whether he and the secretary were debating foreign policy or about to go in for a kiss. As the vice president headed for his office, Secretary Baker shouted about their recent meeting on foreign policy implications of the Trans-Pacific Partnership trade agreement: "Now, this is a big fucking deal!"

"Thank God my mother isn't around to hear that!" the vice president shot back.

At this point, I realized two things: my guests were getting a pretty solid rogue tour, and I hadn't checked my BlackBerry in about five minutes, which is about four minutes too many. After typing my password, usually *Hoagie* and a number, I saw a flurry of unread emails about an ongoing situation in Paris. Each email was made up of copy-and-pasted tweets from our media monitor to the entire communications department, as well as senior advisors and the chief of staff and his deputies. Something about a shooting. Maybe in multiple locations.

The producers' eyes nearly popped out of their heads as Henry Kissinger, Madeleine Albright, and Colin Powell made their way out of the Roosevelt Room and passed us, but I was focused on my phone. More tweets flooded my in-box. I told Tim and Matt that whatever was going on in Paris was turning into something real. You get pretty good, reading thousands of headlines and tweets per day, at determining what's about to be a major story—about what matters and what doesn't.

We were only a few minutes in, but this seemed huge and horrific; it seemed like it was going to matter for a long time. And sure enough, as Secretary of Defense Ash Carter filtered out of the Roosevelt, the Situation Room sent a blast email about the attack on Paris. That's the way it typically worked at the White House; unfolding tragedy revealed through a gush of tweets, punctuated by emails from the Situation Room. Often, they were false alarms. As we know, this was not.

Still, it wasn't entirely clear yet what was happening in Paris. And as the president made his way to the State Floor, we hurried to the Oval, where Tim and Matt took in Barack Obama's office. I hung in the Outer Oval Office. Pete was there. The statement on his friend had gone out a few hours earlier, and he thanked me for helping with it. He said he thought it would mean a great deal to the family.

Josh arrived to wait in the Outer as Tim and Matt finished exploring the Oval Office. Evidently, the attack in Paris had reached a level where it might be appropriate for the president to speak publicly on the issue. Josh needed to get word from President Obama that he agreed that was the right course before alerting the press to expect something.

For these types of quickly-pulled-together statements, which were usually in response to varying degrees of national or international tragedy, we used the Brady Press Briefing Room because it required minimal setup. The cameras are ready to go twenty-four hours per day. And the presidential seal takes only seconds to hang on the permanent podium. We allowed about a half hour for those members of the press who were off campus to rush in.

As Josh continued to wait for the president to return, we moved into the Cabinet Room, which is adjacent to the Outer Oval Office. Every member of the president's cabinet, from the small business administrator to the secretary of state, has his or her own brown leather chair—each slightly shorter than the president's seat—that bears his or her title on the back. Following a cabinet member's tenure, he or she is offered the opportunity to *purchase* the chair.

As a fall afternoon turned to evening, we looked at the Colonnade and into the darkened Rose Garden through a series of four matching glass doors—windows onto the president's path. I rattled off a few additional useless facts for Tim and Matt. I was never very good at giving tours; I didn't appropriately memorize the facts and figures. But by 2015, I'd been around long enough to feel more comfortable leading folks, mostly friends and family, around the building. Felt like I belonged. But even as I mined my limited repertoire of White House information for my guests, my mind was elsewhere: worried about what news might pop into my BlackBerry next.

We heard a commotion and watched as Secret Service agents scurried on the other side of the doors, a telltale sign that "Renegade" was "on the move."

It was getting dark this night of November 13, but before long, the president strode by slowly. As clear as day.

He was alone, or as alone as he ever is. He looked increasingly serious with each frame he occupied; it was like I was watching a movie reel. He was silhouetted as he crossed our final frame—an oddly cinematic moment in front of these two film producers, who had just wrapped a movie that included a set with a reconstructed version of the very area where we were standing.

Shortly after my friends left, it was obvious: the shootings in Paris were coordinated; it was a terrorist attack.

The president made his way past Upper Press, through Lower Press, and into the Briefing Room, where he announced: "This is an attack not just on Paris, it's an attack not just on the people of France, but this is an attack on all of humanity and the universal values that we share."

It was filmic language, but this wasn't Michael Douglas; and we weren't on the set of Tim's and Matt's movie.

This was the unreal meeting the very real.

But that's the way of the White House. From silly to serious in an instant. From a presidential pep talk to the passing of a friend. From Larry David to Henry Kissinger. And a president who spent his morning celebrating a remarkable year with a small team and his evening mourning a tragedy with the world.

I guess that's why Tony Snow said, "The White House, with all its pressures, intrigues, triumphs, betrayals, joys, and disappointments, is the most special place you ever will work." Hell, it was the only place I had really ever worked, but walking out late that night—on my way home to eat Oreos and watch *House Hunters*—I knew he was right.

There I was, back where I started the day: on the sidewalk with the other folks. And as I looked up at that grand place—a little less mysterious to me now, but no less glorious—I glanced at my glowing phone. Pete had forwarded me a note that knocked me back. It was from his friend's daughter, who wrote of the president's statement on her father:

"It's so perfect. That's my dad."

So while *humbling* isn't the word I would use to describe walking into the White House, maybe that's exactly what walking out of it is.

• • •

A year and a half later, I walked out of those gates one final time—humbled for a whole host of reasons. It was dark; a bit dreary. And very quiet. I was wearing my tan summer suit; my nod to the nonsense. But in the January darkness, my thoughts turned to the more meaningful, briefly beyond the here and now.

On his first day in office, a year and a half before I arrived, President Obama sent a note to his staff. He wrote: "However long we are keepers of the public trust we should never forget that we are here as public servants and public service is a privilege . . . Public service is, simply and absolutely, about advancing the interests of the American people."

I told you I'm a worrier. Tend to wish or worry away the weekend. *What's next?* I too often wonder most moments. On Memorial Day, I'll lament, "Summer's over!" I'll fret a vacation's close as soon as I land.

But that didn't happen at the White House. I had this sense that it wasn't going to end. That we were on some endless loop. That this was home; my coworkers, family. It's partly why things hit me so hard when it ended the way it did, and it's why I still feel like I'm on a long vacation—that any day, I'll throw on my suit, trek down the streets of DC, past Lafayette Park, and into those imposing gates.

Leaving the last time, I was uneasy. I hadn't wished away my time, but did I appreciate it? I didn't know that as I trudged up the EEOB steps at twenty-two years old, my parents absurdly yet sweetly watching from beyond the fence, that I wouldn't walk out until I was twenty-nine, that this place would help define me.

Dan Pfeiffer did two things before he left the White House. First, he came into Upper Press one night—only this was a different Dan. A nervous Dan. For a moment, our roles were reversed. He sidled up to a free desk next to Howli's, anxious to tell me something: he and Howli were dating!

Stephanie and my family often remind me that I can be dense, but I had thought I had my pulse on this place better than this. I was shocked—in the best possible way—to learn about this budding presidential romance, brewing unbeknownst to me.

Suddenly his frequent visits to Upper Press to make small talk, even after he moved across the hall to senior advisor, made more sense. Theirs wasn't the only relationship forged in the White House. I would attend Dan and Howli's wedding, along with plenty of other staffers who met their husbands and wives through President Obama. Josh met his wife, Natalie, on the campaign—they had their first date the Saturday after Inauguration Day. Marie met her husband, Andrew, while working for Vice President Biden. Bobby met his wife, Ellen, through Obama, too. Cody had his speeches rigorously fact-checked by a woman named Kristen, who would become his wife. Clark and Caroline—Obama spokespeople who are now married—met in Lower Press. And Matt and Stephanie, a talented White House researcher who would go on to work at the State Department, found each other and got married as well.

I thought back to my own wedding on a balmy July evening in downtown Philadelphia. Like most surreal events, I now see my wedding through a series of flashes—what I saw, stories I heard—that congeal to form a sense of the night: Stephanie turning the corner of the aisle with her dad. My inability to get through the ceremony—crying from the moment I saw her until we both said, "I do." My brother Alex, in his tux with the bridesmaids, leaping into the fountain at Logan Circle—and then demanding, dripping wet, that the receptionist call Taylor Swift, who was apparently staying on our floor. Marie and Antoinette presenting me with a framed photo of my engagement in the Rose Garden, with a note from the president.* My dad's moving speech, told in bicycle terms, and my pop-pop dancing in his seersucker suit.

I thought about the faces of the people, my family and lifelong friends, dancing alongside so many guests—my White House family—who were unknown to me just a few years before. Young people I didn't grow up with from across the country who came

* Brian found out about our illicit use of the Rose Garden only when they brought the photo to the Oval to be signed.

together around an idea embodied in a skinny guy with a funny name from the South Side of Chicago. They weren't friends I had my whole life, but that didn't matter, because you get to know people quickly in the White House, where stress is high, days are long, and everything's accelerated in the foxhole.

Seeing the different people from disparate parts of our lives come together to party was one of the most rewarding facets of our wedding. We didn't look alike. Hadn't grow up in the same way. But my White House family and I had something important in common, highlighted by Dan, the second thing he did before he left the White House.

I read hundreds of obligatory "goodbye" emails from departing staff during my years at the White House, but something Dan wrote stood out. He said that no matter where we went or how many years passed, we would forever be known as "Obama people." I took comfort in that as I walked out of the gates for the last time.

I thought about a million little moments. Asking Matt, "What's a POTUS?" Getting red-zoned. That absurd photo of me on a horse in the ocean regularly circulated by Velz and others. Swing states and debates. I thought about Susan Rice opening that horse email and Josh replying to the whole White House, "Giddy-up!" The thrill of 2012. Proposing to Stephanie in the Rose Garden. Lester Holt at Nelson Mandela's funeral. The despair of 2016. Bringing my mom and dad, Stephanie, Harry, and Alex into the Oval Office to meet the president. The Pope sneeze and Seinfeld's squeaking sneaks. Shaq. I thought about walking my nana and my pop-pop through the West Wing, before they could no longer travel. The Door of No Return. Watching an inauguration from the Atlantic Ocean. Then, the Blue Room. These were the moments that marked my time winging it. *West* winging it.

After all, a presidency is defined by a series of moments, for better or worse. Some of those moments flashed through my mind: Signing the Affordable Care Act into law. SEAL Team Six and a red line in Syria. Reaching over the sneeze guard at Chipotle. A baseball game in Cuba. A beer summit and Trayvon Martin. Announcing that America would wind down two wars. Wearing a tan suit. An attack in Paris. "Amazing Grace" in Charleston, and Aurora, and Newtown, and Orlando. Hope and hard-won change.

• • •

But I was drawn to the quieter moments as I drew closer to the gates one last time. I thought back to five years earlier, when I had wrangled my first late-night Marine One arrival. In the middle of the night, the White House takes on a haunting, midnight melancholy. Stillness replaces frenzy. Suddenly from above, three points of light—Marine One and its two decoy helicopters—become visible from the South Lawn. Watching the chopper carrying our forty-fourth president throttle past the glowing monument to our first president, I was struck by the thought: one day Obama will be a monument.

That same idea would occasionally pop into my mind in the

Oval Office: I'm talking to a battleship, likely a bridge, too—an international airport, as well as countless future high schools. But for now, he was the person landing before me on his backyard.

The strong winds of Marine One leave an impression. At once, everything is tossed about, but at once, you're confident everything will be all right.

Obama bounds up the South Lawn, across the drive, and into the Dip Room. The doors close behind him, and the helicopter, no longer Marine One, lifts away into the night. The stillness returns. And the anxieties of the world seem to hold in abeyance until the sun peeks over the tidal basin by Jefferson when the White House comes back to life. By the time the sun reaches the top of Washington, the day is in full swing. And as the sun sinks beyond Lincoln, calm sets back in.

• • •

I think about Obama people, about granite and grace and generations to come—their kids, my kids—as today's Obama people become tomorrow's Obama family, and we expand beyond the gates of the White House. I think about monuments. How they remember people and events. And I think about those kids who might stop by an Obama monument many White Houses from now. They may not see it at first, but if they look closely, somewhere in the smallest veins of the granite will be the people who worked there, winged it there, laughed there, fell in love there, cried there, and served there.

On January 17, 2017, as the iron gates locked into place behind me for the final time, my blue badge gone, I thought back to Antoinette's overly earnest, corny-as-hell daily goodbye: "It's been a pleasure serving the American people with you."

Yes, it had been.

EPILOGUE

. . . Of the End

She's not going to get there.

A lump formed in my throat the instant I heard it, but I was determined not to cry.

"Okay, then . . ."

The West Wing was emptying out. And I thought it was time to leave. The party was over. I departed the White House grounds knowing that walking into work would never be the same but unwilling to grapple with what it all meant at midnight. A crowd had gathered on Pennsylvania Avenue. Somebody asked me if they had called it. I yelled back "No!" and kept moving.

Typically, I'll check my work phone ten times in the brief time it takes to walk home, but I had nothing to look at this night. Both phones dead. I peered creepily into somebody's window from the sidewalk to see if the worst had become official, but all I could make out were the blues and too much red of election night coverage. I kept moving. It was unseasonably warm. I slapped myself hard on the cheek, which I regretted immediately as cliché.

I was relieved to find that the election had not been called when I arrived home, the campaign granted a stay of execution. Stephanie, still in her Hillary T-shirt, and I watched John Podesta, who used to pop in and out of Upper Press often, walk into frame. He asked the group of thousands, assembled under the glass ceiling of Manhattan's Jacob Javits Center, to head home.

The day after the election, we woke up to a gloomy, rainy day. It was fitting, but also a bit much—like we were living a movie with a lazy script. In the basement of the West Wing, I heard a White House aide plead facetiously with a counterterrorism staffer, "Please tell me it was the Russians."

I wasn't ready for the gallows humor and remained stoic until my mom called. She had won big the night before, but I heard her crying on the other line. Aubrey had just called her on the way to preschool. Aubrey liked to imitate Trump by shouting "Blah blah-blah blah-blah!" She had seized on his lack of substance and took her imitation to anyone who would listen. She even delivered the spot-on impression to the Clintons, after asking about the trash in the park. They were delighted. "We've got to get you on TV," President Clinton said with a smile.

I loved the Trump impression, but I was ready to be done with it, to move on from his candidacy. So was Aubrey, who had wanted to talk to her grandmother as soon as she heard the news about

Donald. She was confused and upset, but, still, she was sure it would be okay: "Hillary can win next year, right?"

She thought that in part a presidential race was like a regular race. "Hillary just ran a little slower than Donald last night."

I choked back tears thinking of the eternal hope and brightness of a child, as I filtered into Josh's office with dozens of other shell-shocked staffers. We were back where we had begun to celebrate the night before.

Jen Psaki reminded us of the important work that lay ahead, and Cody previewed the remarks he had worked on with the president, to be delivered in the Cabinet Room. The president's assistant, Ferial, dropped in and asked for Josh. A moment later, she was back:

"The president would like to see all of you in the Oval Office."

I've given countless White House tours for friends and family, most of whom comment on how small and cramped everything is. Not so with the Oval, where the drab carpet of the West Wing gives way to beautiful hardwood and a rug with the president's favorite quotes emblazoned along the outer edge. The light is brilliant, crisp.

Our group of communications staffers, from the press secretary down to the media monitor, made our way in. For some, this was their first time in the Oval Office. We spread out along the edge of the room, and I took my place between Kennedy's "No Problem of Human Destiny Is Beyond Human Beings" and Roosevelt's "The Welfare of Each of Us Is Dependent Fundamentally Upon the Welfare of All of Us." President Obama began to speak, but staffers kept filtering in; he punctured the tension, calling the procession "like a clown car." He and the vice president stood in front of the Resolute desk. The president started again. He talked about hope and about the importance of doing things the right way—now more than ever. "This is not the apocalypse," he said. The vice president shook his head.

I had seen this format before, even set it up myself sometimes. The president speaking, with the vice president at his side, reaffirming with a smile or underscoring the importance of the moment with a nod. We used it to powerful effect throughout the presidency. I hadn't ever been its intended audience, though.

This is not the apocalypse.

At this point, I broke down. This was not the poised sniffling that the moment called for. I was full-blown ugly crying in the Oval Office as the president gave us a pep talk.

I was upset for my niece, who didn't understand that Hillary couldn't win in a year. And for my mom, who worked so hard on Hillary's behalf. And for my wife, who wore her Hillary shirt to work and around town. And for my nana, who thought she would finally see a woman president. I was selfishly upset for myself. This wasn't how it was supposed to end.

I hadn't even begun to think about the people across the country—the vulnerable, the disadvantaged, the different—for whom a Trump presidency could have real, tangible effects. Still, the president highlighted something that Ben Rhodes, who was standing off to the side, had emailed him when the outcome seemed clear the night before. "History doesn't move in a straight line. It zigs and zags."

In the Oval, desperately trying to compose myself in front of my Obama family, this was a hard zag.

I had to turn away and try to get it together. The president reminded us that most of the folks in the room were young and that this was just our "first rodeo"—that we had known only winning, but hope is called for most in our losses. Then he said that he didn't want to do the televised speech in the Cabinet Room. He looked to the windows; the rain had stopped. "Look, it's sunny out," he said, and suggested he give the speech in the Rose Garden. It was more optimistic. He asked if we agreed.

Yes, we did.

Acknowledgments

Writing a memoir when you're twenty-nine is a little absurd. So first, thank you David Larabell, Jonas Brooks, and everybody at CAA for taking this idea seriously from the start, and believing I had a story to tell.

Thank you to Gallery Books for, well, buying the story. But more important, to the team that made *West Winging It* an actual thing. Natasha Simons, you are a superb editor and you made the book better. I also thank Jen Bergstrom, Jen Robinson, Hannah Brown, Jean Anne Rose, Theresa Dooley, Monica Oluwek, Alexandre Su, and Lisa Litwack.

Thank you to my Obama family: the folks who welcomed me into the fold, who mocked me mercilessly, and who helped make me a better person. Dan and Howli Pfeiffer, Matt Lehrich, Liz Allen, Marie Nesi, Bobby Whithorne, Eric Schulz, Antoinette Rangel, Brian Mosteller, Jeff Tiller, Amy Brundage, Clark Stevens, Hannah Hankins, Desiree Barnes, Crystal Carson, Jen Psaki, Jen Palmieri, Josh Earnest, Jay Carney, and Peter Velz (who dealt with more questions from me while writing this book than anybody else).

There are Obama people never mentioned in my book—some of whom I didn't know well, but whose accomplishments and competence, their own remarkable stories, shaped the way I think about the Obama White House. People such as Deesha Dyer and Gary Lee and Brandon Lepow. Thank you.

Importantly, I thank my family and friends who've put up with me and helped me, from my uncle Bob Dean and neighbors Sean and Anne to my cousin Johnny Buonomo. My in-laws, Jim and Debbie Genuardi; Victoria, Owen, and Dan Edwards; and Kevin and Maureen Genuardi, who I've bugged about buying this book for months. Thank you to my nana and pop-pop, who play a crucial role in the book and an even more vital role in my own life.

And to my immediate family, whose quirks and smarts made an indelible mark on the stories I chose to tell and the way I chose to tell them, thank you: my brother Harry, Juliet, and niece Aubrey. My brother Alex. Each of you is weird and wonderful. And this book wouldn't have been as much fun without your influence.

To my parents, Madeleine and PJ: more than anyone else, this book would not be possible without you. Mom, you're one of the best writers I know, and your help on this book was invaluable. Dad, you work more—and harder—than anyone I've ever known. Whenever I didn't feel like writing a page or two, I'd think of you and get to typing. Thank you both for knocking some sense into me, reminding me not to leave the White House until they forced me out.

To Stephanie: thank you for your support and unwavering kindness. I realize fully that I'm the lucky one in this equation. I would say I couldn't have imagined when we met in the second grade that we'd fall in love and get married. But I could and I did. I love you.

Oh—and thanks, Obama.